Praise for *Americans and the Holocaust*

"This remarkable book shatters the myth that Americans lacked information about the dangers of Nazism. These diverse, historical sources from multiple voices across the United States leave us with troubling questions about the national will to respond to discrimination, war, and genocide."

— Ken Burns, Lynn Novick, and Sarah Botstein, Florentine Films

"This book is an important and exceptionally useful resource for the classroom. Any teacher or student who wants to get a feel for the prevailing sentiments in America during the prelude to World War II and during the war itself will be immensely aided by this important collection of voices. If you want to know what did people know and when did they know it, this collection will help provide the answer."

— Deborah E. Lipstadt, author of *Antisemitism Here and Now*

"This wide-ranging, representative, and deeply absorbing selection of American commentary on the plight of Europe's Jews during the 1930s and 1940s both informs about the past and prompts reflection on the present. Readers will come face to face with the best and the worst of our country's reflexes, both then and now."

— Peter Hayes, author of *Why?: Explaining the Holocaust*

"Kudos to Daniel Greene and Edward Phillips for producing this searing collection of contemporary news stories, government reports, and other documents contradicting the common belief that the American government and people had little access to information about the Holocaust as it unfolded. With its haunting parallels to the deep strains in our society today, this is an essential read."

— Lynne Olson, author of *Those Angry Days: Roosevelt, Lindbergh, and America's Fight Over World War II, 1939–1941*

"This expertly curated array of primary sources—newspaper clippings, State Department memos, photographs, and more—explores the persistent question: What did Americans know about the Holocaust? The answer—an astonishing amount!—deepens our understanding of the past and challenges what we think we know about our own times."

— Doris Bergen, author of *War and Genocide: A Concise History of the Holocaust*

AMERICANS AND THE HOLOCAUST

AMERICANS
and the
HOLOCAUST

A READER

Edited by

DANIEL GREENE *and* EDWARD PHILLIPS

Published in association with the
UNITED STATES HOLOCAUST MEMORIAL MUSEUM

RUTGERS UNIVERSITY PRESS

New Brunswick, Camden, and Newark,
New Jersey, and London

Library of Congress Cataloging-in-Publication Data

Names: United States Holocaust Memorial Museum. |
Greene, Daniel, editor. | Phillips, Edward, editor.
Title: Americans and the Holocaust : a reader / edited by
Daniel Greene, and Edward Phillips, in association with the
United States Holocaust Memorial Museum.
Description: New Brunswick : Rutgers University Press, [2022] |
Includes bibliographical references and index.
Identifiers: LCCN 2021015446 | ISBN 9781978821682 (paperback) |
ISBN 9781978821699 (hardback) | ISBN 9781978821705 (epub) |
ISBN 9781978821712 (mobi) | ISBN 9781978821729 (pdf)
Subjects: LCSH: Holocaust, Jewish (1939–1945)—Foreign public opinion,
American. | Holocaust, Jewish (1939–1945)—Influence. | World War,
1939–1945—Press coverage—United States. | World War, 1939–1945—
Public opinion. | National socialism in popular culture—United States. |
Mass media—Political aspects—United States—History—20th century.
Classification: LCC D804.45.U55 A485 2022 | DDC 940.53/180973—dc23
LC record available at https://lccn.loc.gov/2021015446

A British Cataloging-in-Publication record for this book is available from the British Library.

References to internet websites (URLs) were accurate at the time of writing.
Neither the editors nor Rutgers University Press is responsible for URLs that
may have expired or changed since the manuscript was prepared.

♾ The paper used in this publication meets the requirements of the
American National Standard for Information Sciences—Permanence of Paper
for Printed Library Materials, ANSI Z39.48-1992.

www.rutgersuniversitypress.org

Manufactured in the United States of America

Contents

Foreword

During the spring of 1945, as US troops first encountered Nazi concentration camps in Germany and the hostilities of World War II in Europe ended, descriptions and images of the full horror of Nazism quickly filled US newspapers, magazines, and movie theater newsreels. In the ensuing months, Americans in large numbers came face-to-face for the first time with the extensive and shocking visual evidence of the massive crimes that we now call the Holocaust. As Americans learned more about these atrocities, some asked important questions about the response of the international community and especially their own nation: *What did the US government and the American people know about the threats posed by Nazi Germany? What could have been done to stop the rise of Nazism in Germany and its assault on Europe's Jews? What should have been done?*

This book enables readers to delve deeply into those questions by gathering together primary sources—evidence from the time that reveals what Americans knew about Nazism and how they debated their responsibility to respond. It draws on groundbreaking research conducted for the exhibition *Americans and the Holocaust*, which opened at the US Holocaust Memorial Museum in 2018 to commemorate the Museum's twenty-fifth anniversary. Like the exhibition and multiple educational resources created to accompany it, this book reminds us of the challenging circumstances in the United States during the 1930s and 1940s, including profound economic crisis, fear of communism, pervasive antisemitism and racism, and weariness from fighting in World War I that led to widespread isolationism. These attitudes are clearly documented in the public opinion polling conducted in this period. This domestic context played a critical role in shaping Americans' responses to crises abroad. During the twelve years that Nazis were in power, Americans disagreed vehemently about whether to admit refugees from Nazism, intervene in the war, or aid Jews targeted for murder. The primary sources included here give us insight into the choices made by government leaders and ordinary people alike, allowing readers to take a broad, panoramic look at how Americans responded to Nazism.

By the time Nazi Germany launched World War II with its invasion of Poland in 1939, democratic civilization itself was at stake, yet Americans overwhelmingly wanted the country to remain neutral. After the attack on Pearl Harbor in 1941, the US military fought for almost four years to defend democracy, and more than 400,000 Americans died defeating Nazism in Germany and imperialism in Japan. The American people—soldiers and civilians alike—made enormous sacrifices to free Europe from Nazi oppression. Yet saving Jews and others targeted for murder by the Nazi regime and its collaborators never became a priority. In asking why rescue never became a main objective for the US government, it is natural to focus on leaders at the highest levels. There is no doubt that President Franklin D. Roosevelt and his administration could have done much more on behalf of Europe's Jews. The United States could have admitted many more Jewish refugees, publicized all the information it knew about Nazi crimes, pressured the Allies and neutral nations to help endangered Jews, and more actively supported resistance against the Nazis. These acts together would likely have reduced the death toll, but they would not have prevented the Holocaust: by the time of the D-Day invasion in 1944, five million Jews had been murdered.

In the 1979 Report to the President of the United States that established the vision for the US Holocaust Memorial Museum, Holocaust survivor Elie Wiesel wrote, "Americans have a distinct responsibility to remember the Holocaust." The responsibility, he explained, stems in part from that the fact that some American families have ties to victims of the Holocaust; it extends to honoring the millions of American soldiers who fought in World War II and recognizing the sacrifices made by their families at home. Wiesel also urged that we have a responsibility to learn what made the Holocaust possible, why it happened, and how it could have been prevented. Delving deeply into what Americans knew and asking what more might have been done is the purpose of this book. By engaging with the complexities of the past in this way, we are better able to understand the present and think about our own role in shaping the future.

Sara J. Bloomfield
Director, United States Holocaust Memorial Museum

Preface

On March 8, 1923, the *Chicago Daily Tribune* newspaper made its first mention of the "Bavaria Fascisti Chief" Adolf Hitler. Reporter Raymond Fendrick of the paper's Foreign News Service noted three particulars about Hitler: his fervent antisemitism, especially his admiration for the antisemitic American automaker Henry "Heinrich" Ford; his 6,000-man force of militarist "shock troops"; and his rising reputation as an outspoken nationalist. But for most of the remaining 1920s, Hitler and his National Socialist (Nazi) German Workers' Party remained on the fringes of German politics, and American press coverage about them was at best sporadic. Only during the early 1930s, as the Great Depression ravaged the world's industrial nations, did some Americans begin to pay attention to the meteoric rise of Hitler and the Nazis in Germany and to ask questions about its possible significance.

Americans and the Holocaust: A Reader includes a sampling of the information available to Americans about the Nazi persecution and murder of European Jews between 1933 and 1945. Presented in relatively strict chronological order, the selections intend to prompt readers to consider three essential questions in confronting this history: *What did Americans know? When did they know it? What did they do with that knowledge?* We urge readers to continually push against hindsight from their twenty-first-century knowledge about the Holocaust. We seek to show the ways the US government and American people responded to Nazism by wrestling with the rationales behind their actions and inactions in the context of the moment, which was defined by economic crisis, fear of communism, and widespread views that were isolationist, antisemitic, anti-immigrant, and racist.

These sources also help to overturn the incorrect but commonly held assumption that Americans had little access to information about Nazism during the 1930s and 1940s. Even if it was not always front-page news, information about discrimination against Jews was available to the US government as well as the American public. But the contemporary responses to this information show that the real threats of Nazism and the murderous nature of the regime toward Jews were not comprehended. The relatively wide gap between information and understanding—an essential theme here—directly influenced how Americans responded to Nazi Germany and, eventually, to its annihilation of six million European Jews.

A second animating theme at the heart of this book is the gap between many Americans' disapproval of the Nazi regime's treatment of Jews and a will to action among the American people and within the US government to help Jewish victims. The sources included here reveal actions both taken and not taken, especially as some Americans debated whether to provide refuge for those persecuted by the Nazi regime. In doing so, we challenge overly simple, inaccurate statements such as: *Americans didn't do anything to respond to Nazism* while also raising an additional critical question: *What more could have been done?*

Focusing on action and inaction opens this narrative to include many actors—governmental leaders and elected officials, faith leaders, grassroots organizations, culture makers, journalists, "ordinary" people—who faced critical choices about when and how to act, or not to act, in response to Nazism during the 1930s and 1940s. Reading sources that capture these multiple and diverse voices within the context of their times advances our understanding of the range of Americans' responses to Nazism.

Following a Prologue that describes the United States and Germany in the aftermath of World War I, the four main chapters of this book are defined by historical topics and enduring questions:

"Fear Itself, 1933–1938." How did Americans respond to the rise of Nazism? As the Nazis established a dictatorship, the regime developed new laws to give the appearance of legitimacy to their anti-Jewish policies. Some Americans had access to information about these events and organized protests but could not coalesce their efforts into a sustained anti-Nazi movement.

"Desperate Times, Limited Measures, 1938–1941." How did Americans respond to a refugee crisis? German territorial expansion and increasingly harsh persecution of Jews intensified a refugee crisis as Jews in Nazi-controlled lands sought to flee. Many Americans were forced to face the tensions of living up to the "humanitarian ideals" that portrayed the United States as a nation of immigrants while recognizing the political realities of its isolationism, xenophobia, discrimination, racism, and profound economic insecurity.

"Storm Clouds Gather, 1939–1941." How did Americans respond to the war in Europe? Germany drove Europe into war, quickly occupied much of eastern and western Europe, and following the invasion of the Soviet Union in June 1941, began the mass murder of eastern Europe's Jews. In America, the European war sharply divided the nation between those who believed the United States should stay out of the overseas conflict and those who advocated joining the fight against Germany.

"America at War, 1942–1945." How did Americans respond to Nazi atrocities in the context of war? Japan's attack on Pearl Harbor thrust the United States into war. After learning of Nazi Germany's plans to "exterminate" the Jews of Europe, the United States only belatedly looked for ways to prevent the systematic murders. Not until the final days of the war, as American troops came across the concentration camps in defeated Germany, did most Americans become aware of the scale of Nazi crimes against civilians.

Americans and the Holocaust ultimately intends to broaden readers' knowledge of how Americans responded to the Holocaust by taking a panoramic look at American society and culture during the 1930s and 1940s as it faced the Nazi threat.[1] This book also speaks to realities in American history that are profoundly relevant in our own times. Challenges regarding national security fears, economic instability, responsibilities to immigrants and refugees, racism and antisemitism, and America's role in the world—both as a member of the international community and as a haven for the oppressed—were as urgent in the 1930s and 1940s as they are today.

Wrestling with the complexities of the past should sit at the center of our engagement with it. As historian Peter Hayes counsels in his book *Why? Explaining the Holocaust,* we should not treat the Holocaust as somehow outside the realm of historical inquiry, by thinking of it as "'unfathomable,' 'incomprehensible,' and 'inexplicable.'"[2] Moreover, our engagement with the history of the Holocaust, and the history of Americans' responses to it, should foreground context. As these sources demonstrate, the international and domestic situations shaped attitudes and decisions in the United States as Americans faced the threat of Nazism.

1. Robert Abzug's *America Views the Holocaust, 1933–1945: A Brief History* (Boston: Bedford/ St. Martin's, 1999) offers an excellent selection of primary sources, but the book is currently out of print, and the sources included here differ almost entirely from those in Abzug's book.

2. Peter Hayes, *Why? Explaining the Holocaust* (New York: W. W. Norton & Co., 2017), xiii.

Note on Sources

Newspaper Wire Services

During the 1930s and 1940s, the American media landscape included daily newspapers, weekly and monthly magazines, radio broadcasts, and newsreels shown in movie theaters. Television was in its infancy and, of course, the internet did not exist. Most newspaper coverage of international events was written by journalists who worked for the Associated Press (AP) or the United Press (UP), two wire services that distributed their reports nationwide to papers large and small. Such wire service stories gave Americans throughout the entire country, not just in major metropolitan areas, access to significant information about Nazi Germany, the plight of Europe's Jews, and responses to both by national leaders in the United States.

Many of the articles included in this book are wire service stories that ran in multiple newspapers—usually with variant headlines and, for reasons of page space, greater or lesser portions of the original wired report. Wire service stories here are identified as such, and they have been drawn from a range of local newspapers.

Journalism, it is often said, is the "first rough draft of history" and, like most first drafts, may contain errors. Some of the contemporary reporting of events included here has been shown to be incorrect by subsequent historical research. In some cases, factual errors or erroneous statements in original sources have been excised.

Gallup Polls

Modern public opinion research originated in the early 1900s as a tool for advertisers. By the 1920s, many firms had dedicated research departments that utilized a sampling method to learn about how to appeal to customers. Within a decade, pollsters began using this technique to measure public opinion on a range of other topics. Pollsters attempted to be scientific; however, those polled, usually in face-to-face interviews, tended to be "likely voters" from middle- and upper-class White households.

One of the leaders in this field was George Gallup, who founded the American Institute of Public Opinion in 1935. This book includes a number of "Gallup polls" among its sources, which are intended to serve as snapshots of how Americans viewed events throughout the 1930s and 1940s.

General Comments

Some of the primary sources in this book originally had typographical or other minor errors. In most cases, these obvious errors have been corrected without calling them out. When misspellings or other errors in the original sources were significant, we have added "[*sic*]" to signal that the mistake is reproduced from the original, historic source. Note also that many of the sources here have been edited for length and clarity; removed passages are indicated with "[. . .]."

Finally, this book makes no attempt to include everything that Americans could have known about Nazi Germany and the persecution of Europe's Jews. Nor can it comprehensively cover significant initiatives undertaken by many American Jewish and non-Jewish organizations and individuals. We have combed through hundreds of sources and selected a range to focus on key Holocaust-related topics, with a breadth and depth that we hope will engage readers and prompt them to want to learn more.

Abbreviations

FDRL   Franklin D. Roosevelt Presidential Library and Museum, Hyde Park, NY

NACP   National Archives and Records Administration, College Park, MD

USGPO   United States Government Printing Office, Washington, DC

USHMM   United States Holocaust Memorial Museum, Washington, DC

Timeline

United States	Germany/Europe

CHAPTER 1

January 30, 1933	German president Paul von Hindenburg appoints Adolf Hitler chancellor (head of government).
March 4, 1933 — Franklin D. Roosevelt is inaugurated as 32nd president following his landslide election in November 1932.	
March 23, 1933	Germany's parliament, the Reichstag, passes the Enabling Act, granting Hitler's government authority to rule without the Reichstag, a crucial step toward establishing the Nazi Party dictatorship.
May 10, 1933	Students in universities across Germany burn more than 25,000 books that the Nazi Party considers "unGerman."
August 31, 1935 — Congress passes a Neutrality Act prohibiting the export of "implements of war" to foreign nations at war.	
September 15, 1935	The Reichstag (composed entirely of Nazi Party delegates) enacts the "Nuremberg Laws" that strip German citizenship from Germany's Jews and ban marriage and sexual relations between "Aryans" and Jews.

	United States	*Germany/Europe*
August 1–16, 1936		The 11th Summer Olympics is held in Berlin.
November 3, 1936	Franklin D. Roosevelt wins re-election in a second landslide.	
May 1, 1937	In response to civil war in Spain (1936–39), Congress passes a second Neutrality Act that forbids the transport of arms on US merchant ships to countries at war and authorizes the president to bar all belligerent ships from US waters.	

CHAPTER 2

March 12, 1938		Germany occupies and annexes Austria (the *Anschluss*), endangering the lives of the nearly 200,000 Austrian Jews.
July 6–15, 1938		An international refugee conference meets in Évian, France, with delegates from thirty-two countries.
September 29, 1938		The Munich Agreement between Germany, United Kingdom, France, and Italy permits Germany's annexation of the Sudetenland, an area in western Czechoslovakia.
November 9–10, 1938		On Kristallnacht, the "night of broken glass," Nazi paramilitary forces and civilians carry out an attack against Jewish-owned businesses, homes, and synagogues, throughout Germany, Austria, and the Sudetenland.

	United States	*Germany/Europe*
February 9, 1939	Senator Robert Wagner (Democrat-NY) and Representative Edith Nourse Rogers (Republican-MA) introduce the Wagner-Rogers Bill, which proposes admitting 20,000 European refugee children to the United States. The bill never becomes law.	
March 15, 1939		Germany occupies the Protectorate of Bohemia and Moravia in Czechoslovakia, putting some 120,000 Czech Jews in peril.
August 23, 1939		Germany and the Soviet Union sign a treaty of nonaggression (the Molotov-Ribbentrop Pact), secretly defining "spheres of influence" over lands between the two countries (including the Baltic States) and a plan to partition Poland.

CHAPTER 3

September 1, 1939		Germany invades Poland. France and the United Kingdom declare war against Germany on September 3, starting World War II in Europe. Under occupation, Poland's 3.3 million Jews are immediately at risk.
October 8, 1939		The Nazi regime opens the first ghetto for Jews in German-occupied Poland. During World War II, Germany would establish more than 1,100 ghettos to separate Jews from non-Jews.
November 4, 1939	Congress passes a third Neutrality Act, lifting the arms embargo and putting all trade with belligerents on a "cash-and-carry" basis. US ships are banned from transporting goods to belligerent ports.	

TIMELINE

	United States	Germany/Europe
June 14, 1940		The first transport of prisoners arrives at the Nazi-operated Auschwitz concentration camp, a former army barracks complex near Oświęcim, in German-occupied Poland.
June–July 1940		The Nazi regime constructs the first crematorium at Auschwitz to burn the bodies of dead prisoners. Later, a large gas chamber that operated into 1942 was added to murder prisoners.
April 9, 1940		Germany invades Denmark and Norway; its occupation is complete by June 10.
May 10, 1940		Germany's invasion and occupation of France, Belgium, Luxembourg, and Netherlands begins. It is complete by June 25.
June 22, 1940		France signs an armistice with Germany, which then occupies north and west France. A collaborationist government controls southern France from the city of Vichy.
September 16, 1940	Congress enacts the first peacetime draft in US history. All men between the ages of 21 and 45 are required to register for military service.	
November 5, 1940	Franklin D. Roosevelt is reelected president for an unprecedented third term.	
March 11, 1941	The US government enacts the "Lend-Lease" policy to supply food, oil, and armaments to Allies in exchange for leases on army and navy bases in Allied territories. This policy effectively ends US neutrality.	

	United States	Germany/Europe
June 22, 1941		Germany invades the Soviet Union ("Operation Barbarossa") on three fronts. Germany's so-called mobile killing squads begin the mass murder of Jews in occupied lands.
June 1941		Germany orders the closing of all US consulates in Nazi-occupied territories, essentially ending immigration from most of Europe to the United States.
Fall 1941		Construction of the Chełmno killing center in occupied Poland begins. It becomes operational in December 1941.
October 1941		Construction of the Auschwitz-Birkenau killing center begins. Its first two gas chambers become operational in early 1942 and replace the killing operations at the Auschwitz concentration camp.
November 1941		Construction of the Bełżec killing center in occupied Poland begins. It becomes operational in March 1942.

CHAPTER 4

	United States	Germany/Europe
December 7, 1941	The US naval base at Pearl Harbor, Hawaii, is bombed by Japanese warplanes. The United States declares war on Japan on December 8. US military activity through most of 1942 focuses on the Pacific theater.	
December 11, 1941		Germany declares war on the United States, which responds by declaring war on Germany.

	United States	*Germany/Europe*
January 20, 1942		Nazi leaders meet at the Wannsee Conference to coordinate the implementation of the "Final Solution to the Jewish Question," the systematic murder of Europe's Jews.
By early 1942	*The Nazi regime and its collaborators have murdered more than one million eastern European Jews in mass shootings. Tens of thousands more have died of disease, starvation, or mistreatment in ghettos.*	
February 19, 1942	President Roosevelt signs Executive Order 9066, which is used to authorize the forced relocation of people of Japanese ancestry from their homes on the West Coast. Two-thirds of the approximately 120,000 people moved are American citizens.	
March 1942		Construction of the Sobibór killing center in occupied Poland begins. It becomes operational in May 1942.
March 1942		The Nazi regime constructs gas chambers at the Majdanek concentration camp in occupied Poland. They become operational in September 1942.
April 1942		Construction of the Treblinka killing center in occupied Poland begins. It becomes operational in July 1942.
November 8, 1942	US troops land in North Africa ("Operation Torch"), marking the entry of the United States into the European theater of war.	
November 24, 1942	Rabbi Stephen S. Wise tells the American press that the Nazi regime has a plan to murder all the Jews of Europe. The story appears in newspapers across the United States the next day.	

	United States	*Germany/Europe*
December 17, 1942	The United States and eleven Allied nations issue a joint declaration that denounces the "cold-blooded extermination" of Europe's Jews and promises to punish those responsible for the crimes.	
By February 1943	**The Nazi regime and its collaborators have murdered some 4.5 million Jews.**	
February 2, 1943		After six months of fighting and at a cost of nearly two million men, Germany's advance into the Soviet Union is stopped at Stalingrad; the Soviet counteroffensive from the east begins.
March 1943		Nazi officials close the Chełmno killing center. All the victims' bodies are exhumed and burned.
April 1943	Delegates from the United States and the United Kingdom meet in Bermuda to discuss the Jewish refugee crisis. The meeting fails to produce any plan to rescue Europe's Jews.	
Spring 1943		The Nazi regime constructs four large gas chambers and crematoria at the Auschwitz-Birkenau killing center. Fully operational by June, they replace the original two facilities.
End of June 1943		Nazi officials close and destroy the Bełżec killing center. An estimated 434,000 Jews were murdered there during its operations.
July 9, 1943	US and British troops land in Sicily ("Operation Husky") to begin the campaign to liberate Italy.	

	United States	Germany/Europe
Mid-October 1943		Nazi officials close and destroy the Sobibór killing center. At least 170,000 people and as many as 250,000 were murdered there.
October 19, 1943		The Treblinka killing center is also closed and dismantled, and its grounds are ploughed over to conceal its operations. At least 750,000 and as many as 925,000 people were murdered at Treblinka.
January 22, 1944	President Roosevelt signs Executive Order 9417 to establish the War Refugee Board, charged with the rescue and relief of victims of Nazi Germany's oppression.	
By June 1944	*The Nazi regime and its collaborators have murdered more than five million Jews.*	
June 4, 1944	US forces occupy Rome.	
June 6, 1944	Allied troops land in Normandy, France ("D-Day").	
June 23–mid-July, 1944		Nazi officials reopen the Chełmno killing center in order to murder some 25,000 Jews deported from the Łódź ghetto in occupied Poland.
July 24, 1944		The Majdanek concentration camp is captured nearly intact by the Soviet Army. Approximately 80,000 people were killed at Majdanek, 60,000 of whom were Jews.
August 15, 1944	Allied troops invade southern France.	
August 25, 1944	Allied troops liberate Paris.	
November 7, 1944	Franklin D. Roosevelt wins election to his fourth term as president.	

	United States	*Germany/Europe*
Early November 1944		Nazi officials cease use of the gas chambers at the Auschwitz-Birkenau killing center and begin to demolish them.
December 16, 1944– January 25, 1945		Germany begins a counteroffensive (which Americans call the "Battle of the Bulge") against the western Allies' advance on Germany.
January 18, 1945		The Nazi regime murders the last prisoners at the Chełmno killing center. At least 172,000 people were killed at Chełmno.
January 27, 1945		Soviet troops liberate the Auschwitz-Birkenau killing center. Some 960,000 Jews and 125,000 other victims (including non-Jewish Poles, Roma, Soviet POWs and civilians, and other Europeans) were killed before the Germans destroyed the last crematorium on January 20, 1945.
March 25, 1945	The US Army crosses the Rhine River into Germany.	
April 12, 1945	The Supreme Commander of Allied Forces in Europe, US General Dwight Eisenhower, tours the concentration camp at Ohrdruf, a subcamp of the Buchenwald network, which US troops had encountered on April 4.	
April 12, 1945	President Roosevelt dies of a cerebral hemorrhage; Harry S. Truman becomes president.	
April 16, 1945		Soviet troops begin the battle to capture Berlin. The Nazis surrender Berlin on May 2, 1945.

	United States	Germany/Europe
April 25, 1945	US and Soviet troops meet at the Elbe River in western Germany.	
April 30, 1945		Hitler commits suicide.
May 7, 1945		Germany surrenders. All official German military operations cease on May 8. The unconditional surrender is formally signed May 9, 1945. The war in Europe ends.
By war's end	*The Nazi regime and its collaborators have murdered six million Jews.*	

POSTSCRIPT

August 15, 1945	After the United States drops atomic bombs on Hiroshima (August 6) and Nagasaki (August 9), Japan announces its surrender, ending the war in the Pacific.	
November 20, 1945–October 1, 1946	The four-nation International Military Tribunal tries twenty-one "major war criminals" in Nuremberg, Germany.	
December 22, 1945	Truman Directive grants "displaced persons" preference under the quota immigration system.	

AMERICANS AND THE HOLOCAUST

Two Nations, 1918–1932

World War I—the "war to end all wars" (1914–18)—reshaped the Western world. Some sixty-five million men from sixteen countries were mobilized for military service. More than 8.5 million—perhaps as many as 9.5 million—died in battle or from disease; 21 million were wounded.[1] The "Great War" destroyed the three European empires of Austria-Hungary, Russia, and Germany, while witnessing the emergence of the United States as an international financial and industrial power. The victorious allies—France, the United Kingdom, Italy, and the late-to-enter United States under Democratic president Woodrow Wilson—laid full blame for the ruinous war at Germany's feet. The humiliation would mark Germany for a generation.

Recovery, 1918–1929

United States

America's relationship to Europe's war had been complicated from the outset. Initially, President Woodrow Wilson insisted on neutrality, but neutrality did not preclude assistance. During the first years of war, the United States made extensive loans to the embattled Allies who, in turn, bought vast quantities of US-produced munitions, raw materials, and food. As a result, the war created an economic boom. But in 1917, when Germany's fleet of submarines attacked and sank American merchant ships carrying war supplies to Great Britain, public opinion quickly turned in favor of joining the Allies, and President Wilson pushed for a declaration of war in April. During the following year and a half, millions of federal dollars poured into the wartime economy and more than 4.3 million US soldiers mobilized for service abroad. Their presence as much-needed replacements for diminished British and French forces proved critical in the final campaigns that defeated Germany and its

---

1. War Department, General Staff, Statistics Branch, "Military Casualties–World War–Estimates," February 25, 1924, box 4, Campbell B. Hodges Papers, Archives & Special Collections, US Military Academy Library; Adam Hochschild, *To End All Wars: A Story of Loyalty and Rebellion, 1914–1919* (Boston: Houghton Mifflin, 2011), xv, 347.

allies. Hostilities came to an end on November 11, 1918, by which time the United States had established itself as a formidable actor in international relations.

For the next eight months, President Wilson worked with the other Allied leaders to set terms for a lasting peace in the Treaty of Versailles, which was signed on June 28, 1919. The treaty included a proposal for a new international body, the League of Nations, intended to work collectively to resolve disputes among nations. Many Americans, however, saw the League as a reversal of the nation's traditional isolation from international politics and even as a threat to its sovereignty. The legislative bill to ratify the treaty and join the League of Nations failed to get the two-thirds majority vote for approval from the US Senate, a stunning defeat for Wilson. The United States quickly became isolationist again.

The push to return to a peacetime way of life was immediately challenged by the onset of a significant economic recession as the demand for armaments vanished. But peacetime production gradually was restored by 1923. For the rest of the "Roaring Twenties," the US mass-production economy of automobiles, radios, airplanes, and a host of new consumer products grew steadily.

The renewed isolationism was accompanied by another wave of warnings about foreign influence on the United States, especially fear of immigrants. Many Americans focused on the perceived negative social and cultural impact that immigrants from central, southern, and eastern Europe—particularly Jews, Catholics, and Slavs—was having on the historically Anglo-Saxon Protestant US culture. (Between 1900 and 1910, nearly 7.5 million people, 80 percent of all European immigrants to the United States, came from those regions.[2]) This increasingly xenophobic climate also saw the spread of widely believed "scientific" notions of eugenics. In particular, the assertion that northern and western European ethnic groups or "races" were inherently superior to the "undesirable" southern and eastern Europeans took hold among many influential Americans and aligned with racist attitudes more generally. Moreover, the collapse of the Russian Empire in the 1917 Bolshevik (Communist) Revolution raised fears that Russian agents intended to radicalize US workers and political anarchists into a violent overthrow of the government.

In May 1921, Congress passed and President Warren G. Harding signed the so-called Emergency Quota Act. For the first time, the government set numerical limits, a quota, on immigrant admissions to the United States from each country in Europe. (Existing immigration restrictions from parts of Asia and Africa continued.) The act drastically cut European immigration to just 356,000 persons per year.[3] This

2. US Department of Commerce, Bureau of the Census (with the cooperation of the Social Science Research Council), *Historical Statistics of the United States 1789–1945* (Washington, DC: USGPO, 1949), 33.

3. "An Act to limit the immigration of aliens into the United States," *US Statutes at Large* 42 (Washington, DC: USGPO, 1923): 5–7. The 1921 quotas were set at 3 percent of the number of foreign-born US residents per nation as tallied in the 1920 census.

temporary act was renewed and made even more restrictive with the Immigration Act of 1924[4] (signed by President Calvin Coolidge) that further reduced immigration, roughly by half. This 1924 law—also known as the National Origins Act or the Johnson-Reed Act—stipulated that total annual immigration would be reduced to approximately 150,000 after July 1927.[5] This final count dramatically favored western and northern Europeans, providing them with two-thirds of the allowable immigration quotas and allocating just one-third to central, southern, and eastern European nations. By 1929, Germany's yearly quota was 25,957 visas, 17 percent of the annual total, and the second highest of any nation.[6]

These urges to restrict immigrants from entering the United States were, of course, nothing new. The nation's majority White Anglo-Saxon Protestant culture included deeply ingrained discrimination and persecution of African Americans, Jews, Catholics, and Indigenous peoples. Post-Civil War "Jim Crow" laws throughout the American South legally separated Black Americans from Whites and denied equal opportunity under the law. Racial discrimination enshrined in law was regularly enforced by gruesome public lynchings. Property-ownership documents banned Blacks, Jews, and Catholics from entire neighborhoods across the nation, North and South, and members of these groups were either restricted or prohibited from participating in a wide range of public social institutions. Antisemitism was on the rise throughout the 1920s and into the 1930s, manifesting in questions about Jews' loyalty to the United States, efforts to brand them as Communists, and vicious lies about imagined, secret Jewish conspiracies to control the world.

Germany

The last weeks of World War I for Germany were calamitous. The war had caused extreme burdens and worsened social tensions among classes, raising the specter that a revolution, like the 1917 Russian Revolution, might occur. On November 9, 1918—two days before an armistice ended the war—leaders of the nation's parliament

4. "An Act to limit the immigration of aliens into the United States, and for other purposes," *US Statutes at Large* 43 (Washington, DC: USGPO, 1925): 153–69. This law restructured the quota formula to limit immigration to 2 percent of the foreign-born residents by nation in the 1890 census, which predated—and thereby removed from the calculations—the huge wave of immigrants from southern and eastern Europe.

5. *Ibid.*, Sec. 11(b), 159. The formula was again changed, to a proportion of the 150,000-person limit based on the national origin of *all* US residents—not just the foreign-born—as enumerated in the 1920 census.

6. *Ibid.* The 1927 quotas were not enacted until March 22, 1929, by executive order of President Herbert Hoover, just weeks into his new administration (1929–33). Total "national origin" counts were to be determined from historical immigration and emigration records and census data. Herbert Hoover, *Proclamations and Executive Orders: Herbert Hoover, March 4, 1929 to March 4, 1933,* vol. 1 (Washington, DC: USGPO, 1974), 7–10.

declared Germany to be a republic. Emperor Wilhelm II was forced to abdicate, ending the empire's federal monarchy.[7] The recovery would be long and difficult.

Defining the nature and operation of the new republican government fell to nationally elected representatives who assembled in the city of Weimar in spring 1919 to draft a new constitution. As events in Germany between 1919 and 1933 would prove, the new structure contained elements that became critical weaknesses. The Weimar Constitution established the executive office of Reich president, elected for a seven-year term, who would appoint a chancellor to direct the numerous government ministries responsible for administering national law. The new constitution permitted proportional representation to the Reichstag for all political parties that won a minimum threshold of votes. In practice, this allowed parties with as few as 60,000 votes to gain a seat in the legislature. As a result of this segmentation, no single party ever won a majority of seats during the Weimar era, and the coalitions of dissimilar blocs necessary to govern were often too fragile to be sustained.

As Germany wrote its new constitution, the Allies determined the peace. The Treaty of Versailles compelled Germany to cede territory to Poland, Czechoslovakia, Belgium, and France and limit its army to 100,000 men. Germany and its allies were deemed responsible for the war and required to pay reparations for the Allies' costs. German leaders who refused to accept the defeat rallied opposition to these terms.

Postwar Germany faced debilitating economic problems as it struggled to return to peacetime production and absorb millions of demobilized soldiers into the workforce. The government turned to printing more money, yielding a hyperinflation that devalued the *reichsmark* (RM) from 320 RM to one US dollar in mid-1922 to 4.2 *trillion* RM to one dollar by late 1923. Reparations alone did not cause Germany's economic woes—the debt was reduced and eased by substantial loans from the United States, and Germany ended up paying only a small part of the bill—but reparations remained a bitter subject within Germany.

Fundamental differences about politics, ideology, and the economy fractured the Weimar Republic. From the earliest days, the radical left attacked the new system, stressing the solidarity of the German "proletariat" in the international class struggle against capitalist exploitation. But increasingly it was the right, which envisioned a "superior" Germanic nation, that threatened the democratic regime. For opponents of Weimar, widespread discontent with the Treaty of Versailles and the restrictions it imposed became a potent political weapon.

In Munich, Bavaria, one fringe right-wing group formed the German Workers' Party in January 1919. Among its adherents was a thirty-year-old former army corporal named Adolf Hitler, who proved to be a persuasive spokesman. By 1921, Hitler

7. A federation of states, either monarch-led (kingdoms, principalities, duchies) or not, with a single monarch as overall head.

became leader of the party, renamed the National Socialist German Workers' Party (Nationalsozialistische Deutsche Arbeiterpartei, NSDAP, or "Nazi" for short).[8]

Continuing economic challenges reached a crisis point in January 1923, when France accused Germany of defaulting on its reparation payments and sent troops to occupy the industrial Ruhr region and seize its coal mines for payment "in kind." France's action led to an upsurge in Germans' nationalist sentiment, which benefitted the Nazi Party. Emboldened by growing popular support for his outspoken opposition to the Treaty of Versailles, Hitler and his political ally, war hero General Erich Ludendorff, led an attempted coup (*putsch*) in Munich on November 8–9, 1923. They hoped to overthrow the Weimar democracy and gain support from the Bavarian state government. Weimar government forces quickly quashed the revolt. Two days later, Hitler was arrested and charged with treason. During the much-publicized trial, Hitler seized moments to expound on his political views before a national audience. The court found Hitler guilty of high treason and sentenced him to five years in Landsberg prison. But his imprisonment lasted only eight months and provided him the opportunity to write *Mein Kampf* ("My Struggle"), a manifesto outlining his political and antisemitic views for the future of Germany.

After his imprisonment, Hitler moved his party from a strategy of revolution to seeking power from within the government he hated. Slates of Nazi Party candidates ran in four Reichstag elections between 1924 and 1928, but never won more than a handful of seats. Nevertheless, the NSDAP had established a foothold in Germany's national politics.

The Great Depression, 1929–1933

United States

The collapse of the US stock market in late October 1929 began the years-long, worldwide Great Depression. The booming economy of the Roaring Twenties had encouraged overly optimistic speculation in the stock market. When stock prices began to fall in September, panic selling set in. During the four-day crash (October 24–27), the key market indicator, the Dow Jones Industrial Average, dropped by 25 percent, losing the equivalent of nearly $450 billion in 2020 dollars. By early July 1932, the market was down 90 percent from its peak. Banks and businesses failed in great numbers, unemployment rose to nearly 30 percent—12.8 million workers—by 1933, and wages for those still working dropped precipitously.[9]

8. On Hitler's early career, see Michael Burleigh, *The Third Reich: A New History* (New York: Hill and Wang, 2000), 84–121.

9. "Great Depression Facts," FDRL, https://www.fdrlibrary.org/great-depression-facts.

Republican president Herbert Hoover, inaugurated in March 1929 before the crash, sought to engage businesses and corporations in voluntary financial programs rather than push for government intervention to stabilize the economy. But the programs failed to substantially raise the production and consumption necessary to offset the economy's significant weaknesses. Hoover's administration enacted Republican-backed protectionist tariffs on a range of foreign goods in hopes of stimulating consumption of American goods, but these tariffs instead yielded retaliatory tariffs from other nations that further damaged the already deteriorating international trade.

Facing continuing high unemployment in mid-1930, Hoover returned to the postwar policy of limiting immigration. He informally suggested Congress consider cutting the existing quotas by half for a year, but Congress took no action.[10] At a press conference in September 1930, Hoover announced he had instructed the State Department "to tighten up" on the 1924 immigration law's "exclusion of those who are liable to become public charges."[11] Under Hoover's direction, the State Department would more vigorously exclude immigrants who might become dependent on public or private assistance after arriving in the United States. Thereafter, applicants for immigration visas had to present evidence of sufficient personal financial means or, later, present an affidavit from a US citizen who would provide any necessary support. The requirement resulted in a 90 percent drop in European immigrants from 1930 to 1933, far below the available annual legal quotas.[12]

By the time Hoover sought a second presidential term in fall 1932, public opinion had turned strongly against him for ineffectively addressing the widespread despair. He lost the presidency in a landslide to Franklin Delano Roosevelt, the Democratic governor of New York, on November 8, 1932.

Germany

The Great Depression came more slowly to Germany, reaching a crisis point in May 1931. The collapse that month of the most important bank in central Europe precipitated its spread. Like in the United States, banks and businesses failed rapidly. German unemployment, still at somewhat high levels after its own postwar depression, skyrocketed to nearly 30 percent—at least 5.5 million workers—by early 1932. Declines in consumer goods production brought about scarcities, and wage drops for the employed workers contributed to the much-lowered standard of living. State welfare

10. Department of State, Report on Immigration, released at a Hoover press conference on September 9, 1930, in Herbert Hoover, *Public Papers of the Presidents of the United States: Herbert Hoover, 1929–33*, vol. 3 (Washington, DC: USGPO, 1976): 365.

11. *Ibid.*, p. 363. This exclusion had been specified in all US immigration laws since 1882 but without uniformly close enforcement.

12. Department of Commerce, *Historical Statistics 1789–1945*, 33.

services proved incapable of providing more than minimal aid to the suffering German people. The economic dislocations hit men between ages 18 and 30 particularly hard; to fill their free time, many took to various political activities, including the militarily disciplined fighting organizations for the Nazi Party (the *Sturmabteilung*, or S.A.) on the far right, and for the Social Democratic Party and the German Communist Party on the left. Street fighting among these groups, and with the local police, along with political agitation for revolutionary change gave meaning to tens of thousands of young peoples' lives.[13]

In contrast to other nations, Germany's depression triggered a major political crisis that threatened the Weimar Republic and constitution. From mid-1930 to early 1933, the Weimar government lurched through four chancellor resignations, three dissolutions of the Reichstag that required new national elections, and the conclusion of President Paul von Hindenburg's first seven-year term as president. German leaders struggled to manage the continuing crisis, but the nation gradually slid toward authoritarianism as democracy and cooperative coalition-building among the deeply divided political parties failed.

Article 48 of the Weimar Constitution played a central role in this collapse. It granted the German president extraordinary powers to rule without the consent of the Reichstag:

> In case public safety is seriously threatened or disturbed, the Reich President may take the measures necessary to reestablish law and order, if necessary using armed force. In the pursuit of this aim he may suspend the civil rights described in Articles 114 [individual liberty], 115 [inviolability of a person's home], 117 [privacy of personal correspondence], 118 [freedom of speech], 123 [freedom of peaceable and unarmed assembly], 153 [freedom to own property], partially or entirely.[14]

The article was tested in the summer of 1930, when the Reichstag rejected a government-proposed budget program. In response, the chancellor—with the president's tacit blessing—dissolved parliament, called for new elections, and put its plan into effect by decree.[15] The September 1930 Reichstag elections fundamentally weakened its ability to function. While the center-left Social Democratic Party won the plurality of the Reichstag's seats, the far-right Nazi Party became the second largest bloc in the body, while the far-left Communist Party finished third. The several nonradical parties that together had enabled the Reichstag to function lost their working majority. And neither the Nazis nor the Communists were willing to work with other parties.

---

13. Detlev J. K. Peukert, *The Weimar Republic* (New York: Hill and Wang, 1993), 252–55.

14. "The Reich Constitution of August 11th 1919 (Weimar Constitution)," translation by the Deutsche Historisches Museum–Berlin, https://www.zum.de/psm/weimar/weimar_vve.php.

15. Peukert, *Weimar Republic*, 258.

As a result, both the president and the chancellor gained a freer hand to use Article 48 to rule.

Economic damage spread throughout Germany in 1931 and 1932, and two more elections revealed the popular will for more radical political solutions—including astounding support for Hitler and the NSDAP. In spring 1932, Hitler and two other candidates sought the national presidency against incumbent Hindenburg. Hitler barnstormed the country on an airplane and spoke before hundreds of enthusiastic rallies in a modern, well-targeted, and highly effective campaign.[16] In the March 1932 election, Hitler won 30.1 percent of the popular vote; Hindenburg's 49.6 percent was just shy of the majority needed to win. In the April run-off election, Hitler increased his tally to 36.8 percent, but fell well short of Hindenburg's 53 percent. A new Reichstag election in July 1932 dramatically reinforced the Nazi Party's growing political position: in that race, the NSDAP gained the largest plurality in parliament at nearly 38 percent.

While the 1932 elections were not outright victories for Hitler, they nevertheless gave his party enormous influence that President Hindenburg and his advisers could no longer ignore. Hitler was twice offered positions in the government (as vice-chancellor in August 1932 and as chancellor in November), but he refused because accepting would have put limits on his authority. Hindenburg again offered Hitler the chancellorship in 1933, hoping that the Nazi leader and the NSDAP members of the Reichstag could be controlled. That expectation turned out to be badly mistaken.

Milestones for both the United States and Germany came in early 1933—the starting point for the main focus of this book. On January 30, Adolf Hitler was named Germany's chancellor, the head of its government. Six weeks later, on March 4, Franklin D. Roosevelt took the oath of office as the 32nd President of the United States, famously telling Americans that the only thing they had to fear was "fear itself." Nobody who observed these two new national leaders could have known then that the actions of Chancellor Hitler and Germany would pose such profound challenges to President Roosevelt and the United States. Nor could Americans—or even Nazi ideologues themselves—have predicted that the Nazi regime eventually would implement a plan to murder all the Jews of Europe.

Adolf Hitler: Bavaria's Rebel

Adolf Hitler received intermittent attention from the American press well before he became Germany's chancellor in 1933. The two newspaper articles below, written by foreign correspondents for the *New York Times* and *Chicago Daily Tribune* respectively,

---

16. Steven Luckert and Susan Bachrach/USHMM, *State of Deception: The Power of Nazi Propaganda* (Washington, DC: USHMM, 2010), 48–61.

report on Hitler's growing popularity in the southern German state of Bavaria in the early 1920s, noting especially the party's efficient use of propaganda and effective organization, as well as Hitler's hatred for Jews. The *Tribune* correspondent also focuses on the inspiration that Hitler took from American automobile industrialist Henry Ford. Hitler especially lauded Ford's "anti-Jewish platform" and, for that reason, admired his influence in America.

1.

NEW POPULAR IDOL RISES IN BAVARIA

Hitler Credited With Extraordinary Powers of Swaying Crowds to His Will.

FORMS GRAY-SHIRTED ARMY

Armed With Blackjacks and Revolvers and Well Disciplined, They Obey Orders Implicitly.

LEADER A REACTIONARY

Is Anti-Red and Anti-Semitic, and Demands Strong Government for a United Germany.

By Cyril Brown.

MUNICH, Nov. 20.—Next to the high cost of living and the dollar, "Der Hitler" and his "Hakenkreuzlers" [swastika-men] are the popular topic of talk in Munich and other Bavarian towns. This reactionary Nationalistic anti-Semitic movement has now reached a point where it is considered potentially dangerous, though not for the immediate future.

Hitler today is taken seriously among all classes of Bavarians. He is feared by some, enthusiastically hailed as a prophet and political economic savior by others, and watched with increasing sympathetic interest by the bulk who, apparently, are merely biding the psychological moment to mount Hitler's bandwagon. Undoubtedly the spectacular success of Mussolini and the Fascisti[17] brought Hitler's movement to the fore and gained popular interest and sympathy for it. Another condition favorable to the outburst of the movement is the widespread discontent with the existing state of affairs among all classes in the towns and cities under the increasing economic pressure. [. . .] As a highly placed personage put it:

"Hitler organized a small insignificant group of National Socialists two years ago, since when the movement has been smoldering beneath the surface. Now it has eaten

---

17. Benito Mussolini (1883–1945): founder of Italy's National Fascist Party, prime minister in the Italian government in 1922, and fascist dictator after 1925 who controlled Italy until his dismissal, arrest, and execution in April 1945.

its way through, and a conflagration of course is not only possible but certain if this now free flame of fanatical patriotism finds sufficient popular combustible material to feed on."

Hitler [. . .] is wasting no time working out political programs, but devotes his whole energy to recruiting fresh forces and perfecting his organization.

Blackjacks Silence Opposition.

[. . .] His simple method is, first, propaganda, and secondly, efficient organization. He personally conducts patriotic revival meetings for this purpose, often descending from his stronghold, Munich, on other Bavarian towns with special trainloads of followers. He has the rare oratorical gift, at present unique in Germany, of spell-binding whole audiences regardless of politics or creed. The new converts made at these rallies, those who absolutely and unconditionally pledge themselves to Hitler and the cause, are carefully sifted through and the pick of them who pass the standard military muster are organized into "storm troops" with gray shirts, brassards [armbands] in the old imperial colors, [a black and] anti-Semitic Swastika cross in a white circular field on red; [they are] armed also with blackjacks and, it is popularly whispered, revolvers.

Hitler, in addition to his oratorical and organizing abilities, has another positive asset—he is a man of the "common people" and hence has the makings of a "popular hero," appealing to all classes. It is reported that he was a worker before becoming leader of the Bavarian Social Nationalists. He served during the war as a common soldier and won the Iron Cross of the First and Second Classes, which for a common soldier is distinctive evidence of exceptional bravery and daring. To Bavarian mentality he talks rough, shaggy, sound horse sense, and according to present Bavarian public opinion a strong, active leader equipped with horse sense is the need of the hour.

Chief Points of His Program.

Hitler's program is of less interest than his person and movement. His program consists chiefly of half a dozen negative ideas clothed in generalities. He is "against the Jews, Communists, Bolshevism, Marxian socialism, Separatists, the high cost of living, existing conditions, the weak Berlin Government and the Versailles Treaty." Positively he stands only for "a strong united Germany under a strong Government."

He is credibly credited with being actuated by lofty, unselfish patriotism. He probably does not know himself just what he wants to accomplish. The keynote of his propaganda in speaking and writing is violent anti-Semitism. [. . .] But several reliable, well-informed sources confirmed the idea that Hitler's anti-Semitism was not so genuine or violent as it sounded, and that he was merely using anti-Semitic propaganda as a bait to catch masses of followers and keep them aroused, enthusiastic and in line for the time when his organization is perfected and sufficiently powerful to be employed effectively for political purposes.

A sophisticated politician credited Hitler with peculiar political cleverness for laying emphasis and over-emphasis on anti-Semitism, saying, "You can't expect the masses to understand or appreciate your finer real aims. You must feed the masses with cruder morsels and ideas like anti-Semitism. It would be politically all wrong to tell them the truth about where you really are leading them."

The Hitler movement is not of mere local or picturesque interest. It is bound to bring Bavaria into a renewed clash with the Berlin Government as long as the German Republic goes even through the motions of trying to live up to the Versailles Treaty. For it is certain the Allies will take umbrage at the Hitler organization as a violation of the military clauses of the treaty and demand disbandment. [. . .]

—*New York Times*, November 21, 1922, 21.

2.

"HEINRICH" FORD IDOL OF BAVARIA FASCISTI CHIEF
Anti-Jewish Articles Circulate by Millions.
By Raymond Fendrick.

MUNICH, March 7.—"Heinrich" Ford of Detroit will have 100 per cent moral support of Adolf Hittler's [*sic*] Deutschen Arbeiterpartei [German Workers' Party] if he runs for President.[18]

"I wish that I could send some of my shock troops to Chicago and other big American cities to help in the elections," the young leader of the Bavarian Fascisti party said grimly. "We look on Heinrich Ford as the leader of the growing Fascisti movement in America. We admire particularly his anti-Jewish policy which is the Bavarian Fascisti platform. We have just had his anti-Jewish articles translated and published. The book is being circulated to millions throughout Germany."

"The International Jew."
The articles which Herr Hittler referred to evidently were from the Dearborn Independent. They have been published in two volumes by Hammer-Verlag of Leipzig and are displayed in every bookshop in southern Germany. The title is "The International Jew," with Henry Ford's name on the front page as the author.[19]

18. Ford's success as an industrialist led to unsuccessful efforts to recruit him to run for the US presidency in 1924.

19. *The International Jew*, a four-volume reprint (Dearborn, MI.: Dearborn Publishing Company, 1920–22) of a series of articles that appeared in *The Dearborn Independent* newspaper, published by Ford, in 1920.

"It is not true that Mr. Ford is backing the Fascisti movement in Germany financially," said Herr Hittler, but "Heinrich's" picture occupies the place of honor in Herr Hittler's sanctum.

If Mr. Ford is not the angel of Herr Hittler's Fascisti, in spite of story [*sic*] of the Bavarian government to the contrary, huge sums are coming from somewhere.

House Painter's Dream.

The Bavarian Fascisti party, officially known as the Deutschen Arbeiter-partei, apparently is made up of all the idlers and others with an adventurous heart in Munich and other Bavarian towns. It probably would have remained obscure, if hatred had not been stirred up again in Germany. The French occupation, however, has proved a boon for Herr Hittler, who is becoming a national hero, although actually he was a house painter from Vienna and a former Austrian citizen.

Herr Hittler's organization, which includes 5,000 shock troops uniformed in gray, is spreading by leaps and bounds throughout Germany. He has a large organization in Munich sending out Mr. Ford's books and other Bavarian Fascisti propaganda by the car loads.

The nationalist wave has put the movement on a much higher plane.

Why He Opposes Jews.

"We are against the Jews because they are responsible for internationalism, and we have already chased all Jews from Munich, except the more serious nationalistic Jews," Herr Hittler added.

"I wish to become a German citizen, but I do not intend to ask the Jewish government in Berlin for this favor.[20]

"We are opposed to swarms of Americans and other foreigners raising prices throughout Germany while millions of Germans are starving because of the increased prices. We are equally opposed to German profiteers, and we are demanding that all be imprisoned."

Against Ruhr Armies.

The character of Herr Hittler's movement originally was socialistic and pacific, but the success which was brought by the nationalistic movement in Germany following the occupation has given it a strongly military character directed against France and Belgium.

—*Chicago Daily Tribune*, March 8, 1923, 2.

20. Austrian-born Hitler moved to Munich, Germany, in 1913 and served in the German Army during the war. In 1925, he petitioned to be released from his Austrian citizenship and became officially "stateless" until he was granted German citizenship in February 1932.

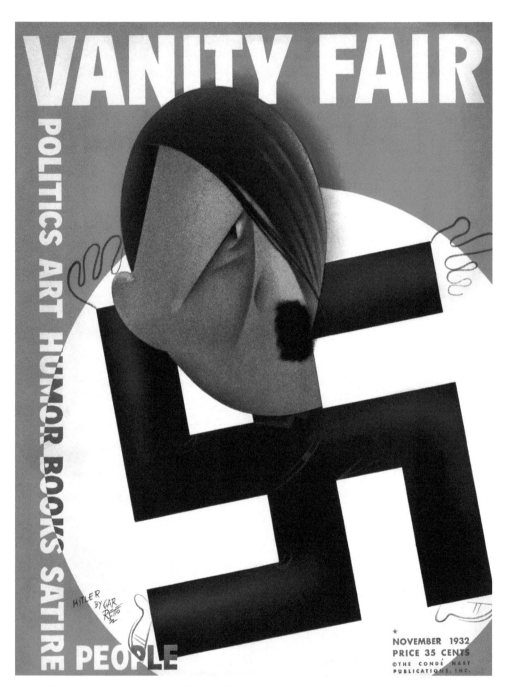

Paolo Garretto, caricature of Adolf Hitler for *Vanity Fair*, November 1932.

CHAPTER 1

Fear Itself, 1933–1938

The presidential inauguration of Franklin Roosevelt in March 1933 coincided with the lowest point of the Great Depression in the United States. Most of his administration's time and attention for the next five years focused on addressing the nation's devastating economic woes and the resultant miseries of unemployment, poverty, and hunger. The demands for massive, innovative government domestic policies—known as the "New Deal"—led Americans to look inward, pushing most action on foreign affairs to the sidelines and reinforcing the tradition of isolationism.

Nevertheless, Roosevelt, a firm believer in internationalist solutions to the world's problems, made some careful foreign policy moves to aid the domestic recovery through the opening of new markets for US goods. But Congress, wary of rising militarism in Germany, Italy, and Japan[1] and gripped by isolationism, passed a series of Neutrality Acts in 1935, 1936, and 1937 that prevented the United States from providing support, either materially or financially, to foreign nations involved in war.

Despite the profound isolationism of the mid-1930s, world events did remain on view to the broad American public if and when they chose to observe them. At several moments in the 1930s, reports from within Nazi Germany about the regime's persecution of Jews generated concern and even public outcries from Americans for action. Yet despite some important acts of protest, Americans did not mount a sustained anti-Nazi movement between 1933 and 1938.

American Jewish leaders hoped to persuade the US government to condemn the Nazi persecution of Jews in Germany but disagreed on tactics. Some favored public demonstrations such as rallies or marches, but others advocated working more quietly behind the scenes, perhaps concerned about playing into widespread antisemitic stereotypes that grossly exaggerated Jewish influence in the United States. (Jews

---

1. Germany had covertly begun rebuilding its military in violation of the Treaty of Versailles throughout the 1920s, but in March 1935, Hitler made public a massive expansion of the rearmament efforts. Fascist Italy invaded and colonized Ethiopia in 1935 and established Italian East Africa. In 1931, Imperial Japan invaded Manchuria in northeast China, an act of aggression that in 1937 became a war between the two nations.

made up less than 4 percent of the American population during the 1930s.[2]) With antisemitism in the United States at a historic high, few Americans took an interest in the concerns of the nation's small Jewish community or a persecuted Jewish minority in a foreign country.

Popular American newsmagazines reported almost weekly on Hitler and Nazi Germany throughout 1933. Some articles questioned whether Hitler would remain in power. Others claimed that his ambitions for Germany were truly dangerous, especially for the 525,000 Jews living there.

This *Newsweek* magazine article, published less than two months after Hitler became Germany's chancellor, includes a number of "striking themes" that would define the Nazi Party's twelve-year rule: the dismantling of Germany's democracy, propaganda spread by Germany's leaders, rule by terror, the plight of refugees, and the threat of murder in retaliation for disobedience to Nazism.

1.

A Week's Vignettes of Nazi-Land
Hitlerite Raids Less Frequent, but Attacks on Marxists and Anti-Semitic Campaign Still in Full Force

Striking themes in the German news medley were these:

Before the new Reichstag elected Mar. 5 met in the Garrison Church at Potsdam Tuesday, it was revealed that the Hitler government would ask it for the powers of a dictator.

No one doubted that they would be granted, though that means the end of parliamentary democracy in Germany and the creation of another Fascist State essentially similar to Italy.

The bill which Hitler requested the Reichstag to pass consists of five articles.[3] The first and second authorize the Hitler cabinet to enact laws within the constitution and, except when they violate rights of the President, Reichstag or Reichsrat (Upper Chamber), without it as well.

The third specifies when laws drafted by the Chancellor shall take effect, empowers him to sign laws previously signed by the President and junks most of Germany's

2. H. S. Linfield, "Jewish Communities of the United States," *American Jewish Year Book* 42 (Philadelphia: Jewish Publication Society of America, 1940): 222.

3. The Law to Remedy the Distress of the People and Reich, generally called the Enabling Act, was passed by both houses of the German legislature and signed by President Hindenburg on March 23, 1933.

law-making machinery. The fourth enables the government to make treaties without the Reichstag's consent. The fifth states that the whole measure shall remain in effect until Apr. 1, 1937, unless another Reichstag succeeds this one meanwhile.[4]

Invited

In short, Hitler invited Parliament to legislate itself out of existence. Under his policy, it would meet only when he directed. [Fascist Italian dictator] Mussolini could ask no more.

• A fourth Nazi entered the Nazi-Nationalist Cabinet when President von Hindenburg made Paul Joseph Goebbels Minister of Public Enlightenment and Propaganda. National Socialists rank him only a step below Hitler. He is their propagandist-in-chief.

A strange figure, frail and undersized, with a clubfoot, he seems chiefly composed of nose, nerves, and energy. He is 35 years old. Fire-spitting spell-binder, ex-poet, ex-playwright, editor of a blazing Nazi newspaper in Berlin, Dr. Goebbels, Ph. D. Heidelberg, will be the Hitler government's glorified press-agent.

Henceforth

Henceforth, he says, "the press must be the keyboard on which the government can play." One of his plans is to broadcast a daily "cultural" radio program to the United States, featuring music and "objective" news flashes.

• Little by little Nazi violence ebbed, leaving appalling high water marks behind it. Wilhelm Frick, Nazi Minister of the Interior,[5] ordered State governments to curb bands of Brown Shirts[6] who have been bedeviling retail stores. Nazi hostility toward department and chain stores is to be sublimated into a special tax.

Hermann Wilhelm Goering, Nazi Minister of the Interior for Prussia,[7] forbade Nazis to interfere unofficially with municipal activities, courts, theaters, and opera houses. Last week the interfering was done officially. Both the Dresden State Opera and the Berlin Civic Opera were compelled to replace employees with National Socialists.

---

4. The law was renewed in 1937 and 1939 by the all-Nazi Reichstag, renewed by Hitler's decree in 1941, and made "perpetual" by Hitler in 1943.

5. Wilhelm Frick (1877–1946): Reich Minister of the Interior from Hitler's accession to the chancellorship in January 1933 to 1943. He developed many of the Nazi regime's major laws.

6. The "brown shirts" (named for the color of their uniforms): members of the Nazi Party's paramilitary "storm troops," the *Sturmabteilung* or SA. The party's use of this often violent and undisciplined force against political opponents was a major factor in the Nazis' rise to prominence. The SA remained a politically important and independent organization until 1936, when it was incorporated under the Nazi Party's SS (*Schutzstaffel*), the protection squad for Hitler.

7. Hermann Goering (Göring in German; 1893–1946): an early member of the Nazi Party and a participant in the failed "Beer Hall Putsch" of 1923. After 1933, he held a number of major posts in government, including president of the Reichstag, founder of the Gestapo, and commander of the Luftwaffe, the German air force.

Bruno Walter, Jewish conductor, fresh from a season in New York, was forbidden to direct concerts in Leipzig, Berlin, and Frankfurt.

• More acts of terrorism interrupted the trend back to order. In Cologne, Nazis entered the home of a German merchant, forced him to open his safe and fled with 800 marks. Three of them, seized by other Nazis in compliance with Hitler's recent manifesto, were stripped of their brown shirts and turned over to the police.

Ransacked

In Berlin, another Nazi band ransacked the apartment of Frau Ebert, widow of Friedrich Ebert, first President of the Republic,[8] demanding her "mustard (Republican) flag." President von Hindenburg deplored their "unchivalrous" conduct and ordered an investigation.

In Berlin, too, it was learned last week, Nazis raided the house of Lion Feuchtwanger, Jewish novelist, making off with his automobile and the manuscript of a novel, the sequel to "Josephus." Prudently, Doctor Feuchtwanger, now in Switzerland, had not returned home from his recent trip to New York, where, deriding Hitler, he had declared that the Chancellor's book, "My Struggle," contained 139,900 mistakes in its 140,000 words.

On Monday, police and Brown Shirts raided Albert Einstein's country home outside Potsdam.[9] Incredibly, they were searching for arms and ammunition. They found a bread knife.

• Details of the Nazi reign of terror following Hitler's Mar. 5 election triumph[10] filtered out as thousands of refugees reached neighboring countries. Vienna became a clearing house for their stories of horror as they swarmed into Austria. They told of Communists, Socialists, Liberals, and Jews who had been jailed, beaten, and tortured. Other refugees streamed into France with further details, still others into Poland, where Jews began to boycott German goods. [. . .]

"We are going to extirpate Marxism," shouted Captain Goering last week. "I am going to keep my fist on the neck of these creatures until they are finished. We . . . are going to tear the word Marxism out of every book."

By his own testimony there are now "from 80,000 to 100,000" political prisoners in Germany. On Monday it was announced that they would soon be placed in concentration camps.

Political prisoners who are National Socialists, however, are being paroled and will soon be pardoned. [. . .]

8. Friedrich Ebert (1871–1925): prominent leader of the Social Democratic Party of Germany, the Weimar Republic's first chancellor (1918–19) and first elected president (after 1919) until his death.

9. Albert Einstein (1879–1955): perhaps the most famous physicist of the twentieth century. He was visiting the United States when his home was ransacked. He quickly renounced his German citizenship, obtained a position at Princeton University, and in 1940 became an American citizen.

10. In the March 5, 1933, national Reichstag election, the Nazi Party won 44 percent of the seats and became the largest bloc in the parliament, though it fell short of a majority.

• According to Chief of Police Himmler of Munich,[11] three men, who escaped after an automobile chase through the city, planned to assassinate Chancellor Hitler Monday as he left his Munich home to fly to Berlin. At the first shot fired at Hitler, Herr Himmler says, "Such fury would overcome most of the people that we should witness a massacre and pogrom such as the world has never seen."

—*News-Week,* March 25, 1933, 13–14.

Images of Adolf Hitler and other Nazi Party leaders appeared on many popular American magazine covers during the 1930s. The July 10, 1933, issue of *Time* magazine featured German Minister of Public Enlightenment and Propaganda Joseph Goebbels above the caption, "Say it in your dreams: 'THE JEWS ARE TO BLAME.'"

11. Heinrich Himmler (1900–1945): an early member of the Nazi Party's SS. He expanded it and gained total authority over Germany's police organizations until the end of the Nazi regime in 1945. He became a key figure behind the implementation of Germany's racial policies and, after 1941, the mass murder of Europe's Jews.

2.

Foreign News
GERMANY
"WE DEMAND!"

[. . .] Resurgence. Overlooked or minimized by many a foreign reporter in his distaste for Nazi bluster and brutality is the great German fact of RESURGENCE, the lifting up in heart and soul of a people tired of remembering their defeat in 1918, their impoverishment under inflation and the feeling ever since that Germany had ceased to be a Great Power.

In unlacing this strait jacket of a national inferiority complex no Nazi has helped Adolf Hitler so much as the taut, vivid, sometimes hysterical, little man whom all Germany knows as "The Doctor," famed Dr. Paul Joseph Goebbels, now Minister of Propaganda and Public Enlightenment. To an amazing degree Herr Hitler and Dr. Goebbels possess in common the trick of talking to grown Germans as if they were children, yet with such furious fire, conviction and intensity that the soul of the German listener is uplifted and soars in joy.

"Germany can no longer be ranked as a second class power!" cries Hitler. "Be proud of Germany!" shouts Dr. Goebbels with his curious but effective gesture of clenching both fists close to his bosom as though about to tear his chest. "Be proud of a Fatherland for which millions sacrificed their lives! Strike a rogue more than once! Believe in the future—then only can you be a victor!"

Profoundly the resurgent German does believe in the Fatherland's future and nothing helps him more than the Goebbels-Hitler method of explaining away all Germany's defeats and trials in terms of the Jew. True Germans were not defeated in the War, so runs the Nazi tale for grown-up children. They were betrayed by Jewish pacifists. [Karl] Marx[12] was a Jew: In the welter of German revolution the Jews fomented a German Republic essentially Marxist. Under inflation "which only the Jews understood," they bled true Germans white by their scheming speculation. Somehow or other they had something to do with the mountain of debt the Allies piled on Germany. All these "facts" are profoundly important in the Germany of today. They are at the root of national resurgence. By blaming everything on their Jewish fellow men, other Germans are escaping from their mental prison of inferiority. Louder and louder the Minister of Propaganda dins with clenched and pounding fists the exhortation he has thundered from half the platforms and over all the radios in Germany: "Never forget it, comrades, and repeat it a hundred times so you will say it in your dreams—"THE JEWS ARE TO BLAME!" [. . .]

---

12. Karl Marx (1818–1883): German philosopher, historian, and political theorist whose most famous works, *The Communist Manifesto* (1848) and *Das Kapital* [Capital] (1867–83) underpinned the radical leftist politics of communism.

[. . .] Today Minister of Propaganda Goebbels plays on the entire German press, stage, screen and radio (to use his own expression) "as upon a vast keyboard." In lieu of solid Nazi achievements, for which Germany must wait, the Government provides sensation after sensation, from the burning of un-German books to threats (not as yet carried out) to sterilize Jews.

"Ours is a program without compromise," is his rallying cry, "backed by men who will carry it out passionately! A watchword without formula, but with living energy! WE DEMAND!"

—*Time,* July 10, 1933, cover (Werner Hopmann, artist) and 16–18.

Protesting the Nazi Dictatorship

Rabbi Stephen S. Wise, president of the American Jewish Congress,[13] helped to organize one of the first anti-Nazi rallies, held at New York's Madison Square Garden on March 27, 1933. Representatives of Protestant, Catholic, and Jewish groups, as well as leadership of the American Federation of Labor, spoke to a packed crowd in the arena. Similar anti-Nazi protests took place in more than sixty-five locations across the United States in spring 1933 during the first few months of Nazi rule in Germany.

In this speech, reprinted by the *New York Herald Tribune,* Rabbi Wise insisted that protest should be directed against supporters of the Nazi Party rather than against the German people writ large. In making this distinction, Wise may have underestimated the extent of support for Nazism among the German people by 1933.

3.

Wise Explains Jewry's Plea to Garden Crowd

Outlines Four Demands on Hitler

Government for Protection of the Right

Denies He Is Reich's Foe

Germany Herself Mistreated, He Tells Hearers

The American Jewish Congress has called but not caused this protest meeting of tonight. The American Jewish Congress has not aroused this protest against anti-Jewish

---

13. Founded by Rabbi Stephen Wise and other leaders of the American Jewish community in 1918 to promote equal rights for Jews and other minorities. Throughout the 1930s and 1940s the American Jewish Congress spearheaded relief efforts for Jews endangered by the Nazi regime in Europe.

wrongs in Germany, but has brought within the bounds of law and order an oceanic tide of indignation against the outrages inflicted upon Jews in these days under the Nazi government.

Not out of the bitterness of anger, but out of the deeps of sorrow and the spirit of compassion do we speak tonight. For Germany we have asked and we continue to ask justice and even magnanimity from her erstwhile foes. We demand in the sight of humanity the right for Germany from the nations and the right from Germany for the Jewish people. No wrong under the heavens could be greater than to make German Jews scapegoats because Germany has grievances against the nations. We who would secure justice from the nations for Germany and justice to Jews from Germany affirm tonight that Germany cannot hope to secure justice through injustice to its Jewish people.

This protest of tonight is not against the German people, whom we honor and revere and cherish. How could we, of the household of Israel, fail to cherish and honor the German people, one of the great peoples of the earth, a people that has made monumental, indeed eternal, contributions to human well-being in the domains of religion, literature and the arts? How could we fail to cherish and to revere the people of Goethe and Schiller,[14] Immanuel Kant and Hegel,[15] Beethoven and Wagner,[16] Heine[17] and Einstein?

Denies "Deutschfeindlich" Campaign

This protest of tonight is not against the political program of Germany, for Germany is master within her own household, but solely against the present anti-Jewish policy of the Nazi government. [. . .] We are not against Germany, and it is an unforgivable calumny to declare that we are "Deutschfeindlich" [anti-German]. We are the friends of and believers in Germany. Germany at its highest, Germany at its truest, the German nation at its noblest! Because we are the friends of Germany, because we have inextinguishable faith in the basic love for righteousness of the German people, we appeal to Germany, representing as this meeting does, Protestants, Catholics, Jews, in the name of America, which has been stirred as rarely before against wrongs perpetrated upon Jews. [. . .]

We understand the plea and the plaint of our brother Jews in Germany. They are German patriots who love their fatherland and have had reason to love it. Some of

---

14. Johann Wolfgang von Goethe (1749–1832) and Friedrich Schiller (1759–1805): among the most famous German writers in the eighteenth and nineteenth centuries.

15. Immanuel Kant (1724–1804) and Georg W. F. Hegel (1770–1831): major thinkers in the field of philosophy.

16. Ludwig van Beethoven (1770–1827) and Richard Wagner (1813–1883): leading composers whose many works remain among the standard musical repertoire.

17. Heinrich Heine (1797–1856): internationally renowned poet.

their leaders are under the impact of panic and terror; others under some form or compulsion, in any event, the compulsion of a great fear, if not actual coercion. [. . .]

To those leaders of German Jewry who declare that the present Jewish situation in Germany is a local German question we call attention to the word of Abraham Lincoln. Defenders of slavery urged and excused slavery on the ground that it was local. Lincoln's answer was "Slavery is local, but freedom is national." The conscience of humanity has made a world problem of the present situation of the Jews in Germany. We lay down no conditions tonight, we make no stipulations, we do not even urge demands. But we do affirm certain elementary axioms of civilization. The Jews of the world, no more than the Jews of Germany, do not demand exceptional treatment or privileged position or favored status for themselves. We do not even ask for rights. We ask only for the right. We demand the right.

What are these elementary maxims of civilization as we call them? The immediate cessation of anti-Semitic activities and propaganda in Germany, including an end to the policy of racial discrimination against and of economic exclusion of Jews from the life of Germany. That is Jewish life and the human rights of Jews must be safeguarded. One other absolutely reasonable and just axiom, rather than demand: The revocation of all special measures already taken against Jewish non-nationals (Ostjuden) [east European Jews] and their equal treatment with all other non-nationals in Germany. [. . .]

[It] must be made clear in the hearing of men that even if life and human rights are to be safeguarded, there must not be substitution of the status of helotry [enslavement] for violence. Such substitution will not satisfy us nor satisfy the aroused conscience of humankind, even though Jews in Germany must sink into the horror of seeming acquiescence. Every economic discrimination is a form of violence. Every racial exclusion is violence. To say that there will be no pogroms is not enough. A dry and bloodless economic pogrom remains violence and force. [. . .]

I close as I began. We are not met in the spirit of bitterness, hatred or revenge. We do not desire the German people be punished because of the unwisdom of the measures and the injustice or some practice of its government. Whatever nations may ask in the spirit of reparation and reprisal, we who are Jews know that our spirit must be in consonance with the high tradition of Jewish forbearance and Jewish forgiveness. But there must be no further reprisals against our fellow-Jews, no penalizing them as German hostages because the conscience or the world utters its mighty protest. God help the German people to be equal to themselves.

—*New York Herald Tribune*, March 28, 1933, 2.

The following wire-service article from the Associated Press draws on US State Department reports that predicted the "physical mistreatment" of Jews in Germany had come to an end in late March 1933. Following expressions of concern by leading

American Jewish organizations, US Secretary of State Cordell Hull[18] assured them that physical assaults on Jews had lasted for a "short time" but seem to have been "virtually terminated." But as events played out in the coming months, the State Department had obviously misjudged these assurances from the Nazi government.

The description of Jews as a "race" in this article points to an important difference between racist Nazi ideology and American Jews' self-understanding during the 1930s. Nazis viewed Jews as an inferior race, with biologically innate characteristics that made them, paradoxically, both weak and dangerous. By contrast, before World War II, some Jewish communities in the United States and elsewhere used the term "race" much more neutrally when describing themselves and their community. It later became more common to speak of Jewish "culture" or "ethnicity," rather than of a Jewish "race."

4.

MISTREATMENT OF JEWISH RACE IN GERMANY ENDS

———

REPORT MADE TO STATE DEP'T IN WASHINGTON

———

Is Based on Investigation by American Consulates

———

LEADING AMERICAN JEWS INFORMED

———

Telegram From Secretary Hull Is
Addressed to Rabbi Wise and Others

WASHINGTON, MARCH 26—(AP)—The State Department tonight reported that an official investigation of conditions in Germany indicated that "whereas there was for a short time considerable physical mistreatment of Jews, this phase may be considered virtually terminated."

The finding, based on reports from the Berlin embassy and American consulates throughout Germany, was telegraphed by the State Department tonight to leading American Jews who had requested the government to verify reported mistreatment of members of the race at the hands of Hitlerites and to take appropriate action.

While State Department officials did not amplify the telegram, it was understood authoritatively that an official protest to the Hitler government is planned in view of the embassy's report.

———

18. Cordell Hull (1871–1955): US congressman and senator (Democrat-TN) for more than 25 years before President Roosevelt named him secretary of state. He held the post from 1933 to 1944, when he resigned due to ill health.

Secretary of State Hull said the embassy felt "a stabilization appears to have been reached in the field of personal mistreatment, and there are indications that in other areas the situation is improving."

American Jewry had been aroused to a high pitch of indignation by the reports of harsh measures against members of their race by Brown-shirted followers of Adolf Hitler, chancellor and now dictator. Protest meetings have been called in various parts of the nation. The State Department has been flooded with telegrams asking appropriate diplomatic action.

Following is the secretary's telegram, addressed to Rabbi Stephen S. Wise, New York; Bernard Deutsch,[19] New York, president of the American Jewish Congress; and Cyrus Adler, Philadelphia:[20]

"You will remember that at the time of your recent call at the department I informed you that in view of numerous press statements indicating wide-spread mistreatment of the Jews in Germany, I would request the American embassy at Berlin in consultation with the principal consulates in Germany to investigate the situation and submit a report.

"A reply has now been received indicating that whereas there was for a short time considerable physical mistreatment of Jews, this phase may be considered virtually terminated. There was also some picketing of Jewish merchandising stores and instances of professional discrimination.

"These manifestations were viewed with serious concern by the German government.

"Hitler in his capacity as leader of the Nazi party issued an order calling upon his followers to maintain law and order, to avoid molesting foreigners; disrupting trade; and to avoid the creation of possibly embarrassing international incidents.

"Later, (vice chancellor) Von Papen[21] delivered a speech at Breslau in which he not only reiterated Hitler's appeals for discipline but abjured the victors of the last election not to spoil their triumph by unworthy acts of revenge and violence which could only bring discredit upon the new regime in foreign countries.

"As a result, the embassy reports that the authority of the regular police has been reinforced.

"The feeling has been widespread in Germany that following so far-reaching a political readjustment as has recently taken place, some time must elapse before a state of equilibrium could be reestablished.

19. Bernard S. Deutsch (1884–1935): president of the American Jewish Congress from 1928 to 1935.

20. Cyrus Adler (1863–1940): an American educator and Jewish religious leader and scholar.

21. Franz von Papen (1879–1969): German chancellor in 1932, then Hitler's vice-chancellor from 1933 to 1934, when he became Germany's ambassador to Austria.

"In the opinion of the embassy such a stabilization appears to have been reached in the field of personal mistreatment, and there are indications that in other phases the situation is improving.

"I feel hopeful in view of the reported attitude of high German officials and the evidences of amelioration already indicated, that the situation, which has caused such widespread concern throughout this country, will soon revert to normal. Meanwhile I shall continue to watch the situation closely, with a sympathetic interest and a desire to be helpful in whatever way possible.

(Signed)   Cordell Hull
                                 Secretary of State."

—Associated Press, *Bangor (ME) Daily News,* March 27, 1933, 1 and 12.

The US State Department received hundreds of petitions like this one from civic groups, churches, and Jewish organizations from across the United States asking the government to investigate and act upon Nazi Germany's treatment of its Jewish citizens.

Although tens of thousands of Americans signed such petitions of protest, the US government made no official statement against the German regime at the time.

5.

The United Churches of Lackawanna County
312 CHAMBER OF COMMERCE BLDG.
SCRANTON, PENNA.

March 27, 1933.

Hon. Cordell Hull
Secretary of State
Washington, D. C.

Dear Sir:

The following resolution has been adopted by the Good Will Commission of the United Churches of Lackawanna County (Pennsylvania) and I have been instructed to forward the same to you. Our organization represents a large proportion of the Protestant churches of our county:

WHEREAS, certain sinister reports concerning anti-Semitic persecutions in Germany, under the new Hitler dictatorship, are most disturbing; and

WHEREAS, even though conflicting reports are at hand, the policy of anti-Semitism has been repeatedly affirmed as part of the Nazi program, thus giving us cause for credence; and

WHEREAS, on Christian grounds we protest against all forms of racial and religious intolerance and feel impelled to plead the cause of its victims; be it hereby

RESOLVED, that we convey our sentiments to the Secretary of State of the United States calling upon our Government to make any necessary investigations and to employ its good offices in the interests of those whose basic human rights are being denied.

Very truly yours,
[*signed*] George L. Ford
Executive Secretary.

—Petition, March 27, 1933, RG 59, Records of the Department of State Central Decimal File 1930–1939, 862.4016/184, NACP.

Soon after coming to power, the Nazi Party staged an economic boycott against Jews in Germany. On April 1, 1933, local Nazi Party chiefs organized community actions intended to intimidate Germany's Jews and to discourage non-Jews from shopping at Jewish-owned stores. The boycott lasted only one day and many individual Germans even ignored it, yet it marked an important turning point in Germany's treatment of Jews.

Wire-service reports published in American newspapers also noted additional forms of persecution aimed at removing Jews from professional life in Germany and restricting the attendance of Jewish children in schools.

Nazi Minister of Enlightenment and Propaganda Paul Joseph Goebbels orchestrated many of these measures and boasted of them. A report nearly one month after the boycott from the Jewish Telegraphic Agency, a wire service for the American Jewish press, quoted Goebbels's claims that Germany was being too mild on Jewish "enemies."

6.

NAZIS START JEWISH BOYCOTT

———

Troops Clear Berlin Law Courts of
Jewish Judges and Attorneys As Beginning

———

WILL LAST ONLY ONE DAY

———

Charges Jews Responsible For World War
Made In Justification For Movement

BERLIN, GERMANY, MARCH 31.—(UP)—The nationwide boycott against Jews in Germany, which will start at 10 a.m. tomorrow, will last only day, it was announced officially tonight.

COURTS ARE CLEARED

BERLIN, GERMANY, MARCH 31.—(AP)—Nazi storm troops today cleared the Berlin law courts of Jewish judges and attorneys.

Reports to the United States that Chancellor Hitler's Nazi party might be persuaded at the last minute to refrain from launching the drastic economic war on Jewry tomorrow, seemed only to add fuel to the fire today.

A new proclamation defines the action as beginning war on the entire Jewish race of the world.

The Jews, backs to the wall as the last appeal for mercy fell on deaf ears, envisioned ultimate ruin and isolation from German cities and towns.

Nazi charges that the Jews of the world were responsible for the world war, and Nazi declarations that repressive measures against Jews continue "until victory is ours," set the tone today for the nationwide boycott which is to begin at 10 a.m. tomorrow.

The central boycott committee of the National Socialist party issued fiery appeals to followers of Chancellor Hitler throughout the nation, instructing them in the part they are to play in the boycott against Jewish businessmen, attorneys and physicians.

"Jews Stab Germany"

In the proclamation, made public at Munich and printed in the Voelkischer Beobachter, the Hitlerite organ, the committee said:

"Judah is stabbing Germany in the back with the same methods it employed to perpetrate the criminal world war. Again Judah is at work calumniating the German people as huns and barbarians."

Will Be Reprinted

Local committees were ordered to see that the instructions were reprinted prominently in the entire German press. Among other things, these instructions call for outdoor demonstrations and the public display of posters which accuse German Jews of having enlisted the aid of foreign Jews against Germany.

Beginning tomorrow, Jewish stores will be obliged to hang out black placards with yellow paint, announcing that they are owned by Jews.

The newspaper Angriff, edited by Joseph Goebbels, government propaganda chief, said tonight that the threat of a boycott "has had no visible effect up to now on Jewish instigators of atrocity reports published abroad."

On the contrary, said Angriff, "in some sections of the American press Germany's counter measures are being answered with a renewed demand for a boycott of German goods."

Passports Seized

The authorities at Breslau ordered all Jews to turn in their passports, making travel for them impossible.

The Nazi group in the Prussian diet proposed that Jewish children be restricted to 1 per cent of each school's enrollment.

Nazi headquarters directed members of the party to refrain from interfering with the business of the Woolworth chain stores.[22]

—United Press and Associated Press, *Santa Cruz (CA) News,* March 31, 1933, 1.

7.

Germany Is Too Easy On Jews, Goebbels Asks Stronger Attack

(Jewish Telegraphic Agency)

COLOGNE. APRIL 25—Stronger persecution of the Jews was urged by Dr. Paul Goebbels, the Reich's Minister of Propaganda and Popular Enlightenment, in an inflammatory address before a mass meeting here last night. "We exercise too great mildness toward the Jews," Minister Goebbels declared. "They do not deserve it. Jews are our enemies."

The chief propagandist of the Nazi administration pointed out that the government's weakness in permitting itself to be gentle toward the Jews was evidenced in the fact that the complete boycott of Jewish business was only conducted for a single day. The brevity of the boycott was pictured as indicating a regrettable leniency in the German temperament. More stringent measures were urged for the future.

—*Jewish Daily Bulletin,* April 26, 1933, 1.

American diplomats in Germany were well aware of the Nazi persecution of Jews and political opponents in 1933. Yet the accepted rules of international diplomacy obliged them to respect Germany's national sovereignty—its right to govern its own citizens—and to not intervene on behalf of those being targeted.

In this memorandum, US Secretary of State Cordell Hull documents his meeting with Germany's ambassador to the United States, Hans Luther. Secretary Hull reports mentioning the "vast heaps" of protests received from Americans regarding Germany's treatment of Jews. But Hull specifically emphasizes that he made no "complaint" to Luther about the treatment. Luther does not deny that discrimination against Jews had occurred. Instead, he seeks to assure Hull that "the worst has been over for some time" even as he blames Jews for Germany's problems and endorses the idea of a revolution to ensure that the "best pure German element" controls Germany.

22. Woolworth's, a popular department store, was frequently thought by Germans to be Jewish-owned. Store management in Germany went to great lengths to publicize that it was not.

8.

DEPARTMENT OF STATE
THE SECRETARY

May 3, 1933.

MEMORANDUM OF CONVERSATION BETWEEN SECRETARY HULL AND THE GERMAN AMBASSADOR, DR. HANS LUTHER.

Mistreatment of Jews in Germany.

The German Ambassador came in at my request [. . .] in order that I might ascertain from him in person whether it would be agreeable for me to discuss with him in the most unofficial, personal and friendly manner the Jewish situation in Germany, and to make full and emphatic representations to him in this tone and manner of the state of sentiment in the United States, both among the Jews and the general public, relative to the reported atrocities and mistreatments of the Jews in Germany either by individual groups or by the Government, or both. I stated that my purpose in thus talking with him was to make fully possible the preservation of our friendly relations with the German Government by thus keeping up as clear understandings as possible.

I then called the attention of the Ambassador to the vast heaps of memorials, letters and other solemn and earnest protests by groups of American citizens of all religious denominations and racial persuasions earnestly protesting the reported mistreatment of Jews in Germany and urging our Government to take all possible steps to terminate such treatment, even to the extent of making very definite and more or less peremptory demands of the German Government itself. I stated that I have been doing all within my power to carry out this spirit by exercising every possible resource to bring about a cessation of the reported acts or mistreatments in Germany and, gradually at least, to encourage a return to normal conditions but, since this problem was an internal problem within Germany and under the immediate jurisdiction of the German Government, I did not undertake bluntly or definitely to make complaint directly to the German Government. I did, however, in various representations and dispatches endeavor to draw out the German Government, and in a favorable direction, towards the satisfactory treatment of this reported uprising against the Jews in Germany so that the Government would thereby be most disposed and calculated to assert its efforts to compose this situation and bring it back to normal.

The German Ambassador, although I did not request him to make reply to my statements unless he felt justified in doing so, proceeded with an elaborate statement, the central point of which was that a general civic revolution is taking place in Germany in which the young Germans are undertaking to bring into control the best pure German element. He stated that the mistreatment of Jews was only one segment of the conflicting conditions that developed under this revolution, against groups; that it included certain other groups, as well as Jews; that the Government is not a party to the Jewish antagonisms or persecutions, as the case may be considered; that the Jews comprise one per cent of the population of Germany, but that many hospitals are manned exclusively by Jews; that of four thousand lawyers in Berlin, three thousand are Jews; that Jews occupy key positions in all important walks and avocations entirely disproportionate to their relative population in Germany, and that in the general movement to equalize the condition of the various groups and even nationalities, including certain other groups that poured into Germany following the War, it was not unnatural that these groups became a target for more or less rough treatment as a necessary part of this plan or general readjustment of the organic political structure of the German Government, of their organized Society, and of their general economic situation.

The Ambassador insists that the worst has been over for some time, so far as it relates to the Jewish troubles in Germany; that the situation is constantly improving; that there is no purpose to expel the Jews as a race from Germany; that many laws and court agencies are from week to week becoming more and more available for the protection of Jews and Jewish rights and property, and that it will only be a question of a reasonable time when normal conditions and relationships will, to a measurable extent, be brought about.

I repeated with much emphasis the deep-seated feeling in this country and expressed the earnest hope that every possible step be taken to alleviate and relieve the acute situation in Germany as it relates to the treatment of the Jews. The Ambassador showed every disposition thus to confer personally and unofficially, both now and hereafter, relative to any subject where there might be a chance to promote better understanding and more friendly relationships between the Governments and the peoples of this country and Germany.

[initials] C[ordell] H[ull]

—Memorandum of Conversation, May 3, 1933, RG 59, Records of the
Department of State Central Decimal File 1930–1939, 862.4016/691, NACP.

On May 10, 1933, university students on campuses across Germany burned more than 25,000 volumes of "unGerman" books in an effort to bring German culture in line with Nazi Party goals. The students threw books onto large bonfires with great ceremony, band-playing, and so-called fire oaths that denounced the works. At Berlin's book burning, some 40,000 persons gathered to hear Nazi Minister of Propaganda and Enlightenment Joseph Goebbels speak.

The book burnings were a direct affront to one of America's most treasured freedoms, the right to the free expression of ideas. Following on the heels of a procession of abuses against Jewish citizens, the book burnings—widely covered in US newspapers, with a focus on American authors—evoked protests among the American press and public.

The American Jewish Congress chose May 10, 1933—the preannounced date of the book burnings—to coordinate massive, nationwide street demonstrations against the burning of books and the Nazi persecution of Jews. In New York City, 100,000 people marched for more than six hours. Similar events took place in cities across the country, including Philadelphia, Chicago, and Cleveland.

9.

German Students Burn Books Of Noted American Authors

BERLIN (AP).—Books of Helen Keller, Franz Boas and Jack London,[23] as well as hundreds of German authors, went up in smoke throughout Germany Wednesday night.

University young men and women, pronouncing judgment on world literature considered as contravening German spirit, started huge bonfires of the volumes shortly before midnight.

Dr. Joseph Goebbels, minister of public enlightenment and propaganda, pronounced the government's blessings and declared that "the period of Jewish intellectualism now has ended."

The weird glow illuminated Opera square opposite Berlin university, as students, garbed in the picturesque costumes of their fraternities, the Nazi brown or the steel helmet grey, threw a thousand torches on the pyre, then seized the books from trucks and hurled them into the blaze amid cheers. [. . .]

Doctor Goebbels declared, "As you had the right to destroy the books, you had the duty to support the government. The fire signals to the entire world that the November revolutionaries[24] have sunk to earth and a new spirit has arisen."

—Associated Press, *(Boise) Idaho Daily Statesman,* May 11, 1933, 1.

In reaction to Germany's persecution of Jews, the American Jewish Congress and other Jewish and labor organizations in the United States—including the Jewish War Veterans, Jewish Labor Committee, and American Federation of Labor—tried to persuade consumers to boycott stores that stocked German-made goods. Some of the efforts were led by women, as evident in this resolution from the Women's Division of the American League for the Defense of Jewish Rights.

Although efforts to boycott German goods lasted throughout the 1930s, they never gained as much national attention or had as much impact as its organizers hoped.

23. Helen Keller (1880–1968): author and political activist; Franz Boas (1858–1942): anthropologist and opponent of "scientific racism"; Jack London (1876–1916): novelist and social activist.
24. Reference to the founders of the Weimar Republic in November 1918.

10.

NEWS *from the* AMERICAN LEAGUE
for the DEFENSE OF JEWISH RIGHTS

RESOLUTION ADOPTED at the CONFERENCE
HELD UNDER THE AUSPICES OF THE WOMEN'S DIVISION OF THE
AMERICAN LEAGUE FOR DEFENSE OF JEWISH RIGHTS.
at the Hotel Astor, on June 27, 1933.

The advent of Adolf Hitler and his party, the National Socialists, to power in Germany marked the inauguration of a reign of barbaric anti-Semitism un-paralleled in the history of modern civilization. The Jews of Germany, domiciled for over a thousand years in that country to whose cultural development and economic prosperity they have contributed out of all proportion to their numbers, have of a sudden been declared aliens and undesirables and subjected to every persecution, violence and indignity on the sole ground of race and religion.

Hordes of Nazis have, with the blessing of government officials, perpetrated upon defenseless Jews atrocities of unspeakable horror, in which hundreds have lost their lives, thousands have been wounded and maimed, and thousands incarcerated in detention camps and prisons.

Parallel with physical violence, the Nazi government has put into effect a policy of economic and spiritual repression aimed at the annihilation of German Jewry. In pursuance of this policy, the Hitler government expelled all Jews from public office; drove them from the professions, the arts, literature and the stage; compelled employers to discharge Jewish employees; forced German Gentiles to divorce their Jewish business enterprises; closed the schools and universities to Jewish students; expelled Jewish children from the schools and subjected them to insults and degradation.

As a result, the 600,000 Jews of Germany have been driven to utter despair and complete economic ruin. The number of suicides among German Jews has been assuming frightful proportions. Erstwhile well-to-do, cultured men and women have been driven to begging in the streets.

The universal and unqualified condemnation by civilized mankind has failed to affect the ruthless rulers now in control of Germany. The Nazis have remained deaf to all appeals to conscience and humanity. The only means, therefore, left to humane, liberty-loving and just men and women the world over, is an economic boycott of goods, products and services emanating from Germany.

Now, therefore, We, delegates of organizations of Jewish women, representing the majority of consumers of our people, convened by the Women's Division of the American League for the Defense of Jewish Rights in conference at the Hotel Astor, New York City, this 27th day of June, 1933, alive to our responsibilities as Americans and Jewesses and profoundly deploring the necessity of taking this action,

<u>Do Hereby Solemnly Proclaim</u> that it is the duty of every Jewess in the United States of America to boycott all goods, materials or products manufactured, raised or improved in Germany, or any part thereof, all German shipping, freight and traffic services, as well as all German health, pleasure and other resorts, and generally, to abstain from any act which would in any manner lend material support to the present regime in Germany.

It is specifically understood that the foregoing measures are directed exclusively against the goods, products and services of the German Reich proper, and shall continue until all the anti-Jewish laws, edicts and policies have been wholly repealed and renounced. We trust that this movement will find sympathetic response in the heart of all American women who stand for the best there is in civilization. [. . .]

> —Resolution, June 27, 1933, Records of the Non-Sectarian
> Anti-Nazi League to Champion Human Rights, Rare Book
> and Manuscript Library, Columbia University.

Americans Assaulted in Germany

Members of the Nazi Party's SA militia physically attacked Americans in Germany at least thirty-five times during 1933 alone. The Associated Press published a list of twenty-eight separate incidents that occurred between March and October 1933.

As US consul general in Berlin, George Messersmith was responsible for assisting and protecting US citizens in Germany.[25] In a report to the State Department about the matter, he wrote: "In every one of these cases the attack upon the persons and homes of these Americans was unprovoked and brought about through the assumption that they were Jews. It is not believed that the attacks were made upon them as Americans or as foreigners, but on the grounds that they were Jews."[26]

Messersmith, US Ambassador to Germany William Dodd,[27] and other members of the embassy staff protested these attacks vigorously to the German government. During their first meeting in October 1933, Hitler assured Ambassador Dodd that attacks on Americans in Germany would end, and many fewer occurred after 1933.

---

25. George S. Messersmith (1883–1960): entered the US foreign service in 1914 and was stationed in Berlin from 1930 to 1934.

26. George Messersmith, "Molestation of American citizens domiciled or temporarily in Berlin," March 14, 1933. RG-59, Central Decimal File, 1930-1939, Box 6782, 862.4016/156, p. 6, NACP.

27. William E. Dodd (1869–1940): a University of Chicago history professor for twenty-five years prior to his appointment as ambassador to Germany in June 1933, where he served until December 1937.

11.

Nazi Attacks on Americans

By The Associated Press.

BERLIN, OCT. 12.—United States Consul General George S. Messersmith said tonight that nearly three-fourths of the cases in which Americans had been attacked by Nazi representatives were on file with the Consul General in Berlin in the form of sworn affidavits. The rest, he said, were in different consular offices in Germany. A list of the cases follows:

March 3—Leon Jaffe, attacked by brown-shirted troopers in Berlin.

March 3—Henry H. Sattler, attacked by fifteen storm troopers in Berlin.

March 4—Nathaniel S. Woolf, approached by six brown shirts who entered his Berlin apartment, drew revolvers and struck him in the face, later conducting him to a Nazi hang-out and thence to Gruenwald Woods and ordering him to leave Germany immediately.

March 4—Edwin F. Dakin, threatened in his Berlin quarters by storm troopers with pistols.

March 7—Solomon Friedman, attacked by three storm troopers.

March 7—Mrs. Max Schussler, molested in her Berlin home by storm troopers, who, showing revolvers, compelled her husband to sign documents while she stood nude before them.

March 8—Louis Berman, attacked on a Berlin street by four brown shirts who threatened him with pistols and stole $285 and some personal papers.

March 10—Herman I. Roseman, attacked in front of a department store, struck in the face.

March 11—Mrs. Klauber, assaulted in her home at Munich by storm troopers.

March 11—Julian Fuhs, attacked in his wife's restaurant in Berlin by a civilian and several storm troopers, who knocked him down.

March 11—Edward Dahlberg, attacked and struck in the face in Berlin by storm troopers.

March 13—Max Mayer Hausman, attacked by storm troopers at Mannheim.

March 29—Julian Fuhs again attacked by same civilian and storm troopers in a restaurant; knocked down, kicked, threatened with revolvers. The consulate was informed a storm trooper had been discharged from the organization while Mr. Fuhs's assailant, Oskar Joost, was fined 50 marks.

April 1—Bernard S. Lustig taken to a storm troopers' hang-out in Berlin, detained and subjected to indignities.

April 1—Louis S. Chase molested and struck by storm troopers in Berlin while in company of his sister; later taken to a Nazi hang-out.

April 3—Hirsch Roth taken by storm troopers from his apartment, threatened, detained and subjected to indignities.

April 3—Mrs. Lilly Steinlauf Blutinger molested in her residence, threatened.

April 19—Herbert Baer arrested without cause at Karlsruhe, detained in custody without being informed as to the reason or permitted to communicate with the consulate; finally released May 10 on representations of the Stuttgart Consulate.

June 21—Dr. Joseph Schachno severely beaten and maltreated at Koepenick.

July 1—Walter Orloff arrested at the University of Greifswald for alleged Communist activities on mere denunciation and confession extorted through maltreatment.

July 11—Samuel Danzig, university student at Halle, attacked by a storm trooper while leaving a restaurant.

July 11—Thorsten Johnson, arrested at Stettin in a seaman's drinking place for an alleged derogatory remark concerning the Chancellor. Although the prosecuting attorney assured the consulate the case was not serious Johnson was sentenced to jail and finally released Sept. 8 on representations by the Berlin Consulate.

Aug. 15—Harold B. Dahlquist, attacked in Berlin; struck in the face by a storm trooper.

Aug. 15—Dr. Daniel Mulvihill, struck on the head by a storm trooper in Berlin.

Aug. 16—Samuel G. Bossard, assaulted by five Hitler youths: knocked down.

Aug. 16—Philip Zuckerman, attacked at Leipzig by a group of storm troopers, knocked down, stamped upon and removed to a hospital in Berlin, where he has been under constant medical treatment ever since.

Sept. 1—Rolf Kaltenborn, hit in the face in Berlin while accompanied by his father, mother and sister.

Oct. 10—Roland Velz, struck in the face twice by storm troopers at Duesseldorf.

—Associated Press, *New York Times*, October 13, 1933, 15.

12.

HITLER ASSURES DODD YANKS WILL GET PROTECTION
U. S. Envoy Has Talk with German Chancellor.

BY SIGRID SCHULTZ.[28]

BERLIN, Oct. 17.—Ambassador William E. Dodd of the United States emerged from a 45 minute conference with Chancellor Adolf Hitler and Baron Konstantin von Neurath, Nazi foreign minister,[29] today apparently greatly impressed with the German leader's desire for peace.

The chancellor reemphasized to the ambassador the government's peaceful assurances contained in his speech to the nation Saturday. He also assured Mr. Dodd that

28. Sigrid Schultz (1893–1980): the *Chicago Tribune*'s correspondent-in-chief in central Europe beginning in 1926. At that time, no other woman held such a high position for an American newspaper. She remained in Germany until 1941, sometimes risking her life to provide on-the-spot coverage during the Nazi Party's rule.

29. Konstantin von Neurath (1873–1956): German foreign minister from 1932 to 1938.

the era of assaults against Americans for failing to salute the Nazi swastika emblem is over. Hitler said that the government will take every precaution to prevent recurrence of such incidents.

The chancellor further promised that assailants of foreigners will be severely punished. He also said new orders will be issued to safeguard foreigners from attacks.

Two Sent to Jail.

Shortly before the visit a so-called speed court sentenced Paul Eskardt, a glass-blower, and Friedrich Wilbertz, a chauffeur, to six months in prison for assaulting Roland Velz, a native of Meriden, Conn. The assailant of Dr. Daniel Mulvihill, another American, also was punished.

The German government is investigating 32 other cases in which Americans complained that they were attacked. A report will be presented to the American embassy in the near future. It is believed, however, it will be impossible to identify most of the assailants. Nevertheless, the embassy is confident that the assaults will end.

Gen. Wilhelm Hermann Goering, Prussian premier and reichsminister, issued an order today that foreigners must not be molested but must be given police protection.

Dodd Tells of Interview.

Prof. Dodd, speaking of his interview with Hitler, declared he felt somewhat better about the general outlook than in the past few days.

"I found the chancellor greatly interested in American public opinion. He desires that there be no misunderstanding between Germany and the United States," he said. "The interview was very cordial. The attitude of a desire for peace contained in Saturday's speech [by Chancellor Hitler] [sic] was reëmphasized in our talk.

"The chancellor is imbued with the hope there will not be war and is tremendously aware of the implications of war.

"All these assaults on Americans are about to come to an end. You have seen Gen. Goering's order. This is approved 100 per cent by the chancellor, who is honestly perturbed over the situation. In the future the assailants will be dealt with severely and summarily."

Studies Foreign Relations.

After devoting the first months of his rule to internal problems, Hitler now is turning his attention to foreign relations. He fully realizes the seriousness of his government's position in international affairs. It is understood in diplomatic circles that he hopes Ambassador Dodd and the United States will help him frame a compromise in which the former allies will recognize part of Germany's claim to equality in armaments.

For the first time Hitler and his lieutenants are evincing considerable interest in the American attitude on European problems. The feeling is prevalent here that only joint pressure by the United States and Italy will help solve Europe's armaments tangle.[30] Berlin is looking to Washington for guidance, judging from an officially inspired news agency which sees in the statement of Norman H. Davis, American ambassador at large at Geneva, evidence of a "similarity of the American and German attitudes toward the disarmament conference which is bound to reduce international tension." The agency added:

"By requesting France and Britain to present disarmament proposals the United States brings pressure to bear upon these nations and compels them to demonstrate their desire for disarmament to the rest of the world. That is all Germany is asking for, too."

—*Chicago Daily Tribune*, October 18, 1933, 7.

Germany's Jews In Danger

At the Nazi Party's annual rally in September 1935, the German parliament (Reichstag) unanimously passed new laws that isolated Jews and other "non-Aryans" from German society.[31] These "Nuremberg Race Laws" (officially known as the Reich Citizenship Law and the Law for the Protection of German Blood and German Honor) excluded Jews from German citizenship and prohibited Jews from marrying or having sexual relations with persons of "German or German-related blood." The law also declared the swastika banner as Germany's official flag.

One week after these laws were passed, *Time* magazine explained the "big doings" of the Nazi regime, even as it continued to poke at Hitler by calling him a "little man."

13.

Foreign News
GERMANY
Little Man, Big Doings

Once a year quaint medieval Nürnberg [Nuremberg] finds its population tripled by the marching, seething squash of Adolf Hitler's Party Congress. Last week on Adolf Hitler Platz [. . .] 800,000 pairs of German boots came pounding in[. . . .] In Nürnberg

---

30. In the aftermath of World War I, the League of Nations, joined by the non-league member United States, began talks toward an international limitation of arms. The Conference for the Reduction and Limitation of Armaments (also called the World Disarmament Conference) met in Geneva, Switzerland, between 1932 and 1934, but ended in failure, in large part because Hitler withdrew Germany from the talks in October 1933.

31. Between March and July 1933, Hitler's government banned all political parties except the Nazi Party. After the November 1933 national elections, all 661 seats in parliament were held by delegates of the Nazi Party. Thereafter, the Reichstag became little more than a rubber-stamp for the Nazi government's decrees.

all neutral observers noted last week the air of respect and reverence for the Realm-leader [Hitler]. At this third Congress since he came to power he seemed to take on a dignity bordering on the religious, enhanced by solemn German chanting in his honor. [. . .]

Approval in Advance. Extremely flattering to the Party Congress was an abrupt order from the Realmleader summoning all Deputies of the German Reichstag to attend him in Nürnberg, this being the first time Herr Hitler has called his Parliament to heel at such a distance from Berlin.

Called to order shortly after 9 p.m. by the No. 2 Nazi, beefy General Hermann Wilhelm Göring among whose countless titles is President of the Reichstag, Germany's 600 Deputies first waived all the Reichstag's rules of procedure and voted to place themselves "under the leadership principle."[32] Thus they approved in advance whatever decrees from Realmleader Hitler might be read out to them by President Göring. [. . .]

"Our Holy Symbol!" In menacing tones General Göring then read out three new decree laws. The first ended the clumsy arrangement under which the German tricolor and the Nazi swastika have been flown together as national flags. Henceforth Germany's sole flag is the swastika. "It is the anti-Jewish symbol of the world!" thundered General Göring amid deafening cheers. "A soldier from the front lines, Adolf Hitler, pulled us out of the dirt and brought us back to honor. . . . The swastika has become for us a holy symbol!" [. . .]

Citizenship, Blood & Honor. The second decree read out by General Göring is the National Citizenship Law. This divides Germans into "citizens" (with such rights as suffrage) and "members" (rights not defined). Jews under this law are automatically "members," and German "citizens" will be degraded to that status if they are found to be Communists or otherwise "unworthy."

The final decree last week is the Law for the Protection of German Blood and German Honor. This permits Jews to fly a racial flag of their own: prohibits them from flying the German flag; bars Jews from marrying outside their race in Germany; bars them, whether married or not, from having sexual relations across the race line; and, as a final deterrent, forbids a Jew to employ a German female servant less than 45 years old.

The implications of this proviso struck the German Reichstag so forcibly that Deputies clutched their quaking midriffs and the whole chamber roared with Homeric laughter until tears of mirth glistened on many a cheek. Banging down his gavel President Göring boomed: "No Jew can insult Germany!"

---

32. *Führerprinzip*: defined Nazi Germany's top-down hierarchy of political authority that placed Hitler's word above written law and demanded absolute obedience from those below.

Party Above State. Far more important than these laws was a brief but epochal announcement to the Party Congress by Adolf Hitler. He declared that hereafter "problems the State is unable to solve will be solved by the Nazi movement!"

This served notice on Germans that direct-action party zealots like Jew-baiting Boss Julius Streicher[33] of Nürnberg emphatically enjoy the Realmleader's confidence and may be expected to take German law more and more into their own hands. At their final meeting last week Herr Streicher appeared exhilarated, Herr Hitler tired.

—*Time,* September 23, 1935, 22–23.

In response to growing concern about Germany's Jews, New York Governor Herbert H. Lehman wrote to President Franklin D. Roosevelt on November 1, 1935, to urge him to admit more Jewish immigrants from Germany than the United States had during the first two years of Nazi rule. Governor Lehman reminded the president that the US Congress in 1924 had established limits (quotas) on the number of immigration visas that could be issued each year. When Lehman wrote, the maximum number of immigration visas available for people born in Germany was 25,957, as the president explains.

In his reply, Roosevelt cites the law that limits the number of immigration visas that could be issued. He also informs Lehman that the US State Department in fact had been issuing thousands fewer visas each year than it could have under the already restrictive law. The president makes no commitment in his response to increase the number of visas issued, nor does he directly answer Governor Lehman's request.

14.

The Honorable
The Governor of New York
Albany.

November 13, 1935.

My dear Governor Lehman:

I have your letter of November 1, 1935, with its enclosed letter of October 10, 1935, from Professor James G. McDonald,[34] High Commissioner for Refugees (Jewish

---

33. Julius Streicher (1885–1946): an early Nazi Party member, a participant in the "Beer Hall Putsch," and after 1925 the regional head of the Nazi Party in Nuremberg. He founded and published Germany's most viciously antisemitic newspaper, *Der Stürmer* [The Stormer]. Widely read in Nazi Germany, the paper was a major outlet for Nazi propaganda against Jews.

34. James G. McDonald (1886–1964): High Commissioner for Refugees for the League of Nations from 1933 to 1935. His public resignation from the post in December 1935 resulted

and Other) coming from Germany to Mr. Felix M. Warburg[35] with reference to the question of the immigration of German Jews into the United States.

I have brought your letter to the particular attention of the Department of State in view of the responsibility placed by law upon its consular officers abroad for the issuance or refusal of immigration visas. In connection with my reference of this important matter to the competent officers of the Department of State, I am informed that the situation as regards the points you have raised is briefly as follows.

With regard to your request that the quota for German Jews be increased from 2,500 to 5,000 per annum, there is no immigration quota fixed for persons in the class described, nor has there been any arbitrary limitation set upon the number of visas to be issued to natives of Germany other than the maximum quota fixed by law, which is 25,957. Consular officers must issue immigration visas, within quota limitations, to all quota applicants who qualify under the law to receive such visas. They cannot of course issue visas to applicants who are found to be inadmissible under the public charge clause or any other restrictive limitation set by existing law.

I am informed that nearly all immigration quotas have been considerably under-issued during the past four years. Although the German quota comprises only 16.9 per cent of the total of all quotas, immigration visas issued under it now represent 26.9 [per cent] of the visas issued under all quotas. While estimates on this point vary somewhat, it is understood that a very large majority of immigration visas under the German quota are issued to Jewish applicants. [. . .]

The following figures, showing the issuance of immigration visas to natives of Germany are therefore of particular interest in relation to your inquiry.

Fiscal year (ending June 30)	Immigration visas issued (exclusive of students and returning residents of the United States)
1932	2,571
1933	1,798
1934	4,715
1935	5,117

As regards your wish that it be made certain that our consular representative show a sympathetic interest in permitting immigration of German Jews into this country, the Department of State has issued instructions to its consular officers, which are now

from his frustration over the absence of support for his efforts to aid German Jews. In the letter Governor Lehman enclosed to Roosevelt, McDonald expressed his "fears about the situation [for German Jews] as it has been developing since the Nuremberg legislation" of September 1935. (Letter, October 10, 1935, Official File 133 Immigration, Box 1 1933–1935, FDRL.)

35. Felix M. Warburg (1871–1937): German-born American banker who, after the Nazi seizure of power, financially aided Jews fleeing Germany.

in effect, that persons who are obliged to leave the country of their regular residency, and who seek to escape from the condition in that country by coming to the United States, should receive, on the part of American consular officers, the most considerate attention and the most generous and favorable treatment possible under the laws of this country. [. . .]

Furthermore, the principal consular officers stationed at Berlin, Hamburg and Stuttgart, which are the only three consular offices in Germany which now issue immigration visas, have all visited the Department of State during recent months and the problems in which you are interested have been discussed verbally and sympathetically with them at the time of their visits. [. . .]

I note that you have made the request to which I have referred above on the condition that these prospective immigrants "fulfill the immigration requirement in every particular." I believe that the Department of State and its consular officers abroad have had no other desire than to carry out the immigration duties placed upon them by the Immigration Act of 1924 in a considerate and humane manner, consistent with a faithful discharge of their responsibilities under the law. I understand that the percentage of immigration visa refusals in Germany has recently been considerably below the average for all countries.

I appreciate your action in bringing these matters to my attention and I can assure you that it is my earnest desire that all consideration and justice shall continue to be shown to the type of immigrants in whom you are interested.

—Letter, unsigned file copy, November 13, 1935, box 1,
1933–1935, Official File 133, Immigration, FDRL.

Boycott the Olympics?

As the 1936 Olympic Games in Berlin neared,[36] Americans debated whether a boycott would be an effective protest against Nazism. Some leaders of American athletic organizations who wanted to see the United States participate in the games insisted that sporting contests should not be influenced by international politics.

Avery Brundage, the American Olympic Committee president, favored participating in the Olympics. Prior to the games, Brundage went on a fact-finding tour of Germany. He did not speak German, and the Nazi ministers of sport did not allow him to meet privately with representatives of Jewish sports clubs. Brundage left Germany convinced by the Nazis' false assertions that Jewish athletes were being treated fairly. Brundage claimed that boycott advocates were injecting political concerns where they

---

36. Germany was awarded both the winter and summer 1936 Olympic Games in 1931, two years before Hitler was named chancellor.

did not belong. He went so far as to imply that a Jewish-led conspiracy of radicals and Communists was trying to keep the United States from participating.

The popular syndicated columnist and sportswriter Heywood Broun (1888–1939) questioned Brundage's penchant for labeling those who disagreed with him "communists" and suggested that anyone who truly cared about fighting fascism should oppose participating in the Berlin Olympic Games.

15.

FAIR PLAY for AMERICAN ATHLETES
THE ISSUE

In accepting the invitation to compete in the 1936 Olympic Games the American Olympic Committee, like the Olympic committees of 48 other nations which have accepted, does not endorse the policies of any government. The committee considered nothing but sport and its requirements. Germany's political policy within or without its borders has no bearing on the subject. The Committee only followed the universal and unbroken Olympic precedent of forty years and ignored irrelevant political, racial and religious affairs. Attempts to twist and distort the unanimous decision of the committee into an endorsement of Nazi policies are nothing but barefaced effrontery.

The future of amateur sport in the United States is now being threatened as a result of the efforts of certain individuals and groups to involve sport in foreign political affairs, and to keep American athletes out of the Olympic Games. It becomes the duty of those charged with the administration of amateur sport to fight off this invasion. "Shall the American athlete be made a martyr to a cause not his own?"

The Olympic Games were revived in order to encourage the development and extension of international amity and good will in a world filled with intolerance, persecution, hatred and war. The great success of the Games is due to the precautions taken to guard them against entanglement in political, religious or class controversies. To involve them in the present Jew-Nazi altercation would completely invert the object of the Games. [. . .]

THE FACTS

The Games of the Eleventh [Summer] Olympiad are an international and not a German enterprise. They are entirely and exclusively controlled by international committees who make all the rules and handle all the competitions. The Games will be held in Germany whether the United States is represented or not, and from present indications will be a brilliant success since more countries and more athletes than ever before are entered.

The International Olympic Committee and twenty-three international federations composed of the impartial, unbiased sport leaders of fifty nations have sanctioned these Games and approved their location. These men, noted for fairness and sportsmanship, are quite competent to weigh the facts and issues involved.

As always the American team will be selected from the best athletes of this country including Jews, with character and amateur standing the only restriction.

Full courtesy and hospitality in Germany are assured to all Olympic athletes and visitors, no matter what race, color or creed.

Berlin was chosen as the site of the Olympic Games long before Hitler became established in power. When the Nazis took over the German Government the International Olympic Committee in no uncertain terms served notice that there must be no political interference. Jews the world over greeted this warning with great enthusiasm. Certain Jews must now understand that they cannot use these Games as a weapon in their boycott against the Nazis.

—Avery Brundage, President, American Olympic Association.

—American Olympic Committee, *Fair Play for American Athletes,* (Chicago: AOC, 1935), 2.

16.

The Olympics Merely an Opportunity for Hitler to Glorify Himself a Bit

"The Olympic Games belong to the athletes and not to the politicians," said Avery Brundage, chairman of the American Olympic Committee. Brundage has stated the problem quite fairly. The games don't belong to the politicians, as he has said. But I cannot agree that they belong wholly to the athletes themselves. After all, the team is supposed to represent the United States and not merely the admirable group composed of those who can run a little faster than the rest of us and jump a good deal higher.

Representation at Berlin would necessarily involve a national gesture. I am not for opposing friendly relations between nations even though they may not see altogether eye to eye. But it is silly to call friendship "friendship" when there is actually a deep abiding enmity in regard to policy.

If we don't send a team to Berlin in 1936 that will be, if you please, a slap at Hitler's leadership. On the other hand, if we do decide to be represented we are flying in the face of the declared opinion of a vast number of Americans.

★ ★ ★

Mr. Brundage has said that the agitation for withdrawal has been carried on wholly by people who "haven't been closer to Berlin than Manhattan Island." Avery Brundage has been in Germany and comes back to report that all conditions there are lovely. Might it not be a good idea for Mr. Brundage to get a little closer to America and a little further away from the Nazi host who showed him a good time?

He falls into the easy error of saying, "Many of the individuals and organizations active in the present campaign to boycott the Olympics have communistic antecedents. Radicals and communists must keep their hands off American sport."

It has been a familiar device recently to call anybody who disagreed with you a communist. It is admittedly true that radical organizations have gone on record against participation at Berlin. But it is equally true that those who support this gesture are by no means necessarily radical.

★ ★ ★

Again, it is untrue to hold that the issue is entirely one of protest against anti-Semitism. Although I must admit that I think that in itself is an excellent issue, still I am in complete agreement with Rabbi William Margolis,[37] who has said, "It is not now and it never was a Jewish issue, unless peace, justice, fair play and tolerance are also purely Jewish issues."

Least of all do I agree with the argument that those of us who would send no team are truculent fellows intent upon making trouble with a foreign nation with which we are maintaining an officially friendly attitude. I think there is grave danger of disturbance if American athletes compete at Berlin. [. . .] The risk of some misunderstanding, let us say, during the progress of the games is too great for comfort.

Moreover, it has been pointed out that Adolf Hitler has taken an attitude which is not traditional in his statement concerning the Olympic games. It is quite evident, and he has said so, that this meeting is to be used as a sort of propaganda occasion for the glorification of Fascist leadership for the youth of the world. If our young men and our young women go to Berlin we will not be preserving a neutral attitude. On the contrary, we will be paying tribute to a man who scorns and defies those democratic principles which are part of our heritage. [. . .]

Frankly, I am against participation because I'm wholeheartedly devoted to the fight against fascism. It has been said that the youth of America will be bitterly disappointed if we stay away. The youth of America has already been called upon to make its grave decision as to that kind of leadership which is symbolized by the swastika. There should be no loss of time in rejecting it emphatically.

Now is the time for all good men, and young persons as well, to come to the aid of liberty and freedom.

—Heywood Broun, Morning Post (Camden, NJ), October 28, 1935, 2.

The *New York Amsterdam News,* a leading African-American newspaper, encouraged track star Jesse Owens and other Black athletes to boycott the Olympics.

---

37. Rabbi William Margolis (1910–?): served at Congregation Ohab Zedek on the Upper West Side of New York City from 1932 to 1937. He was an outspoken critic of the US government's failure to protest Nazism.

Representatives of the National Association for the Advancement of Colored People (NAACP) also privately encouraged Owens to protest intolerance by boycotting.

Some African-American athletes resented being pressured to support the boycott movement over the discrimination against Jewish athletes in Germany while they endured America's pervasive racism and segregationist Jim Crow laws themselves. Others advocated participating in the games in the hope that Olympic victories by African Americans in Berlin would disprove ideas about "Aryan" racial superiority.

Eighteen African-American athletes participated in the Games and dominated the track and field events. Their victories abroad, however, did little to diminish racial discrimination and segregation at home.

17.

The 1936 Olympic Games
AN OPEN LETTER

To Jesse Owens. Eulace Peacock, Ralph Metcalfe, Cornelius Johnson, Willis Ward, James Luvalle [sic], Ben Johnson, and All Leading Negro Athletes in the A. A. U.[38]
The Amsterdam News congratulates you!

Despite the limitations placed upon you as members of a minority group, you have fought your way to the top. You have challenged and vanquished the myths of racial superiority and inferiority. Through sheer ability, determination and courage you have carried the banner of achievement beyond the narrow confines of race and nationalism. Accepting every opportunity, you have become symbols of that internationalism which is the ultimate goal of all civilization.

The Amsterdam News, however, wishes to call your attention to another opportunity—the greatest in your brilliant careers. An opportunity to challenge a force which seeks to destroy everything you have devoted your best years to building. A force which seeks to deny the universal equality you have so laboriously established. And yet, a force which is not above using you and your achievements to strengthen itself so that eventually it may destroy you. This force is Hitlerism as exemplified in present-day Germany—the scene of the 1936 Olympics.

Under Hitlerism, or the triumph in this country of similar forces, you would have had no opportunity to become the international figures you are. Under the barbaric

---

38. Owens, Peacock, Metcalfe, C. Johnson, Ward, and LuValle were members of the US track-and-field team at the Olympics. Ben Johnson was injured the week before the Games and could not participate. The Amateur Athletic Union, founded in 1888, is a multisport organization for the promotion of amateur sports.

rule of the Nazis, you would have become pariahs and have been subjected to the persecution and oppression which another prominent minority group has suffered in Germany. Under Hitlerism, you would have been denied even the limited opportunities which have been yours in America. And this oppression would not have been confined solely to the field of sports. The Nazi philosophy has bludgeoned its way into every field of human endeavor and has extended its poisonous tentacles far beyond the borders of Hitler Germany.

Humanity demands that Hitlerism be crushed. And yours is the opportunity to strike a blow which may hasten its inevitable end. As members of a minority group whose persecution the Nazis have encouraged,[39] as citizens of a country in which all liberty has not yet been destroyed, as leaders in a field which encourages the removal of all barriers of race, creed and color, you cannot afford to give moral and financial support to a philosophy which seeks the ultimate destruction of all you have fought for.

Your appearance there in the 1936 Olympic Games, the use of your magic names to attract thousands of tourists and sport fans to that country would undoubtedly furnish this moral and financial support.

Therefore, as an open protest against Hitlerism and its threat to civilization, The Amsterdam News begs you to refuse to participate in the Olympic Games in Germany in 1936. We beg you to demonstrate a courage which, so far, has been lacking in the guiding spirits of the American Olympic Committee. We beg you to display that spirit of self-sacrifice which is the true mark of greatness.

We make this request not only in the name of the 204,000 Negroes in Harlem, the 12,000,000 Negroes in America and the countless darker exploited colonials throughout the world. We speak in the name of humanity, of civilization, of all the forces of enlightenment which are threatened by the rise of Adolf Hitler and his barbaric National Socialist philosophy.

The world has never had occasion to doubt your courage. We do not believe that you will furnish that occasion now. The Amsterdam News, along with the millions who have followed your achievements, awaits your answer to this most vital question. Will you strike this blow?

Sincerely.
THE AMSTERDAM NEWS.

—*New York Amsterdam News,* August 24, 1935, 1.

39. Nazi Germany persecuted mixed-race children born of White German mothers and fathered by Black soldiers from France's African colonies. The French forces occupied Germany's Rhineland under the terms of the Treaty of Versailles. Beginning in 1937, Germany rounded up and forcibly sterilized several hundred African-German children.

Nazis in America

The German American Bund, established in 1936 as a pro-Nazi organization, encouraged its members to demonize Jews and Communists and dream of a fascist America. Fritz Kuhn, the Bund's leader and a naturalized American citizen, tried to portray himself as the "American *führer*" though he never received the support from the Nazi Party in Germany that he desired.

The Bund's membership, most of whom were Americans of German descent, probably never exceeded 25,000. Yet its pro-Nazi propaganda and mass demonstrations sometimes reached large crowds. At one Bund rally at New York's Madison Square Garden in 1939, more than 20,000 attendees booed any mention of President Franklin D. Roosevelt and cheered "Heil Hitler!" Thousands of anti-Nazi protesters filled the streets outside the arena.

In this article for the *American Magazine,* crime reporter Joseph F. Dinneen provides background on Kuhn and the Bund. Among his topics is the existence of American Nazi camps the Bund established across the United States to train German-American youth in military tactics and the philosophy of Adolf Hitler.

18.

Thousands of citizens shouting, "Heil" . . . Private troops drilling under the swastika . . . Here are the startling revelations about our rising army of goose-steppers

By Joseph F. Dinneen

AN AMERICAN *FÜHRER* ORGANIZES AN ARMY

The American Nazi Storm Troops, first private militia in our history, are prepared, as I write, to muster, this July, in New York for the annual convention of the Nazis in America. A self-styled German-American *führer* is to review them. In the ranks and among the members [. . .] are the combined remnants of the Ku Klux Klan, Gold Shirts, Silver Shirts, Black Legion, Silver Battalion, Pan-Aryan Alliance, and similar organizations.[40] In solemn conclave assembled, they will guarantee to this country "an America for Americans"—a strange and startling paradox.

Nazis in the United States are nothing new. They were investigated as early as 1934 by a congressional committee. Their activities have been widely publicized. But a drilled and uniformed private militia, the "storm troops," not a part of this country's armed force, is a development which presents a serious problem and establishes a dangerous precedent.

---

40. American radical proponents of antisemitism during the 1930s.

The "storm troops," organized within the Nazis on this side of the water, are committed to a form of government alien to this country. They have been permitted legally to arm and drill; to train, in one instance at least, with rifles taken from a New York armory. [. . .]

Nazis operate nine camps across the country where German-American children are drilled in German military tactics, including the goose-step, and in the beliefs and philosophy of Adolf Hitler. They maintain the most formidably organized boycott in the history of the country, issuing sectional business directories directing German-Americans where to buy. They levy a tax for this service upon German-American businessmen. They have instilled such fear into reputable German-American merchants and professional men that they are frankly afraid to criticize or discuss those Nazi leaders. They contribute a large sum annually to the parent organization in Germany. Last summer the American *führer*, Fritz Kühn, was photographed presenting this tithe to Adolf Hitler after Kühn and a uniformed detail of American Nazis had paraded before him.

An independent investigation of Nazi activities in the United States discloses that for purposes of organization this country has been divided into three districts: East, Central, and West. As I write, there are 78 local units in the larger cities. The more important of these in number of members and contributions are in Los Angeles and San Francisco, Calif.; Seattle, Wash.; Portland, Ore.; Detroit, Mich.; Toledo and Cleveland, Ohio; Pittsburgh, Pa.; Boston, Mass.; Baltimore, Md.; Washington, D. C.; Trenton, Newark, and Passaic and Bergen counties in New Jersey; Staten Island, the Bronx, Yorkville, Manhattan, and Jamaica in New York; and in the central district the larger units are in Sheboygan, Schenectady, Buffalo, and Kenosha. [. . .]

After days of negotiation in which there appeared to be at times considerable doubt and question, it was finally agreed that I might interview Fritz Kühn, the American *führer*, and I was to be permitted to make notes. It was raining that night when I presented myself to Wheeler Hill at the headquarters office, and after a short wait Hill escorted me along a corridor to a back room. After a signal knock, we were admitted, and Hill presented me to the *führer*. [. . .]

Kühn, seated at the desk, facing the door, was not alone. At his right sat two men who were not introduced by name, but during the course of the interview one was identified as the leader of uniformed American Nazi storm troops, the other as the comptroller of the American Nazi treasury.

Kühn is large and tall, stands six feet two or three, and weighs about 240 pounds. He is square-faced and heavy-jawed. His hair was clipped closely in the German military style, something like the American crew haircut. He appeared to be in his late forties. [. . .]

Kühn invited to me to sit down facing him, and there was a moment's inspection of me by all three. This, in substance, is the interview:

"What did you say your name is, again, please?" Kühn leaned forward upon the desk and looked at me.

"Dinneen," I told him. "Joseph F. Dinneen."

"How do you spell that?" he asked.

I spelled it for him.

"Are you an Aryan?" he asked.

I smiled. "I presume so," I told him. "My parents were Irish."

"You look Jewish," he told me.

"I know it," I agreed. "I've been told so quite often, but, as it happens, I'm Irish."

Kühn spoke to his associates in German, of which I understand only a little. The conversation became animated, and when quiet returned I gathered that my ancestry was not to be questioned further.

"Who do you write for?" Kühn asked.

"THE AMERICAN MAGAZINE," I told him.

"What is this AMERICAN MAGAZINE?" he asked.

"It's on every news and magazine stand in the country and on most of them throughout the world. Eight to ten million people read it every month. I'm surprised you haven't heard of it."

He shook his head. "We don't read American magazines," he said. "What do you want to know?"

"I want to know all you can tell me about the Nazis in America, their aims and ends, and how you propose to achieve them. As the president of the organization, I presume you are qualified to discuss it."

"I am not president," he said. "I am leader."

"Sorry," I told him. "I stand corrected. Leader!"

"What position are you going to take in your article?" he inquired.

"To tell the truth about it, accurately, impartially, and to the best of my ability."
[. . .]

Every question I asked had to be justified and its purpose explained. Many of my questions led to conferences among the five others now present, all of the conferences were carried on in German. Thus it was revealed that Fritz Kühn was born not far from Munich, Germany, educated at what corresponds to American grade and high schools, and served as a machine gunner in the German army during the World War. [. . .]

The Bund was originally organized as the Teutonia society in 1923 by Fritz Gissibl, a Chicago printing-press-man, newly arrived from Germany. Gissibl, then a boy of twenty, was solicited for membership in the Ku Klux Klan, thought the idea of the Klan was a good one, and adopted it for an all-German society with the same anti-Jewish and anti-Negro commitments. Objection to Catholics[41] was not then adopted, because many of them were admitted to membership.

41. During the early 1920s, the Klan began to target Catholics in addition to African Americans and Jews.

Teutonia was an obscure organization until 1932, when Adolf Hitler was making his first bid for power in Germany. Teutonia promptly climbed upon the Hitler band wagon. Its 500 members, mostly German, with some naturalized Americans, enrolled with Nazi headquarters in Germany as members of the National Socialist Labor Party of Germany. Because the Hitler program was anti-Jewish and anti-Catholic, and Teutonia now embraced it, all of the discredited and exposed apostles of hate in the United States were magnetically drawn to it.

Membership in Teutonia spurted immediately and amazingly. The first associated local was organized in Detroit, and here Kühn came into the American Nazi picture as the associate of Walter Hentchel, first president of the Detroit local. A New York local was organized and the tide of the Nazi party rose steadily.

When Hitler came into power in 1933, Americans became suddenly aware of the existence of an organization and a problem. Teutonia changed its name to "The Friends of New Germany," adopted the Hitler program in its entirety, and elected Heinz Spanknobel leader. The organization immediately became a problem for government investigation. [. . .]

A convention was held in Buffalo on March 29, 1936, and out of it came the new American *führer,* Fritz Kühn. From amid the black trousers and white shirts of the rank and file members, the olive-drab uniforms of the guard, and the green German uniforms of the storm troops he arose, came forward, and raised his hand beneath the swastika flag facing them. In response, they raised their hands in Nazi salute as they chorused, *"Heil Hitler!"*

One of the first official acts of the convention was to change the name of the organization from "the Friends of New Germany" to the "German-American Bund." [. . .]

Nothing succeeds like success, therefore it was all right to tell that the German-American Bund is a profitable, going concern and extensive property owner. Camp Siegfried, at Yaphank, Long Island, acquired three years ago, accommodated 15,000 German-American youths under twenty-one last summer. They drilled there with sticks and wooden guns under the guise of sport, attended numerous lectures every day, learned to admire, and almost adore Adolf Hitler, and were instructed in Nazi politics and policies.

The same course was provided at the Efdende Camp in Detroit, a twelve-year-old organization acquired by the Bund; at Northland, about 35 miles outside Paterson, N. J.; at the German Centrale in Cleveland; at Deutchborst, 50 miles out of Philadelphia; and at camps in Chicago, Buffalo, Los Angeles, and Portland, Ore. [. . .]

"How could I become a member of this organization?" I asked the *führer.*

"You'd have to file an application blank," he told me.

"May I have one?" I asked.

There was some doubt about that, but, after a conference in German, [Bund office manager] Wheeler Hill left the room and returned shortly with a blank. Beneath the title, "German-American Bund," and a reproduction of a swastika was the label, "Application for Membership," and the statement in boldface: "I hereby apply for admission to membership in the 'German-American Bund,' *the purposes and aims of which are known to me,* and I obligate myself to support them to the best of my ability. I recognize the leadership principle [*Führerprinzip*], in accordance to which the Bund is being directed. I am of Aryan origin, free from Jewish or colored blood." Beneath this were blanks for my name, occupation, address, year of birth, whether single, married, or widowed, nationality, references, and the question: "To what organizations do you belong?" The initiation fee is $2, monthly dues 75 cents, and there is a provision for donations of from 50 cents up.

"If I filled this out and filed it, what would happen?" I asked.

"You would be investigated by a committee of six members of the unit in your neighborhood. They would inquire into your character, reputation, and your past. It would take about six weeks."

"And as a member what would my duties be?"

"You'd attend all of the meetings. Each unit has one membership meeting a month and throughout the month there are a number of lectures and social and political talks. About every six weeks there is a festival. The biggest festival of the year is Washington's Birthday, which all units are compelled to celebrate. The second big festival is Armistice Day."

"Why do you pick those two days?"

This question brought what sounded like a memorized speech. I recorded it in shorthand and report it herewith:

"Because, although we are of German descent, we are patriotic Americans. The most important thing to us is: We are a group of Americans who only have the benefit of the United States in our minds. We do not like all of these false reports about Germany. We do not like to see these different groups who create hatreds of other countries which will affect diplomatic relationships. There was never such a thing as our attacking the Constitution of the United States. We need it. We are for a clean country, politically and socially. We do not like crookedness in politics. We are fighting Marxian doctrines in any form.

"We bring our German-American boys and girls together and take care of them. We educate them in history—American history. We try to make them all learn the German language, because they ought to know and speak the tongue of the Fatherland. We bring them to the great outdoors in our camps. We are doing a job of Americanism."

Mr. Kühn made this pronouncement striding up and down the room beneath a six-foot silk Nazi flag with its swastika boldly emblazoned. There wasn't an American flag in the room. [. . .]

The announced purposes of the Nazis in America are conflicting. Fritz Kühn has his idea of the purposes of the organization as outlined in his own words which I have quoted. The purposes of the organization at its last convention were outlined in these words:

"As an organization of American citizens it purposes to take a positive attitude in the affairs of the country, while complying unqualifiedly with its duties to the United States. We shall educate the American people to become friends of the new Germany; but, for us, there is no longer a new Germany—for us there is but the one and only Germany, the Germany of today—the National Socialist Germany—the third Reich; to form a protective front against machinations; as American citizens advance our political interests, defend our native land against slander and lies, and to a greater extent do justice to our exalted task of making known the aims and objects of the third Reich.

"The German-American Volksbund," the statement goes on, "is inspired with the National Socialist world concept. National Socialism has given the Germans in foreign countries a unified world view; they cannot survive without a spiritual tie with the homeland. We desire that the spiritual rebirth of the German people at home shall be spiritually transmitted to the Germans of America through the mediums of flaming words and inspiring examples." Otherwise, its announced purposes are to fight Bolshevism and Marxism.

There is nothing in the printed platform of the American Nazis concerning the storm troops. This organization within the party is not mentioned. There are no published or announced aims and purposes of storm troops. The serious menace, the uniformed and trained private militia, has, until now, been overlooked.

—*American Magazine*, August 1937, 14–15, 152–57.

Herblock [Herbert L. Block], "Still No Solution," for national distribution by the Newspaper Enterprise Association syndicate, January 1939.

CHAPTER 2

Desperate Times,
Limited Measures, 1938–1941

Americans' understanding of the Nazi threat changed dramatically in 1938. With bold political and military aggression, Nazi Germany annexed Austria in March. In September, Great Britain, France, and Italy agreed to Germany's demand to take over the Sudetenland, a largely German-speaking region of Czechoslovakia. In return, Hitler pledged peace when he signed the "Munich Agreement"—a pledge Germany would soon violate.

Anti-Jewish policies and violence increased considerably that fall, worsening conditions for Jews in the German Reich. On November 9–10, 1938, in an event known as *Kristallnacht,* the Nazi regime orchestrated a nationwide terror attack against Jews in Germany, the former Austria, and the Sudetenland. These terrifying days were covered extensively by the American press, more than any other news about persecution of Jews during the twelve years of Nazi Party rule.

The events of 1938 suddenly intensified the crisis for hundreds of thousands of Jews in Europe. In spring 1938, President Roosevelt called for an international conference to address the refugee issue. Though the delegates who met in Évian, France, that July expressed sympathy for the refugees, few made commitments of any action on their behalf. For its part, the United States was suffering the effects of another economic downturn in 1938, and increasing fears about national security combined with antisemitism and anti-immigrant sentiment at home contributed to a deep reluctance among most Americans to aid refugees.

When examining the increasing persecution against Jews in Germany throughout the 1930s, it may be tempting to ask: *Why didn't the Jews just leave?* One of the biggest hurdles was financial. In the German Reich after Kristallnacht, all Jewish-owned businesses were forcibly transferred to non-Jews, and new regulations prohibited Jews from most economic activities. The Nazi regime imposed a one-billion reichsmark fine on the Reich's Jews for the damage to property during the pogrom, to be paid as a 20 percent tax on all assets over 5,000 reichsmarks. Would-be emigrants faced an additional, exorbitant "flight tax" (first established in 1934) that seized nearly all remaining personal wealth, putting the price to book ship passage abroad out of reach for many. As impoverished refugees, they were unwelcome in countries still facing economic crises after the Depression. Moreover, to simply suggest that Jews should have "come to America" ignores or minimizes the significant and often insurmountable legal and financial immigration obstacles that had existed since the mid-1920s, well before Hitler came to power, and that continued unchanged by Congress throughout the 1930s. The United States had no "refugee policy" and thus could not offer legal protection to asylum seekers fleeing Nazi persecution during the 1930s. The challenges both to emigrate and to immigrate proved impossible to overcome for many who hoped to escape the horrors of Nazism.

The Refugee Crisis

German troops marched into Austria on March 12, 1938, and to the surprise of many, they received enthusiastic support from the people they met. Austria's leaders succumbed to German demands, and the nation was incorporated into Germany. Weeks later, this annexation—known as the *Anschluss*—was approved retroactively, in a manipulated direct vote that indicated 99 percent of the Austrian people favored Germany's actions. None of Austria's 192,000 Jews, 4 percent of the population, were permitted to vote.

The imposition of the German dictatorship followed quickly. The Nazi regime imprisoned Austria's leading politicians, and anyone who opposed Nazi rule faced arrest and possible torture, even death. Jews were publicly humiliated, their belongings looted and their businesses seized. The immediate implementation of Germany's existing anti-Jewish legislation, often violently enforced by Austrian Nazi collaborators, forced Jews from their jobs and effectively expelled them from Austria's economic, social, and cultural life.

Two days into the Anschluss, the Associated Press explained the events to American readers, focusing especially on the danger faced by the Jewish population.

1.

HITLER ENTERS VIENNA AS JEWS BEGIN TO FEEL WEIGHT OF PERSECUTION

President of Austria Quits; Reich Absorbs Entire German Nation

---

Fuehrer in Triumphal Entry Into Capital—Jews Ejected from Bar Association and From Hospital Organization

---

SWASTIKAS FLY PROUDLY OVER FORMER PALACE OF HAPSBURGS

VIENNA, March 14 (AP)—Adolf Hitler today triumphantly entered Vienna, capital of the German state he has absorbed in his greater German Reich. His motor cavalcade passed the city limits at 4:50 P.M (10:50 A.M. EST).

Hitler, who had changed to an open motor car during his 100-mile journey from Linz, entered his Vienna standing up, bowing, smiling to hundreds of thousands lining the route.

A hundred thousand persons around his hotel roared and demanded his appearance on the balcony.

Once was not enough. Again and again they demanded his return.

They continued to insist that he speak to them until it was announced he would be welcomed officially to Vienna at 11 A.M. tomorrow in the Heroes' Square and that then he would speak.

With Hitler was Heinrich Himmler, chief of all German police, and other high officials of the Reich.

The journey through a smiling countryside from Linz, where he had remained since his coming to Austria Saturday, was like a royal progress, through throngs of the Fuehrer's exultant followers.

An Austrian government of his choice had prepared for his coming by announcing the absorption of Austria into the German nation, now stretching from the North Sea almost to the Adriatic.

Hysteria swept Vienna Jewry.

Hundreds lined up before the Polish and other consulates to ask [for] visas to enable them to leave the country.

A number of Vienna coffee houses were placarded with warnings on doors and windows: "Jews not permitted to enter."

The post office announced every parcel intended for foreign countries would be opened and searched to prevent smuggling of money from the country. [. . .]

As Nazi ecstasy welled up, Austria had approximately duplicated in three days the anti-Semitic measures which required three years for Hitler to effect in Germany.

Vienna Jews grasped at two straws in the whirlwind—escape or the hope that traditionally easy-going Austrian friendliness might soon emerge to curb what they called "German relentlessness."

Suppressive action against the B'nai B'rith lodge was taken yesterday—similar to a move made in Germany three years after Hitler came to power. Storm troopers took over the rooms of the lodge.

Today a crowd of uniformed Nazis invaded a large delicatessen and stripped it bare.

Other storm troopers occupied a fashionable restaurant on the Ring,[1] opposite Nazi headquarters, broke up the furniture, ejected the Jewish proprietor and erected a big sign: "Reopened under Aryan management. No Jews wanted."

Jews were ejected from the Vienna Bar Association. Jewish physicians were barred from the Viennese emergency hospital organization. This was regarded as presaging

---

1. Vienna's Ring Road (*Ringstrasse*): the grand boulevard that encircles the historic center of the city.

firm action against Jewish physicians, who make up a large percentage of the Austrian medical profession. Vienna has been a world medical and surgical center.

The number of wealthy Jews arrested for trying to flee the country with money was multiplying. [. . .]

Hitler made his tour of triumph in a slow procession from Upper Austria while Vienna arranged a conqueror's welcome for him.

He left Vienna, a poor student-laborer, 20-odd years ago.

—Associated Press, *Public Opinion* (Chambersburg, PA), March 14, 1938, 1, 2.

Journalist Dorothy Thompson[2] wrote extensively about the plight of refugees around the world during the 1930s. In 1938, even as she published more than 100 newspaper columns and delivered dozens of radio broadcasts, Thompson also wrote *Refugees: Anarchy or Organization?* Her slim book, published before the Munich Agreement, addressed the growing refugee crisis that resulted from Nazi rule, especially as a result of Germany's annexation of Austria (Anschluss) in March 1938.

Thompson's *Refugees* spelled out the challenges faced by Jewish refugees seeking to flee German-controlled territory. She also put these challenges into a larger context of the migrations of peoples and the increasingly restrictive immigration policies throughout the world that emerged after World War I. She focused especially on the bureaucratic hurdles that immigrants faced as they sought to gather all the necessary papers to document their identity, leave their home country, and enter the United States. Securing this paperwork had become such a significant obstacle that Thompson declared, "It is a fantastic commentary on the inhumanity of our times that for thousands and thousands of people a piece of paper with a stamp on it is the difference between life and death."[3]

2.

Refugees: Anarchy or Organization?

The Problem

As I write this, the news from Europe is distressing in the extreme. Austria has become a district of Greater Germany. Central Europe is in turmoil, as every small state of the Danube Basin feels the increasing pressure of Nazidom. Great Britain and,

2. Dorothy Thompson (1893–1961): a leading American reporter and radio commentator from the early 1920s to the 1950s. Working in Munich in 1931, she interviewed Hitler and wrote a scathing critique of him and his antisemitic Nazi movement. Because of it, in 1934 she was the first American journalist to be expelled from Germany.

3. Dorothy Thompson, *Refugees*, 28. Her statement chillingly continues: " . . . and that scores of people have blown their brains out because they could not get it."

following her leadership, France are considering whether—and if so, how—to protect Czechoslovakia, and whether—and if so, how—to save even a modified League of Nations. [. . .] These chaotic situations cannot fail to add to a problem which is already a world headache—that of dispossessed racial and political minorities.

[. . .] In Germany, more and more Jews are being deprived of the means to continue living in the homes they have had for centuries, while the situation of many Christians, both Protestant and Catholic, is, to say the least, precarious. On the heels of the Nazi victory in Austria there has followed a regime of terror for Jews, for partisans of Dollfuss[4] and Schuschnigg,[5] for still-surviving liberals, for proponents of a Hapsburg restoration[6] and also for Catholics—thus creating a pressing new problem of refugees. [. . .]

In the Danube Basin alone—in Austria, Czechoslovakia, Romania, Hungary and Yugoslavia—live some two million Jews. There are over three million more in Poland. And these figures do not include Christian converts, or men, women and children of part Jewish blood who under the German Nuremberg laws are assigned to the Jewish community.[7] Austria has many such. There are also many in Czechoslovakia and Hungary. If any more countries fall under Nazi domination, or come under Nazi influence, a further growth of anti-Semitism is certain. [. . .] Millions of Jews nevertheless are in danger of becoming pariahs. And at least a part of them will make every effort to leave their homes to escape starvation.

Since the end of the war some four million people have been compelled by political pressure to leave their homes. A whole nation of people, although they come from many nations, wanders the world, homeless except for refuges which may any moment prove to be temporary. They are men and women who often have no passports; who, if they have money, cannot command it; who, though they have skills, are not allowed to use them. This migration—unprecedented in modern times, set loose by the World War and the revolutions in its wake—includes people of every race and every social class, every trade and every profession[. . . .]

The possibility that this number is to be augmented within the immediate future is undeniable. To close one's eyes to it would be ostrichism[8] in an acute form. [. . .]

---

4. Engelbert Dollfuss (1892–1934): chancellor of Austria, 1932–34. In 1933, he abolished the Austrian parliament and seized dictatorial powers to control the government. He was assassinated in a failed Austrian Nazi Party coup attempt.

5. Karl Schuschnigg (1897–1977): succeeded Dollfuss as chancellor in 1934. A firm opponent to Germany's Nazi Party, he was forced by Hitler to resign the day before Germany's occupation in the Anschluss and was imprisoned.

6. The Hapsburg imperial dynasty ruled Austria and its eventual empire from 1278 to 1918.

7. Subsequent additions to the Nuremberg laws categorized "full" and "mixed-race" Jews based on the legally defined "race" of an individual's grandparents.

8. Ostrichism: "burying one's head in the sand," the deliberate avoidance of existing conditions.

President Roosevelt Appeals

Therefore, the appeal of President Roosevelt for international action to aid political refugees[9] is not only timely, generous and imaginative, but it is extremely necessary—not for the sake of the refugees only, but for the sake of all countries that are anxious to prevent further unrest and economic and social disequilibrium.

Obviously what this action needs is a program and efficient organization to deal with the whole matter.

The moment is not politically inopportune. The very urgency of the European crisis provides arguments for such an agency. [. . .] Too long the refugee problem has been largely regarded as one of international charity. It must be regarded now as a problem of international politics. Actually what prompted the President of the United States to take a hand in it was, no doubt, a keen sense of self-preservation. The world, as it is, is a place of unrest and agitation with desperate people taking desperate measures in the attempt merely to survive. And millions of people wandering more or less aimlessly, and battering at every conceivable door, being passed from frontier to frontier, will certainly do nothing to restore world order.

Nor can any democratic country wash its hands of this problem if it wishes to retain its own soul. The very essence of the democratic principle is humanistic; it involves respect for human dignity and human personality; it implies a revulsion against persecution of individuals; it rejects arbitrary edicts; when its capacity for righteous indignation is exhausted by weariness or by callousness, then the democratic principle will die.

It is perfectly true that the problem has not been created by the democracies but by new forms of government which reject the concepts of law and ethics that still rule the democratic world. The burden is not of our making, but nevertheless it is impossible for us not to accept the burden put upon us, and while opposing the political attitudes which have created it, to try to meet it and deal with it.

We have got to face the reality that liberal democracy is the most demanding of all political faiths, and in the world today the most aristocratic. It is a political philosophy which makes painful demands. That is its price. That is also its glory.

And so a defeatist attitude toward the refugee problem, created by the opponents of democracy, becomes a defeatist attitude toward democracy itself.

The Jewish Refugees

When the exodus from Germany started in 1933, the world began to look at the refugee problem as exclusively Jewish.

This is an error. The refugee question is not even essentially Jewish in those countries which make anti-Semitism their leading idea! [. . .] Among those who were

---

9. March 24, 1938; the Évian Conference (July 6–11, 1938) met after Thompson's book was published.

obliged to leave their homeland as a result of legislative measures enacted against them—the so-called Aryan laws—only a fraction are Jews by the standards of any other world than that of Mr. Hitler. [. . .]

Nevertheless, since 750,000 Jews are the foremost victims of persecution in Germany and former Austria; since anti-Semitic propaganda already casts a shadow over the lives of nearly two millions in Hungary, and Romania; since the problem of three and a half million Polish Jews was acute long before Mr. Hitler thought up his Aryan ideology; since thus the number of Jewish refugees within the immediate future will possibly be augmented—it would be ostrichism to close one's eyes to the fact that the question of the Jewish refugee is a major question of international politics.

The challenge is one which the Jews of the whole world must face—and above all the Jews of America, who constitute one-fourth of world Jewry. It is a challenge, moreover, to the prescience and common sense of any racial or religious minority which has ever known persecution or discrimination anywhere in the past; for if these do not now protest the abuse of other minorities what moral grounds will they have for protesting if once again their own rights are threatened?

But it is—even more importantly—a challenge to all responsible political circles, not only to those who condemn persecution for humanitarian reasons but also to those who, taking a purely practical view, fear that starving minorities within the anti-Semitic countries, and an uncontrolled flow of wandering Jews outside, will add further elements of unrest to an already restless world. Nor can the anti-Semitic governments themselves be indifferent, for in the long run—though they may find it gratifying to have the Jews "liquidated"—it is uncomfortable to have in one's midst a body of desperate pariahs.

The Reaction of World Jewry

Up to now, neither the democratic governments, nor the creators of the problem have made an attempt to achieve a constructive solution.

The German Government looks on while a problem is growing up for which mass starvation seems hardly a solution, even for Germany!

Responsible political circles in the world find it too ticklish a problem to tackle because it may imply interference in the internal affairs of other countries, and also because they are afraid that to raise the question of emigration may produce anti-Semitism in their own countries.

As for the Jews of the world, they have made a few gestures of understandable but ineffective protest against Nazi Germany—the boycott the strongest. But the boycott did not substantially weaken the Nazis economically and in any case did not soften their anti-Semitic policy. Instead, the boycott acted as a boomerang against the boycotting Jews in the democratic countries, by awakening anti-Semitism among non-Jews who wanted to do business with Germany, Nazi or not.

In addition, the Jews practiced a magnificently generous philanthropy. They placed huge sums at the disposal of the Jewish organizations which were helping numbers of German Jews to get out of Germany and to find a refuge elsewhere, temporary or permanent. Yet, as anti-Semitic policies spread through Europe it becomes clearer and clearer that charity is not enough. It cannot be too often emphasized that the problem must be regarded and treated as one of international politics. The only approach to a solution must be a political approach.

The Unique Nature of Today's Anti-Semitism

There have been anti-Semitic movements in the world before. Russian pogroms under the Tsar are alive in the memories of many. But the Jewish persecution of our era is peculiar. It is not directed against the ghetto Jew alone, but against the Jewish race as such—against the Jew who has retained his religion and against the Jew who has discarded it.

Moreover a Jewish race is actually created by fiat, disregarding most of the scientific opinion of the world. [. . .] And the Nuremberg laws have even a fundamental lack of logic. For they admit that there is a point in interbreeding where a Jew ceases to be a Jew. They admit the possibility of complete racial absorption, and therefore logic should lead them to solve their problem—if they consider they have one—by racial absorption.

But this artificial creation of a race problem within the white race puts the Jews in a madly impossible position. [. . .]

The assimilated German and Austrian Jews outlawed by Hitler have no separate civilization of their own to fall back on. [. . .]

The German and Austrian Jews are Germans and Austrians. The only civilization they know is the civilization they shared with the German and Austrian nations. When Hitler's laws denied them this civilization, they found themselves in a moral and cultural void. And there was no way out. The aristocrat of the French Revolution could save himself by becoming a *citoyen* [citizen]. The Russian bourgeois could save himself by becoming a *tovaritsch* [comrade]. The German Jew can never become an Aryan. [. . .]

—Dorothy Thompson, *Refugees: Anarchy or Organization?*
(New York: Random House, 1938), excerpted from chapters 1 and 3.

Sympathy without Action

Germany's annexation of Austria in March 1938, the Anschluss, brought nearly 200,000 additional Jews under Nazi rule. In the weeks that followed, thousands of Austrian Jews desperate to emigrate lined up at the US consulate in Vienna. Like German Jews, most ended up on long waiting lists for visas as the number of applicants far exceeded the annual immigration quota. In the immediate aftermath of the

Anschluss, President Roosevelt adjusted American immigration policy by combining the Austrian quota of 1,413 visas with the existing German quota, making 27,370 visas available each year for people born in these two countries, now all considered "German."

Roosevelt also called for an international conference on the refugee crisis. Delegates from 32 countries gathered in Évian-les-Bains, France, July 6–11, 1938. In their statements made throughout the conference, most representatives cited economic concerns to justify their nations' reluctance to let refugees enter. Some spoke bluntly about not wanting to admit Jews.

American newspapers and magazines criticized the participants for their inaction. As *Time* magazine concluded: "All nations present expressed sympathy for the refugees but few offered to allow them within their boundaries."

3.

DEPARTMENT OF STATE

FOR THE PRESS   MARCH 24, 1938

This Government has become so impressed with the urgency of the problem of political refugees that it has inquired of a number of Governments in Europe and in this hemisphere[10] whether they would be willing to cooperate in getting up a special committee for the purpose of facilitating the emigration from Austria and presumably from Germany of political refugees. Our idea is that whereas such representatives would be designated by the Governments concerned, any financing of the emergency emigration referred to would be undertaken by private organizations within the respective countries. Furthermore, it should be understood that no country would be expected or asked to receive a greater number of immigrants than is permitted by its existing legislation. In making this proposal the Government of the United States has emphasized that it in no sense intends to discourage or interfere with such work as is already being done on the refugee problem by any existing international agency. It has been prompted to make its proposal because of the urgency of the problem with which the world is faced and the necessity of speedy cooperative effort under governmental supervision if widespread human suffering is to be averted.

—Press release, March 24, 1938, "Political Refugees
Jan.–May 1938," Official File 3186, FDRL.

10. The proposal was sent to the United Kingdom, France, Belgium, The Netherlands, Denmark, Sweden, Norway, Switzerland, and Italy, as well as to all Latin American countries.

4.

'Yes, But—' Attitude Perils Progress at World Refugee Conference

————

Nations Fear Flow of Jews From Europe

————

All Assert Willingness to Help but Stress Own Inability.

————

Say Immigrants Would Unsettle Economics and Populations.

————

By Gerald G. Gross.

Americans with their homes, their gardens, their jobs, their bathing beaches cannot fully comprehend the situation of "some millions of people" in Europe who but a few years ago felt equally secure but today are unwanted anywhere on the face of the globe.

Jews for the most part, but also including Catholics and Protestants sharing a common misfortune in having been born and reared in lands where Fascist rule was destined to bloom, they are the pathetic pawns for whose sake the Inter-governmental Refuge Conference now is meeting at Evian, France.

"Men and women of every race, creed and economic condition, of every profession and of every trade, are being uprooted from the homes where they have long been established and turned adrift without thought or care as to what will become of them or where they will go," Myron C. Taylor,[11] president of the committee and chairman of the American delegation, said last Thursday at convening of the history making conference.

Attitude of Nations Seems to Be, 'Yes, but—'

What will become of them? Germany and Austria together are estimated to have 1,000,000 citizens, two-thirds of whom are full-blooded Jews and the remainder persecuted Christians, who wish to emigrate.

According to a statement presented to the conference by a German priest, in behalf of Catholic groups, 10,000 members of that faith have fled the Reich and 500,000 are threatened with expulsion. It estimated that Palestine has received 10,000 Jewish refugees from Germany.

By the Nuremberg definition of "Jew," there are upward of 3,000,000 others in Greater Germany who are subject to the same window smashing, professional exclusion, disenfranchisement and other tyrannies, and who must, therefore, be considered within the scope of the Evian parley.

---

11. Myron C. Taylor (1874–1959): an industrialist before turning to international affairs, first as leader of the US delegation to and chairman of the Évian Conference, and then as envoy to the Vatican (1939–50) before he retired from public service.

At Evian it has been a disappointment, if not altogether a surprise, to these millions of unfortunates and their sympathizers in America and elsewhere, that scarcely has the conference opened than delegates take the floor to say, "We feel sorry for refugees and potential refugees but—." [. . .]

Number Coming Here Quite Moderate

When President Roosevelt last March 24 announced his intention of inviting the world's democratic nations to send representatives to a conference on the refugee problem, the idea was acclaimed both at home and abroad. Of the governments in this hemisphere, only little El Salvador is unrepresented at Evian. Funds were allotted willingly to send delegates thousands of miles to the fashionable French watering place across from Lausanne, but most of them, it seems, were instructed to open every statement with a "Yes, but—."

In the United States there exists a sentiment that too many, or at least enough Jews already come here from Europe and the number of new immigrants should be kept to an absolute minimum. To get at the facts, the writer went to the Immigration and Naturalization Service of the Department of Labor.

"We are receiving a large number of protests from people who seem to think a mass migration to the United States of German Jews is under way," said Deputy Commissioner Edward J. Shaughnessy. "Many of these complaints are by citizens who have crossed the Atlantic recently on the steamships Manhattan and Washington.

"Traveling on those liners, it is not difficult to get the impression that Hebrews are pouring into this country by thousands, inasmuch as those two vessels sail directly from Hamburg and accommodate a sizable percentage of the German refugees who have been able to meet the rigid requirements for admittance to the United States.

"Actually, however, the volume of newcomers is quite moderate. It could hardly be otherwise, due to the formidable obstacles placed before would-be emigrants and our own restrictive laws."

Another high official in the Labor Department expressed the opinion that the quota act is sufficient guarantee that America will face no additional economic hazard in accepting refugees. [. . .]

But let us see what story the statistics tell.

For the months of July to November, 1937, inclusive, latest for which official figures are available, the following table is presented:

Previous Residence	Number of Immigrants	Annual Quota
Austria	303	1,413
Czechoslovakia	1,146	2,874
Germany	6,969	25,957
Italy	1,298	5,802
Soviet Union	368	2,712
Spain	209	252

[. . .] When President Hoover, in September, 1930, ordered the State Department to have American consulates tighten up on visa issuances as a measure against the growing depression he effected an appreciable reduction in the number of immigrants, Jewish and otherwise. From a grand total of 241,700 in 1930 there was a drop to 97,139 in 1931, 35,576 in 1932 and 23,068 in 1933. Hebrew arrivals, numbering 11,526 in 1930, had plummeted to 2,372 in 1933. [. . .]

Failure Would Put U. S. 'on the Spot'

Although he tried to elude the honor, Mr. Taylor, former chairman of the United States Steel Corporation, was made president of the Intergovernmental Refugee Conference by acclamation—which puts this country on a prestige spot should the assembly fail, especially since the French parley was President Roosevelt's idea.

Writing last week from Vienna, Vincent Sheean estimated in the New York Herald Tribune that least 50,000 "undesirables" have been jailed in Vienna alone since Austria became part of the Reich on March 12.

He told of 20,000 Jews now in jails and concentration camps and of 15,000 Catholic families eager to leave for other lands. Permission to leave is extremely difficult to obtain and, when that is accomplished, there are still the ever-so strict health, financial and other requirements of the countries to which the refugee might turn.

Problem Requires Intergovernmental Study

"The problem is no longer one of purely private concern," Mr. Taylor said. "It is a problem for intergovernmental deliberation. If the present currents of migration are permitted to continue to push anarchically upon the receiving States, and if some governments are to continue to toss large sections of their populations lightly upon a distressed and unprepared world, then there is catastrophic human suffering ahead which can only result in general unrest and in general international strain which will not be conducive to the permanent appeasement to which all peoples earnestly aspire."

—*Washington Post*, July 10, 1938, B7.

5.

Foreign News
INTERNATIONAL
Refugees

Around the shores of blue Lake Léman, dividing France and Switzerland, lie historic international conference cities, Geneva, Lausanne, Montreux, Nyon. Last week, the gay [lively] French resort of Evian-les-Bains was added to the list as delegates from 32 nations, including three world powers (U. S., France, Britain), four British Dominions (Australia, New Zealand, Canada, Eire [Ireland]), most of the Latin American nations and several smaller European powers, there set up headquarters in the luxurious Hotel Royal. They came in answer to President Roosevelt's invitation, issued soon after Germany annexed Austria, to see what could be done to provide new homes for racial and political refugees. Germany was not invited; Italy, out of sympathy for the Reich, declined to attend.

Evian is the home of a famous spring of still and unexciting table water. After a week of many warm words of idealism, few practical suggestions, the Intergovernmental Committee on Political Refugees took on some of the same characteristics. Two days of stalling went on before a president was elected. No delegate wanted the post, each fearing that his nation would then be responsible for the conference's all-too-probable failure. Finally stocky, publicity-hating Myron C. Taylor, onetime Chairman of U. S. Steel Corp. and chief U. S. delegate, agreed to accept.

All nations present expressed sympathy for the refugees but few offered to allow them within their boundaries. Britain, France, Belgium pleaded that they had already absorbed their capacity, Australia turned in a flat "No" to Jews, and the U. S. announced that she would combine her former annual Austrian immigration quota with her German to admit 27,370 persons (who can support themselves) from Greater Germany next year. Almost sole note of encouragement came from eight Latin American nations: Argentina, Colombia, Ecuador, Uruguay, Peru, Venezuela, Mexico and the Dominican Republic (which nine months ago massacred 1,000 neighboring Haitians because they moved into her territory[12]), offered to accept a limited number of refugees if they came as agricultural workers.

As each nation presented its views, it became clear that there were two fundamental splits to be bridged before a plan could be put into effect:

1) Britain and France want any plan for transplanting refugees to be carried out by existing League of Nations bodies. The U. S., backed by non-League Latin American nations, feels that since the conference's first move will have to be negotiation with League-hating Germany[13] for removal of her Jewish and anti-Nazi population, a body completely removed from League influence would have more chance of success.

2) Britain and France want to limit proposals to the handling of refugees from Germany alone. The U. S. insists that the conference constitute a permanent body to handle not only the German problem but any other refugee question that may arise, from such potential refugee producers as Italy, Poland and Romania.

—*Time*, July 18, 1938, 16.

12. Estimates of Haitian deaths in this massacre range widely, from this 1,000 figure to as many as 30,000.

13. Hitler withdrew Germany from the League of Nations in November 1933, after a national referendum on the question was approved by 95 percent of voters.

In Search of Refuge: Teenage Pen Pals

Marianne Winter, a fourteen-year-old Jewish girl in Vienna, became pen pals with Jane Bomberger, a non-Jewish girl in Reading, Pennsylvania, in 1935. Three years later, Nazi Germany invaded Austria. The Winter family was desperate to leave, but they did not have any American relatives who could sponsor them to immigrate to the United States. Although the girls had never met in person and the Bombergers were not wealthy, Jane's father, Joseph, agreed to financially support Marianne, her parents, and her younger brother, Stefan.

Despite Joseph Bomberger's generosity, the Winters still had great difficulty obtaining US immigration visas. The letters here from Marianne to Jane document some of these difficulties, as well as her father Max's gratitude to the Bombergers for their sponsorship. (Jane's letters to Marianne were lost when the Winters left Vienna.)

The Winter family finally arrived in Pennsylvania in 1939. Their journey took them from Vienna to Prague, through Switzerland, to the seaport at Genoa, Italy, and finally by ship to New York, where the Bombergers met them. They lived with the Bombergers before getting settled on their own.

The letters underscore that English was not Marianne's first language.

6.

[June 6, 1938]

My dear Jane!

Please, I hope you will excuse that I haven't written sooner. You cannot imagine how happy I was when I got your letter in all that time. It showed me that I really have some real friends who think on me also in bad times. I am sure you follow the papers and so I need not tell you details.

Facts are that we have to immigrate under every circumstances and of course I know that you and your family have not the money to claim for us[. . . .] Now I ask you, my dear, if it would be possible for you to get a connection with any rich man who would be able to give an affidavit. [. . .]

I am quite sure that you will do everything you can, and I know that it is not sure that your efforts will success. Though I cannot write such a good English I want to explain how grateful [*illegible*].

I hope that in your house everyone is quite well. [. . .] Here, I mean at home much has changed. My father is not able to earn what we would need. It is sad to say that he have no one in U.S.A, so that I have to ask you. My father has some other plans for Australia and Brasil too, but we do not see any possibility to come in. We are all well, my brother is just in school and I am in shop. Now we can not swim but we have to get a bath for the summer. I congratulate you for your success at school, and I hope you will spend a fine summer. Please, do not forget me and write very soon for me that is very urgent you know?

> With the best greetings to you, your family, and Quentin, I am
> Lovingly, yours truly,
> [*Marianne*]

Vienna, the 29 of June 1938

My dear, dearest Jane!

You can not imagine how we felt after having received your letter an hour ago. We could not believe that there are such people, who are really so kind to help us. It is not to think that real strangers, as you are, give us so much love. To my mother came the tears when we received the letter, because no one of our family understood our situation as well as you did.

Of course my parents give you the most thanks and would like to accept. We thank you again and again that your yourselves have claimed for us. We have enough money, for to cross, thank you, and my mother has three brothers abroad, who do live in Europe, and so they can-not take us to them, but who promised us to give us a certain amount of money for a start. So that you need not fear that we would fall into your pockets.

We can not imagine, how I feel to think to see you in a short time, do you remember in your first letter you wrote me that you have dreamed I was with you. Now it will be true. But it will last two month till we get the papers for to leave.

I thank you again for your frank question about money, because we can not take any money out of there.

I cannot express, how we feel, everything I write is too little, but I hope that once we will be able to show our thanks, we are so happy.

> Now I dare say, we will, I hope, see each other very soon, I am
> Yours lovingly,
> [Marianne]

Dear Sir [*addressed to Jane's father*],

I beg to express you my deepest thanks for your immense kindness. My wife and I are too happy to see the way of getting out from here. Be convinced that we will do everything not to incommodate [*sic*] you and your family in any way.

> I am also with the best greetings also from my wife,
> Your obedient servant
> [Max Winter]

> —Letters, June 6 and 29, 1938, Winter Family Papers,
> USHMM Collection, Gift of Marianne Selinger.

7.

'Hands Across Sea' Are Joined

Correspondence which Jane Bomberger, daughter of Mr. and Mrs. Joseph Bomberger, of 920 Lancaster avenue, started with an Austrian Jewish girl, while she was a member of the Camp Fire Girls, yesterday had brought deliverance from Nazi persecution to the Vienna girl's family. The 18-year-old friend abroad, seeking desperately to relieve the plight of her family, asked Miss Bomberger if it would be possible for them to come to the United States, and the Bombergers arranged it. Miss Bomberger is pictured at the left. Fearing retaliation on relatives in Germany, the family of four declined to permit their names to be used.

—*Reading (PA) Eagle*, February 5, 1939, Winter Family Papers, USHMM Collection, Gift of Marianne Selinger.

November Pogrom

Nazi Party and government officials, supported by the police, set off a nation-wide riot against Jews in Germany and Austria on the night of November 9–10, 1938. Party leaders claimed that the riots were a spontaneous public response to the assassination of a Paris-based German diplomatic official, Ernst vom Rath, by teenaged Herschel Grynszpan, the German-born son of Polish Jewish refugees. In fact, this unprecedented violence was highly coordinated by Germany's leaders.

The Nazi Party's SA militia and Hitler Youth destroyed hundreds of synagogues and thousands of Jewish-owned shops. Nazi police forces arrested nearly 30,000 Jewish men and sent them to concentration camps, where hundreds died of brutal mistreatment. This event is known as Kristallnacht, the "Night of Broken Glass," for all the shattered windows.

American newspapers covered the Nazi terror attack against Jews with banner headlines on the front pages, and articles about the events continued to appear for several weeks. No other story about Nazi persecution of Jews received such widespread, sustained attention from the American press at any time during the Nazi rule.

8.

Hysterical Nazis Wreck Thousands of Jewish Shops,
Burn Synagogues in Wild Orgy of Looting and Terror

Policemen Refuse To Halt Organized Riots in Germany

Many Non-Aryans Commit Suicide; Goebbels Calls Violence Justifiable As Revenge for Paris Assassination

BERLIN, Nov. 10 (UP).—Mobs of enraged Nazis, ignoring government orders to halt, Thursday night continued a wild orgy of looting and destruction throughout Germany in the worst wave of anti-Semitic terror experienced since Adolf Hitler's rise to power. The terror extended into the night, with bonfires, built from merchandise stripped from Jewish shops, blazing in the streets.

The mobs, in almost every city and town of the Greater Reich, had worked themselves to such hysteria that in many places they paid no heed to Propaganda Minister Paul Joseph Goebbels' orders calling a halt to the destruction.

They demanded that every Jew in Germany be made to suffer for the assassination in Paris of Ernst vom Rath, third secretary of the German Embassy, by a 17-year-old Polish Jew [Herschel Grynszpan] whose parents were expelled from the Reich last month.[14]

It was reported with confirmation that two Jews had been shot and killed in other towns. [. . .]

Shortly before midnight Berlin police and Storm Troopers, patrolling in groups of three, succeeded in dispersing the crowds eight hours after Goebbels' order was issued.

Early editions of morning newspapers disposed of the violence with brief accounts. The Berliner Tageblatt, for example, gave it about 150 words on page 3.

Suicides Everywhere.

In its wake the Nazi terror left:

Between twenty-five and thirty charred and gutted synagogues, fired by torches and dynamite.

Suicides of despairing Jews everywhere. Fifty persons attempted suicide in Vienna alone.

Whole blocks strewn with debris in the finest shopping districts of Berlin, Vienna, Munich and other cities.

An estimated 12,000 Jewish stores in ruin.

Thousands of arrests of Jews.

---

14. The so-called Polish Action, late October 1938: the German security Secret State Police (Gestapo) ordered the arrest and deportation of 17,000 Polish Jews living in Germany in retaliation for the Polish government's refusal to validate their Polish citizenship and readmit them.

Badly battered non-Aryans, beaten and kicked in the streets by jeering Germans while police looked on passively.

An order to all Jews in Munich to leave within forty-eight hours; some were told to leave the Reich.

Goebbels' promise to the mobs that Germany's further answer to Jewry will be in the form of laws and decrees and indications that, after five and one-half years of anti-Jewish measures, Hitler is ready to expel all Jews and confiscate all Jewish property.

Justifiable, Says Goebbels.

The outbreak of the terror, which was sheer madness for eighteen hours, was well organized and, like the police who look on with apathy, Goebbels called it justifiable in view of the assassination in Paris.

The violence was Germany's comprehensible answer to the slaying of Vom Rath, the Propaganda Minister said.

Several hundred persons were arrested for looting in Berlin after police and Storm Troop reserves had been called out, but the crowds' anger continued surging high.

There was not an undamaged Jewish shop in the center of Berlin, along the Friedrichstrasse and Unter den Linden.

Crowds, including Storm Troopers wearing their badges, still surged the thoroughfares near midnight and continued to break into and wreck Jewish-owned businesses that had escaped during the day because of iron-grilled windows and barred doors.

When ordinary wrecking methods failed, steel hatchets and fire did the work.

Police Shrug at Looting.

The looting in some places reached the grab-bag stage.

In a large arcade connecting Unter den Linden with the Behrenstrasse men and women clambered through shattered windows into shops, passing out toys and jewelry.

A policeman shrugged and said:

"We have orders for no more damage or looting, but what can I do?"

Bonfires made from Jewish stocks and prayer books from synagogues cast flickering light on the roving mobs.

As a Jewish basement shop door caved in under the blows of hatchets a woman and her small daughter fled, to the jeers of several hundred persons. Nearby a youth, recognized as a Jew, was beaten almost insensible. A cruising police car moved on, uninterested. [. . .]

Even Homes Destroyed.

[. . .] Truckloads of arrested Jews moved through the streets. A dozen trucks unloaded their prisoners at the Alexanderplatz police station while a crowd of 3,000 shouted: "Send the Jewish dogs to Palestine—send them across the border!"

When the supply of Jewish shops began to run out in many towns, the Nazi mobs turned to the destruction of homes.

Five or six youngsters, the oldest only about 15, attacked a middle-aged man on a quiet residential street, knocking him down and pummeling him while a cheering circle of children chanted "Jude, Jude" ["Jew, Jew"].

In Vienna, where some of the worst terrorism occurred with the arrest of about 10,000 persons, confiscation of merchandise from Jewish stores was authorized by Nazi officials.

"Yes, we have begun seizing the goods of Jewish stores because, sooner or later, they will be nationalized anyway and used to compensate us for the years of damage the Jews have done to the German people," a Nazi leader explained.

—United Press, *Dallas Morning News,* November 11, 1938, 1, 20.

At his press conference one week after Kristallnacht, President Franklin D. Roosevelt said that the attack had "deeply shocked" the American public. The president also announced that he had summoned home the US ambassador to Germany. The United States was the only nation to make this diplomatic response, and there would be no US ambassador in Germany again until after World War II.

Despite the increased threat faced by German and Austrian Jews, the president chose not to ask the US Congress to reconsider the quota system that limited immigration. When a reporter asked the president directly: "Would you recommend a relaxation of our immigration restrictions so that the Jewish could refugees could be received in this country?" he responded: "That is not in contemplation; we have the quota system."[15]

However, Labor Secretary Frances Perkins did persuade Roosevelt to allow approximately 12,000 Germans—most of whom were Jews—then in the United States on temporary visitors' visas to remain in the country indefinitely. As he explained to reporters, "I cannot, in any decent humanity, throw them out."[16]

Roosevelt made an exception to his practice of off-the-record press conferences by allowing newspapers to quote this statement from his November 15, 1938, meeting with reporters. The handwritten edits on this document were made by the president. The initials "C.H." indicated Secretary of State Cordell Hull's approval of the statement.

---

15. Press Conference #500, November 15, 1938, Press Conferences, FDRL.

16. Press conference #501, November 18, 1938, ibid. Between 1913 and 1940, immigration administration was under the Department of Labor. Frances Perkins (1880–1965), the department secretary from 1933–45, was the first woman to serve in the US Cabinet.

9.

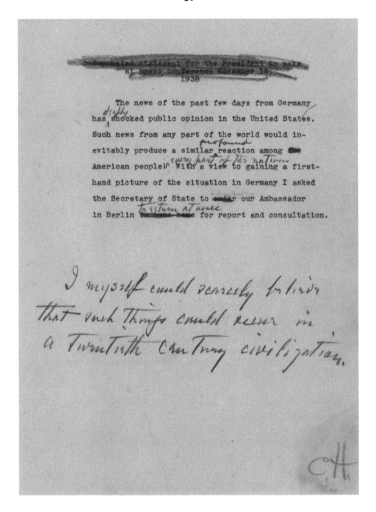

Suggested statement for the President to make
at press conference November 16,
1938

The news of the past few days from Germany has *deeply* shocked public opinion in the United States. Such news from any part of the world would inevitably produce a similar *profound* reaction among American people *in every part of the nation*. With a view to gaining a first-hand picture of the situation in Germany I asked the Secretary of State to ~~order~~ our Ambassador in Berlin ~~to come home~~ *to return at once* for report and consultation.

I myself could scarcely believe that such things could occur in a Twentieth Century civilization.

—Draft Statement, November 16, 1938, The President's
Secretary's File, Box 31 Germany, 1933–38, FDRL.

10.

Treatment of Jews "Shocks U.S."

———

President Takes Lead In Bitter Denunciation Of Nazi Dictatorship

———

Vast System Of Defense Is Pictured

———

WASHINGTON, NOV. 15.—(AP)—President Roosevelt denounced the German dictatorship's treatment of Jews today as almost beyond belief, and then pictured a vast two-continent defense system in which all the Americas would present a united front against aggression from abroad.

His remarks on the Jews, given out at a press conference, were as follows:

"The news of the past few days from Germany has deeply shocked public opinion in the United States. Such news from any part of the world would inevitably produce a similar profound reaction among American people in every part of the nation.

"I myself could scarcely believe that such things could occur in a Twentieth Century civilization.

"With a view to gaining a first hand picture of the situation in Germany, I asked the Secretary of State to order our ambassador in Berlin to return at once for report and consultation."

Thus Mr. Roosevelt disclosed that he himself was back of yesterday's order calling Ambassador Hugh R. Wilson home.[17] Mr. Roosevelt said he could not disclose how long the ambassador would stay here. This gave rise to speculation that the envoy might be kept at home indefinitely.

[The AP report turns to the president's discussion in the news conference about building up military defenses for the Western Hemisphere.]

In commenting on German anti-Semitism, the President adopted the rare procedure of permitting direct quotation of a statement which officials characterized as highly important because a comment from the head of a nation on internal developments in another nation is an extraordinary occurrence.

He said no protest was being made yet to Berlin against the persecution of the Jews.

At the State Department it was said the only protest possibly contemplated at this time would be one based on reported damage to American Jews' property in Germany, on which there are no official accounts as yet.[18] The President said the American embassy in Berlin is checking the reports.

---

17. Hugh R. Wilson (1885–1946): joined the US Diplomatic Service in 1912; named ambassador to Germany in March 1938, where he served until his recall after Kristallnacht in November.

18. The welfare of Americans in Germany continued to be a concern of the US Embassy in Berlin.

Any general protest made on humanitarian grounds, it was said, would await the return of Wilson and his report to the President.

—Associated Press, The Daily Missoulian (Missoula, MT), November 16, 1938, 1, 8.

The gap between Americans' disapproval of the November pogrom and their willingness to act on the behalf of Jewish victims was demonstrated starkly in a pair of public opinion polls just two weeks after Kristallnacht.

11.

Gallup Polls, November 1938

"Do you approve or disapprove of the Nazi treatment of Jews in Germany?"

6% Approve
94% Disapprove

"Should we allow a larger number of Jewish exiles from Germany to come to the United States to live?"

21% Yes
72% No
7% No opinion

—Gallup Organization. 1938. Gallup Poll # 1938-0139: Nazi Germany / Politics. Question 4: USGALLUP.120938.R01A and Question 12: USGALLUP.38-139.Q03. Cornell University, Ithaca, NY: Roper Center for Public Opinion Research. https://doi.org/10.25940/ROPER-31087123.

Admit Refugee Children?

In February 1939, identical bills in the US Senate and the House of Representatives proposed admitting 20,000 German refugee children under the age of fourteen. The bill, sponsored by Democratic senator Robert Wagner of New York and Republican representative Edith Nourse Rogers of Massachusetts, specified that the children would enter over a two-year period as a special group and would not be counted against the restrictive immigration quotas.

Shortly after the Wagner-Rogers Bill was proposed in Congress, Eleanor Roosevelt asked her husband whether he thought she should speak out in support of it. The president replied that she could publicly support the bill but added, "It is best for me to say nothing."[19]

19. President's Official File, Part 1: OF 200 (Trips of the President), Box 48, Folder MMM (Caribbean Cruise—Telegrams and Dispatches, February 17–25, 1939), Telegrams between FDR and ER, February 22, 1939, FDRL.

Senators who opposed the bill introduced amendments that would have counted the refugee children within the existing German quota rather than outside of it. Sen. Robert Reynolds (Democrat-NC) sought a five-year total ban on all immigration in exchange for its passage. Sponsors of the Wagner-Rogers Bill did not accept this offer, and the bill never made it to the floor of Congress for a vote.

12.

"'Please, Ring The Bell For Us,'"

John F. Knott

John F. Knott's political cartoon for the *Dallas Morning News* (July 7, 1939) accompanied an editorial that said admitting refugee children to the United States would be an "act of simple humanity."

Between February and May 1939, multiple organizations issued publications for and against the Wagner-Rogers Bill. Two of these pamphlet's texts are included below.

"Suffer Little Children . . . ," published in 1939 by the Non-Sectarian Committee for German Refugee Children, urged Americans to ask their congressional representatives to support the Wagner-Rogers Bill and directly addressed some of the concerns that it assumed Americans might have about admitting refugee children.

In contrast, the American Immigration Conference Board aimed to severely limit all immigration to the United States during the 1930s. The board's 1939 pamphlet, *America's Children Are America's Problem! Refugee Children in Europe Are Europe's Problem!* opposed the Wagner-Rogers Bill and urged readers to put American children— not refugee children—first, citing the challenges many children faced in the United States during the ongoing Great Depression.

13.

Non-Sectarian Committee for German Refugee Children
"Suffer Little Children . . ."

American Mothers and Fathers - -

Can you imagine yourself willing, even pitifully anxious to say good-by—perhaps forever—to your sons and daughters?

Suppose that you saw your beloved youngsters treated as outcasts—spurned by former playmates, barred from schools, from parks, from every happy activity of childhood. Threatened with physical harm.

Helpless, without funds, despairing for yourselves, you would plead—"At least— save our children." This is now the plea of thousands of German parents.

England, France, Holland, Norway, Sweden and Belgium have heard their cry and have opened their doors to young refugees.

What can we in America do?

Americans Want to Help

The Wagner-Rogers Bill is our answer. This bill would permit 10,000 German refugee children of all creeds to enter the United States in both 1939 and 1940. Once they are admitted to this country, homes await them, homes freely offered by thousands of Americans in every state.

The Wagner-Rogers Bill is a non-partisan measure introduced in the Senate by Senator Robert F. Wagner (Democrat, N. Y.) and in the House of Representatives by Representative Edith Nourse Rogers (Republican, Mass.).

It has the backing of both branches of the labor movement, and of such eminent Americans as Herbert Hoover and Mrs. Calvin Coolidge. Leading Protestant and Catholic clergymen and the Federal Council of Churches support it.

Who are the children?

They will be chosen from the 90,000 now forced by dire need to seek refuge. None will be over 14. These children will be Catholic, Jewish and Protestant.

Where will they go?

To homes already awaiting them throughout the country. Child Welfare agencies in local communities will supervise their placement. Every effort will be made, when possible, to keep the children in touch with their own families, whom it is hoped they may some day rejoin.

Who will be responsible for them?

The Non-Sectarian Committee for German Refugee Children will furnish the financial guarantees required by the United States Government. Funds will be supplied entirely by responsible private individuals and organizations.

How will they be brought here?

Through the cooperation of the American Friends Service Committee (Quakers) and the International Migration Service who are actively engaged in relief and rehabilitation work abroad.

> —Non-Sectarian Committee for German Refugee Children, pamphlet,
> 1939, Archives of the American Friends Service Committee.

14.

America's Children Are America's Problem!
Refugee Children in Europe Are Europe's Problem!

IN THE NAME OF CHARITY;

AMERICAN CHILDREN FIRST

United States Senator Robert F. Wagner (Democrat of New York) has introduced a Resolution calling upon Congress to authorize the admission, for permanent residence, of 20,000 German refugee children into the United States in addition to regular annual quotas. Similar Resolutions have been introduced by Congresswoman Edith Nourse Rogers (Republican, 5th Massachusetts District) and Congressman John H. Dingell (Democrat, 15th Michigan District).

THESE BILLS MUST BE DEFEATED

America's first duty is to feed, clothe and educate her own millions of "ill-fed, ill-clothed, and ill-housed" American children.

This is not the first time such ill-advised proposals have been introduced in Congress. In many sessions of Congress since the World War similar bills have been introduced in an effort to capitalize on the sympathy of the American people and for the purpose of breaking down restrictive immigration. In every case so far, the common-sense of the people has prevailed: not one such proposal has ever been enacted.

HERE ARE THE GRIM FACTS

Every State in the Union has a tremendous number of children in want of proper food, clothing, medical attention and better schooling.

SHARECROPPER CHILDREN

Millions of starving, half-naked children of eight million sharecroppers[20] HERE AT HOME, live in hovels. Their tumble-down shacks have no windows. They sleep on rags. Their clothes are tattered and filthy. They eat thickened gravy and biscuits as a year round diet. They have no medical care. They fall easy prey to disease. They are unschooled. From out of these dingy huts of tragedy comes a reeking army of destitution, while the false idea of humanitarianism and internationalism is wailed by politicians.

Shall We First Take Care of Our Own Children – *OR* Shall We Bestow Our Charity on Children Imported From Abroad?

Mrs. Franklin D. Roosevelt, who has advocated bringing here 20,000 refugee children said in her newspaper column,[21] on January 31, 1939: "I cannot help wondering about the sharecroppers . . . I fear that human suffering is not confined to Europe." . . .

What is American citizenship worth if it allows American children to go HUNGRY, COLD, NAKED, and UNSCHOOLED, and WITHOUT PROPER MEDICAL ATTENTION—while we import and care for children from a foreign country?

SLUM CHILDREN LIVE IN SULLEN POVERTY!

In hundreds of American cities millions of worthy children are growing up in filth, squalor and ignorance in slums. Huddled together in poorly ventilated cramped rooms, these American children of every race and foreign extraction, cry for the right to breathe fresh air, eat good food, and for the right to play and live in the American way.

Shall we sentence these slum children to crime, poverty and hopelessness while we import children from a foreign country?

The Wagner-Rogers-Dingell Bills propose to import TWENTY THOUSAND REFUGEE CHILDREN FROM GERMANY!

---

20. Sharecropping: a farming practice widely used in the American South whereby landowners provided land, housing, seed, and tools to fieldworkers, predominantly African Americans, in return for a share of the crops produced rather than for cash. The sharecroppers were often at a significant economic disadvantage in this arrangement.

21. Eleanor Roosevelt wrote a six-day-per-week column, titled "My Day," that was syndicated to dozens of newspapers nationwide from 1935 to 1962.

These refugee children are to be placed in American homes.

Organized minorities who advocate bringing in these foreign children state that homes already have been provided for them by applications now on file. If that be true—this is America's answer:

If homes are available for the adoption of alien children, Americanism demands that needy American children be adopted into them.

These refugee children are to be "14 years of age and younger".

In almost every State in the Nation, children 14 years of age are allowed to work under certain conditions.

WE CANNOT TAKE CARE OF 20,000 REFUGEE CHILDREN

[. . .] Humanity Demands That American Children Have First Claim To American Charity.

Before we undertake the care for children from other nations LET US TAKE CARE OF OUR OWN!!!

JOHN CECIL
AMERICAN IMMIGRATION CONFERENCE BOARD, Inc.
92 Liberty Street, New York

—Pamphlet, 1939, Florence Mendheim Collection of Anti-Semitic Propaganda, Leo Baeck Institute, Center for Jewish History, New York, NY.

The American Friends Service Committee (AFSC), a Quaker relief organization, created a Refugee Division after the violence on Kristallnacht that helped tens of thousands of individuals and refugees before, during, and after World War II. Clarence Pickett joined the AFSC as executive secretary in 1929 and sought to expand its work abroad in response to the refugee crisis. In this "debate-of-the-month" published by Rotary International[22] in *The Rotarian* magazine six months after the Wagner-Rogers Bill failed in Congress, Pickett argues passionately that admitting refugee children will benefit Americans. He directly rejects the claim that admitting new immigrants will lead to an increase in unemployment.

Democratic Senator Robert Reynolds of North Carolina, who actively opposed the bill, responded to Pickett. Senator Reynolds spoke out frequently about America's unemployment problem and warned that admitting refugees—even children under age 14—would cause more Americans to lose their jobs. He introduced five anti-immigration proposals to the US Senate in 1939 to derail any effort to change the existing immigration laws. Reynolds's maneuvers in the Senate won the day.

---

22. Rotary International: an international service organization of local business professionals.

15.

America: Haven for Refugee Children?
Yes—Let Them Come!

Clarence E. Pickett

Executive Secretary, American Friends Service Committee

For more than 20 years the organization which I serve has concerned itself with children. [. . .]

Whether it is in England, in France, in Germany, in Spain, or in our own country, I have seen no forces at work which so effectively create goodwill abroad, and which so stir public response to existing demands at home, as does coming to the help of children in need wherever they are.

Our great national danger is not starvation or nakedness or lack of shelter. It is unwillingness to share our abundant resources when they are most needed. It is not lack of food but of adequate spiritual purpose from which we suffer. We can provide for our own if we will, and nothing so releases that spirit as an adequate demonstration of it. I look upon the proposal to admit 20,000 children as a test of our quality of life. [. . .]

We are not really being asked a favor—we are being offered a treasure of fine, able-bodied, eager children. We need them to eat our food, to wear our clothes, to liven our sense of human need, to help push back the curtain which now hides from us the ways of bringing about a wider sharing of our rich cultural and economic heritage in America.

I have heard it suggested that in admitting these children we only add to the problem of unemployment. Will not these children grow up to compete with our own? This assumes that greater density of population is a cause of unemployment. But there is not a shred of evidence to show that density of population bears any relation to unemployment. It is something else that creates unemployment.

I am not unconscious that the mechanics of handling such a migration are important. Consular offices are now exercising every precaution prescribed by law to see that only people of mental and physical fitness enter. Plans for aides to accompany each group of ten children on the journey would need to be provided; proper reception homes would be needed at the port of entry; full cognizance of religious affiliation is provided in the plan for placement. Careful studies show that only existing child-placing agencies will be needed for the placement in homes and exercise of supervision. No new services need be set up.

With a declining birth rate and an increasing age level in our own country, stagnation and hardening of our spiritual arteries is our most insidious danger. Because I see a quickening of our response to human need; because I have confidence in the ability of our agencies to handle the technical problems; because I believe a great majority of

Americans, if they saw the whole picture, would respond with open arms; because I believe it is right to do so, I say unhesitatingly—let the children come in.

No—Keep the Bars Up!

Robert R. Reynolds

United States Senator for North Carolina

The time has come for changing the tradition that the United States is an asylum for the oppressed of the world. Our house is full. We must now give first thought to our own citizens, both naturalized and native born. We must find jobs for those who have a rightful claim to the benefits and blessings of American citizenship.

I am opposed to any measure that will provide more competition for the sons and daughters of Americans. If 20,000 boys and girls from abroad are permitted to enter the United States, it will simply mean that in a few years there will be 20,000 more boys and girls here looking for work.

We have in this country today approximately 12 million persons without employment—one-third of whom are under 25 years of age. I think every unemployed man and woman in the United States should be put to work before we allow another foreigner to enter this country.

Since 1820 some 28 million immigrants have entered our gates. Most of these people have made glorious contributions to America. They deserve honor and credit. But times have changed. Our lands no longer need farmers; our mills have too many workers. This appeal to our sympathies in behalf of children might be the entering wedge to break open the immigration floodgates. If we permit special exception to the immigration laws, we will find that within a few years the fathers and mothers of these children will be seeking admission because they wish to reunite their families here on our shores.

It is said that bonds will be made to guarantee that these children will not become public charges. But who will guarantee the bondsmen? They may go bankrupt and become public charges themselves. If we have in this country people who are financially able to take care of children other than their own, then why don't they make financial contributions to unfortunate children here in the United States? [. . .]

Shall we first take care of our own children, or shall we bestow our charity upon children imported from abroad?

What is our citizenship worth if it allows our own children to go hungry and unschooled, without proper medical attention, and without the opportunity for jobs, while we reach out for more children from another country? Let the sympathies and charities of American people begin at home. Our country, our citizens, first.

—*The Rotarian*, February 1940, 11–13.

A Refugee Ship at Sea

16.

Fred Packer's political cartoon "Ashamed!" about the *St. Louis* criticizes the United States for failing to live up to the ideals enshrined on the Statue of Liberty. *New York Daily Mirror,* June 6, 1939.

Between March 1938, when Germany annexed Austria, and October 1941, when Germany banned all emigration of Jews from its territories, transatlantic passenger ships brought to New York Harbor nearly 111,000 Jewish refugees on more than 1,200 trips. Passenger ships carrying refugees also headed to other ports away from Europe. For two weeks in spring 1939, American attention was drawn to the unusual voyage of one of these, the MS *St. Louis.*

On May 13, 1939, the *St. Louis,* a German passenger ship, set sail from Hamburg, Germany, for Havana, Cuba. The *St. Louis* carried 937 passengers, almost all of whom were Jewish refugees. When the ship arrived in Cuba, the passengers learned that the

Cuban government had canceled their landing permits[23] because of recent changes in its immigration policy and would refuse to allow all but 28 of the refugees to disembark.

Despite efforts by US Secretary of State Cordell Hull and US Treasury Secretary Henry Morgenthau Jr. to persuade Cuban officials to accept the refugees, the Cuban government stood firm. Staff from the American Jewish Joint Distribution Committee (a humanitarian organization commonly called "the Joint") flew from New York to Havana to start negotiations on behalf of the refugees. The voyage of the *St. Louis* began to receive significant media attention in the United States and Europe.

After the ship left Cuba, the *St. Louis* lingered off the coast of Miami, Florida, while the Joint attempted to convince officials in the US government to admit the refugees. Because the passengers did not have US immigration visas and had not passed security screening, the US government refused.

As the ship headed back to Europe, Morris C. Troper, the Joint's European director based in Paris, negotiated for the refugees to be admitted by Great Britain, France, the Netherlands, and Belgium. The passengers were relieved to not return to Germany, and they celebrated the Joint's successful efforts on their behalf.

In June 1939, none of the receiving countries were under Nazi control; all but Great Britain would be by the summer of 1940. Ultimately 254 of the *St. Louis* passengers were murdered by Germany and its collaborators during the Holocaust.[24]

17.

REFUGEE SHIP

The saddest ship afloat today, the Hamburg-American liner St. Louis, with 900 Jewish refugees aboard, is steaming back toward Germany after a tragic week of frustration at Havana and off the coast of Florida. She is steaming back despite an offer made to Havana yesterday to give a guarantee through the Chase National Bank of $500 apiece[25] for every one of her passengers, men, women and children, who might land there. [Cuba's] President Laredo Bru[26] still has an opportunity to practice those

---

23. Landing permits, authorized by Cuba's Commissioner of Immigration and distributed by Cuban consulates throughout Europe, allowed for legal entry into Cuba.

24. Sarah A. Ogilvie and Scott Miller, *Refuge Denied: The St. Louis Passengers and the Holocaust* (Madison: University of Wisconsin Press, 2006), 174.

25. The Joint in New York arranged this payment to meet Cuba's new immigration law, which stipulated foreigners may be authorized to enter provided they pay a deposit of 500 pesos ($500).

26. Dr. Federico Laredo Brú (1875–1946): president of Cuba from 1936 to 1940.

humanitarian sentiments so eloquently expressed in his belated offer of asylum after the refugee ship had been driven from Havana Harbor. His cash terms have been met. But the St. Louis still keeps her course for Hamburg.

No plague ship ever received a sorrier welcome. Yet those aboard her had sailed with high hopes. About fifty of them, according to our Berlin dispatch, had consular visas. The others all had landing permits for which they had paid; they were unaware that these permits had been declared void in a decree dated May 5. Only a score of the hundreds were admitted. At Havana the St. Louis's decks became a stage for human misery. Relatives and friends clamored to get aboard but were held back. Weeping refugees clamoring to get ashore were halted at guarded gangways. For days the St. Louis lingered within the shadow of Morro Castle,[27] but there was no relaxation of the new regulations. Every appeal was rejected. One man reached land. He was pulled from the water with slashed wrists and rushed to a hospital. A second suicide attempt led the captain to warn the authorities that a wave of self-destruction might follow. The forlorn refugees themselves organized a patrol committee. Yet out of Havana Harbor the St. Louis had to go, trailing pitiful cries of "Auf Wiedersehen." Off our shores she was attended by a helpful Coast Guard vessel alert to pick up any passengers who plunged overboard and thrust them back on the St. Louis again. The refugees could even see the shimmering towers of Miami rising from the sea, but for them they were only the battlements of another forbidden city.

It is useless now to discuss what might have been done. The case is disposed of. Germany, with all the hospitality of its concentration camps, will welcome these unfortunates home.[28] Perhaps Cuba, as her spokesmen say, has already taken too many German refugees. Yet all these 900 asked was a temporary haven. Before they sailed virtually all of them had registered under the quota provisions of various nations, including our own. Time would have made them eligible to enter. But there seems to be no help for them now. The St. Louis will soon be home with her cargo of despair.

Her next trip is already scheduled. It will be a gay cruise for carefree tourists.

—*New York Times,* June 8, 1939, 24.

After learning that they would not be returning to Nazi Germany, the passengers wrote this message of gratitude to the Joint Distribution Committee in New York for negotiating on their behalf during the tumultuous voyage.

27. A sixteenth-century fortress guarding the entrance to Havana, Cuba, in Havana Bay.
28. In fact, returning to Germany would not be the passengers' fate, as follows.

The arrival of the *St. Louis* in Antwerp was covered by the Associated Press and published in newspapers across the United States. The report closed by remarking on the "relief and joy" among the passengers.

18.

We, the St. Louis passengers about to depart for their various destinations in Belgium, Holland, France and England, wish to thank you from the bottom of our hearts for the part you played in New York in our behalf, and Messrs. Baerwald and Linder[29] for what they did in London, and once again to thank our good friend Morris C. Troper not only for all he did on the Continent in arranging for havens of refuge, but for his self-sacrificing efforts in our behalf during the past few days in order to determine our assignments and to expedite our departure, and we are grateful to all his assistants who cooperated with him so devotedly. [. . .]

Through you we wish to express our deep appreciation to the American Jewish Joint Distribution Committee, to its members and its supporters for having made it possible for these good people to effect the rescue of our wives our children and ourselves

St. Louis Passengers' Committee

> —Telegram draft, June 1939, "Passengers' Committee, 1939," Morris Troper Papers, USHMM Collection, gift of Betty Troper Yager.

19.

REFUGEE SHIP IS AT ANTWERP

907 Jews Happy to Reach End of Trip Filled With Hope and Disappointment.

ANTWERP, June 17 (AP)—The five-week voyage of 907 Jewish emigrants from Germany in search of a new homeland, with eager hopes turned first into tragic disappointment and then desperation, ended happily Saturday as the Hamburg-Amerika liner St. Louis docked in Antwerp.

They still faced a long wait before they may get to the United States, which most of them ultimately hope to reach, after being turned back from Cuba, the land for which they sailed from Hamburg May 15.

---

29. Paul Baerwald (1871–1961): a founder (1914) and chairman (1932–45) of the American Jewish Joint Distribution Committee. Harold Linder was a committee associate (1938–41).

But all were happy at escaping a return to Germany, the prospect of which during the voyage passengers said had led more than 200 to enter a whispered pact to plunge into the ocean as a last resort.

Passengers reported only one of the passengers took his life, a man who slashed his wrists and leaped into Havana Harbor, but said they had been forced to form an anti-suicide pact committee which kept a 24-hour vigil to prevent any attempts at self-destruction.

Waving greetings to welcoming crowds, the refugees were brought into Antwerp harbor shortly before 7:15 p.m. Saturday night.

A special train waited to take 250 of them to Old Marness Castle at Liege; 157 will go to The Netherlands by boats; while two groups of 250 persons each will proceed on another boat to France and Great Britain.

Offered Temporary Homes.

Belgium, The Netherlands, France and Britain agreed to receive the refugees temporarily, while they waited to enter the United States as quota restrictions permit, after the American [Jewish] Joint Distribution Committee furnished a guarantee of $500 each they would not become public charges.

With varying degrees of emotion the passengers told how they left Hamburg full of hope, believing their entry into Cuba was certain, how they waited off Havana vainly for permission to land, and finally heard the St. Louis had been ordered back to Hamburg.

As days wore on and wireless negotiations progressed with the American [Jewish Joint] Distribution Committee in Paris, hopes rose and fell with new prospects and then refusals for them to enter various countries.

"We would sit up far into the night waiting for some news," one woman passenger said.

"When we finally got the message that arrangements had been made for us to land, our relief and joy were indescribable. We threw our arms around each other and danced. It was the happiest moment of our lives."

Captain Is Praised.

From passengers came high praise for the conduct of Captain Gustav Schroeder, the liner's skipper, during their ordeal.

One passenger, speaking from a large group, declared: "He was very sympathetic and understanding and did everything within his power to help us and make us comfortable." All nodded their heads in approval.

Members of the crew at the same time commended the behavior of the passengers.

In the most critical periods, passengers said, the women for the most part remained calmer than many of the men. They explained this was because some of the men had only recently been released from concentration camps and feared what might happen to them if they were returned to Germany.

There were many complete families among the passengers—246 children were aboard—but there were many refugees whose husbands, wives or children already had gone to Cuba or the United States.

Some were well dressed and in other ways showed they came from families of wealth; the impoverishment of others equally was apparent.

A few romances blossomed and Saturday, as relief officials worked aboard the liner deciding their temporary fates, youths and girls strolled the decks with arms linked.

Saturday night they were being separated, some going to one country and others to another, but overshadowing the sorrow at parting were relief and joy at the end of their St. Louis voyage.

—Associated Press, *Fort Worth (TX) Star-Telegram,* June 18, 1939, 3.

Americans Who Dared

A small number of Americans overcame enormous challenges to aid Jewish refugees. Most worked within networks of religious or humanitarian organizations, using both legal and illegal means to confront significant obstacles. They often jeopardized their own safety to assist people in great danger by venturing into areas of Europe that Nazi Germany controlled or occupied. Most of these rescuers did not explain why they took such extraordinary risks beyond simply believing they were doing the right thing. Their efforts helped thousands of Jews survive the Holocaust.

The four sources below describe rescue efforts by Americans: Gilbert and Eleanor Kraus in Austria, Martha Sharp and Varian Fry in France, and Marjorie McClelland in Italy. After the Nazi regime annexed Austria in 1938 and, in 1940, conquered France and allied itself with Italy, it became exceedingly difficult for Jewish refugees to escape from areas under Nazi control.

In January 1939, the Philadelphia Jewish men's organization Brith Sholom asked Gilbert and Eleanor Kraus—a lawyer and a homemaker—to go to Nazi Germany in order to rescue fifty Jewish children. Before leaving their home in Philadelphia, the Krauses persuaded friends to be responsible for the children's affidavits of financial support and solicited cooperation from US State Department officials in both Washington, DC, and Berlin to obtain unused immigration visas.

After interviewing many families in Vienna, the Krauses chose fifty children between the ages of five and fourteen. All of the children's families hoped to leave Austria, but, as obstacles mounted, the parents made the difficult choice to send their children to the United States with strangers.

After traveling from Vienna to Berlin to Hamburg, Germany, the refugee children sailed on the SS *President Harding.* They landed in New York Harbor on June 3, 1939, and were reunited with relatives or placed with sponsor families.

Gilbert and Eleanor Kraus (*seated*, at *center*, with the *President Harding* ship's captain) and 50 children, June 1939, USHMM Collection, courtesy of Liz Perle.

20.

50 Jewish Refugee Tots Are Happy in New Home

Arrival in U. S. Result of Dinner Talk in Philadelphia Lawyer's House Last Year

PHILADELPHIA. JUNE 4—(AP)—Fifty Jewish refugee children from Germany, brought to America by a Philadelphia lawyer as the sequel to a dinner conversation six months ago, romped happy and carefree over an 85-acre suburban estate.

The 25 boys and 25 girls, ranging in age from 5 to 13, docked in New York yesterday. They will remain at the estate, site of a Jewish home for the aged, until foster homes are found for each.

The young refugees came to America on regular visa under the immigration quota.

Their passage was financed by Gilbert J. Kraus, Philadelphia lawyer, and a group of friends as the result of a discussion of the plight of German Jews that took place at a dinner party in the Kraus home early in the year.

Mr. and Mrs. Kraus, who went to Vienna two months ago to bring back the children, were kept busy last night helping nurses and others at the home read bedtime stories and prepare the children for the first night's sleep in America. All the children will be taught English before being placed in foster homes.

—Associated Press, *Pittsburgh Post-Gazette,* June 5, 1939, 2.

On two separate occasions, the American Unitarian Association asked Waitstill Sharp, the religious denomination's minister in Wellesley, Massachusetts, and his wife Martha, a social worker, to travel to Europe to aid refugees. Each time, the Sharps left their own young children in the care of their church community to do relief work abroad.

In German-occupied Prague, Czechoslovakia, in 1939, the Sharps provided moral and financial support for refugees, working closely with British Quakers, a Christian group. They narrowly escaped arrest when the Gestapo closed their office that summer.

In 1940, Waitstill worked in Lisbon, Portugal, and aided Varian Fry's efforts to rescue endangered intellectuals. In Marseilles, France, Martha organized milk distribution to feed refugee children. After Waitstill returned to the United States, Martha remained in France and cooperated with the US Committee for the Care of European Children (USCOM)[30] to arrange a transport of twenty-nine children and eleven adults to the United States in December 1940. Her memorandum from late November reflects the bureaucratic challenges she faced as she worked out the details for this transport out of France through Spain to the seaport in Lisbon.

21.

MEMORANDUM
EMIGRATION FROM FRANCE TO
THE UNITED STATES OF AMERICA.
By Martha Sharp.
November 26, 1940

I have just completed the emigration plans for forty people including twenty-nine children and eleven adults to leave France for the United States of America. The group includes American, French, Russian, Hungarian, German, Austrian, Polish, and Czech citizens. The experience has been so varied that I have been asked to write a memorandum on the steps involved which might assist other people in France planning to emigrate to the U.S.A. The procedure [. . .] for refugee parents wishing to send their children to the United States ahead of them is also included.

The procedure presupposes that the would-be emigrant, adult or minor has been invited by an American Committee or American citizen to visit or to emigrate to the United States of America, and that the interested Committee or American citizen has

---

30. USCOM: cofounded by Eleanor Roosevelt in 1940, operated in southern France to evacuate European refugee children, mainly Jews, to the United States until the November 1941 Nazi occupation of the region.

provided adequate affidavits or financial guarantees for the individual emigrant. These affidavits have either been sent by mail to the emigrant personally and to the nearest United States Consulate or through the State Department of the United States of America to the nearest United States Consulate by cable.

Parents in France (American, French or Refugee) who wish to send their children to the United States of America and who have relatives or friends in the United States should ask them to contact the United States Committee for the Care of European Children[. . . .] This Committee will give them advice about the necessary guarantees, the passage and all procedure having to do with the emigration. [. . .]

[Sharp here details the requirements for citizens of the United States, France, Germany, and other countries to leave France. The following guidelines applied to Jewish refugees from Nazi-occupied nations who were stateless.]

II. AMERICAN VISA.

A. GENERAL INFORMATION.

1. Any prospective emigrant registered on the quota or expecting to go to America as a visitor or in transit should visit the nearest American consulate as soon as he decides to go. American consulates in non-occupied France today are so swamped with letters and work that they cannot possibly answer all the inquiries they receive by mail. It is also impossible for them to notify all the people for whom guarantees arrive not only because of pressure of work but often because of the inadequacy of addresses given from America and the constant inability of refugees to leave adequate forwarding addresses. If there is a chance that the emigrant has received a guarantee he should go in person to the consulate to inquire. An American Consul cannot look over the papers of an applicant and tell him by mail whether or not he will receive a visa. The eligibility of a candidate for an emigration visa to the United States of America depends not only on adequate financial backing in America but also on the physical well being and desirability of the emigrant as an American citizen. For this reason he must appear in person.

2. At the present moment the American visa is not usually given an emigrant without the promise of a visa de sortie [exit visa]. The Consul will look over the papers of a person whose turn in the quota has come and if all are in order he will give the emigrant a letter stating that he will receive his visa for America when the visa de sortie is granted. This paper will form a part of the Dossier for the visa de sortie as described above. [. . .]

B. SPECIFIC PROCEDURE

1. Birth Certificate: An emigrant registered on the quota for immigration or as visitor, whose turn has come for an American visa and whose affidavits of support are adequate must provide a birth certificate. If this is not possible to obtain from

his place of birth because the town has been destroyed or for some other reason, the local Prefecture [regional administrative office] will give an Extrait de Naissance [birth certificate] based on carte d'identité [identification card], marriage certificate, or other identity papers. The American Consulate will usually accept this.

2. Moral & Political Guarantees. Moral and political guarantees must be given for the prospective emigrant by someone who is an American citizen either known to the Consul or well-known in America. This guarantee must state that the prospective emigrant is well known to the writer, that he will not take part in any political activities on arrival in the United States of America and that he is a person of good moral character.

[Sharp here explains procedures for acquiring Spanish and Portuguese visas, as emigrants had to pass through both countries to reach the seaport at Lisbon.]

V.   FINAL SUGGESTIONS

1. The delays incident to sending money from America to Portugal are sometimes great, and sufficient money ought to be sent well in advance of the arrival of the emigrant to take care of his needs while in Lisbon.

2. After all the visas are granted it is necessary to visit the Bank of France to get permission in the emigrant's passport to take money out of France. This is permitted up to the sum of 25,000 [French francs; $500 in 1940] or its equivalent in other money.

3. Finally permission of the local police must be obtained before leaving the city.

—Memorandum, November 26, 1940, Martha and Waitstill Sharp Collection, RG-67.017, USHMM Collection, Gift of Artemis Joukowsky.

Following Germany's defeat of France in June 1940, a newly formed Emergency Rescue Committee. based in New York, recruited thirty-two-year-old journalist Varian Fry to aid anti-Nazi refugees. Fry arrived in France with a short list of people he hoped to assist, but was soon overwhelmed by the number of artists, writers, and intellectuals, many of them Jewish, who sought his help.

Working with networks of like-minded individuals and organizations, and aided by sympathetic US consular officials in Marseilles, Fry and his colleagues used legal and illegal means to smuggle refugees across the Pyrenees Mountains to the neutral countries of Spain and Portugal, and then to the United States. Fry remained in France for thirteen months, operating under constant surveillance and danger. His efforts angered some in the US State Department and officials in Vichy France, an ally of Nazi Germany. Fry was expelled in September 1941.

The title of his memoir, *Surrender on Demand,* published in 1945, refers to the 1940 agreement between France and Germany that required France to turn over any German nationals wanted by the Nazis. Fry's regular refusal to turn over refugees to French officials violated that agreement.

22.

Surrender on Demand

Foreword

This is the story of an experiment in democratic solidarity. The fall of France, in June, 1940, meant not merely the defeat of the French nation; it meant also the creation of the most gigantic man-trap in history. Ever since the Russian Revolution—in fact, even before—France had been the haven of Europe's exiles. Whenever a change of government in another land, or invasion by a foreign power, had obliged men to flee for their lives, France had opened her arms to them. [. . .]

Hitler's invasion of France eliminated the French army as a barrier against Germany and Italy, and the armistice left the German refugees at the mercy of their most relentless foes. Nor had democrats and leftists of any nationality much reason to trust the new, reactionary government which had been brought to power in the wake of the defeat.

When it was learned that the armistice which France made with Germany in June, 1940, contained a clause providing for the "surrender on demand" of German refugees,[31] a group of American citizens, who were deeply shocked by this violation of the right of asylum and who believed that democrats must help democrats, regardless of nationality, immediately formed the Emergency Rescue Committee. The sole purpose of the Committee was to bring the political and intellectual refugees out of France before the Gestapo and the Ovra[32] and the Seguridad[33] got them.

After several weeks of fruitless searching for a suitable agent to send to France, the Committee selected me. I had had no experience in refugee work, and none in underground work. But I accepted the assignment because, like the members of the Committee, I believed in the importance of democratic solidarity. I had seen the democratic governments of Europe go down one by one: first Italy; then Germany; then Austria; then Spain; then Czechoslovakia; then Norway, Holland, Belgium, France; and I was convinced that if democracy was to endure at all it would have to become internationally minded. Thus, quite apart from any sentimental reasons, I accepted the assignment out of deep political convictions.

31. Fry's footnote here cites the language of the armistice text and adds: "'Germans' originally meant all inhabitants of the Greater Reich, i.e., Germans, Austrians, Czechs and many Poles, but was later stretched to include everybody the German government wanted to get its hands on."

32. Fascist Italy's secret police, the Organizzazione per la Vigilanza e la Repressione dell'Antifascismo, founded in 1927. After June 1940, Italy occupied two southeastern provinces in France.

33. Spain's security forces, the Dirección General de Seguirdad, which, with the support of Vichy authorities, had agents in France seeking exiled political opponents of Spain's fascist regime.

But the sentimental reasons were also there; and they were strong. Among the refugees who were caught in France were many writers and artists whose work I had enjoyed: novelists like Franz Werfel and Lion Feuchtwanger; painters like Marc Chagall and Max Ernst; sculptors like Jacques Lipchitz. For some of these men, although I knew them only through their work, I had a deep love; and to them all I owed a heavy debt of gratitude for the pleasure they had given me. Now that they were in danger, I felt obliged to help them, if I could; just as they, without knowing it, had often in the past helped me. [. . .]

I knew, from first-hand experience, what defeat at the hands of Hitler could mean. In 1935 I visited Germany and tasted the atmosphere of oppression which the Hitler regime had brought. I talked to many anti-Nazis and Jews, shared their anxiety and their sense of helplessness, felt with them the tragic hopelessness of their situation. And while I was in Berlin I witnessed on the Kurfuerstendamm[34] the first great pogrom against the Jews, saw with my own eyes young Nazi toughs gather and smash up Jewish-owned cafés, watched with horror as they dragged Jewish patrons from their seats, drove hysterical, crying women down the street, knocked over an elderly man and kicked him in the face. Now that that same oppression had spread to France, I could not remain idle as long as I had any chance at all of saving even a few of its intended victims.

Thus, for a variety of reasons, and through a series of accidents, I left New York in August, 1940, on a secret mission to France, a mission which many of my friends thought a very dangerous one, and which some of them warned me against undertaking. I left with my pockets full of lists of men and women I was to rescue, and my head full of suggestions on how to do it. Altogether, there were more than two hundred names on my lists, and many hundreds more were added later.

I also left believing that my job could be done in one month. I stayed thirteen, and, when I finally came back, against my will, the work was still far from finished. [. . .]

—Varian Fry, *Surrender on Demand* (New York: Random House, 1945), ix–xii.

In August 1940, Roswell (Ross) and Marjorie McClelland traveled to Europe as aid workers for the American Friends Service Committee (AFSC), a Quaker refugee relief organization operating in Europe before, during, and after the Holocaust. Through its Refugee Division, the AFSC worked with other aid organizations to assist tens of thousands of Jewish and non-Jewish refugees who hoped to immigrate to the United States. After 1940, the AFSC also provided aid to Jews and others being held in Vichy France's internment camps and hid Jewish children from the Nazi regime.

34. The most prominent thoroughfare in Berlin.

The McClellands spent a month in Lisbon in the summer of 1940 before traveling to Rome to set up a refugee aid office there. In August 1941, the Rome bureau ceased operations following the forced closure of all United States consulates in Italy. The couple moved to Marseilles, where they joined an existing AFSC office.

Marjorie McClelland wrote this letter to her family one month before leaving Rome. She describes the "dreadful" experience of closing up the AFSC office in Rome and the emotional toll of having to tell people seeking aid that AFSC activities would be suspended. She also expresses her exasperation in this letter about "well-meaning" Americans who resisted admitting Jewish refugees into the United States.

23.

Piazza Trinita Dei Monti 17,
Roma, July 15, 1941

Cara Famiglia [Dear Family],

That address is just to give you a little Italian atmosphere. As we think about leaving Italy I become very fond of the country, its people, and its language. I have been meaning to write for some time reporting about our plans and progress, but they continue [to be] rather vague. After receipt of the cable from AFSC telling us to close up the Rome office and proceed to France if we wanted to undertake this, we were in somewhat of a quandary. [. . .]

These last two weeks closing up the office have really been rather dreadful. The endless number of interviews that Ross has had with people crying on his shoulder, while I wrote endless letters telling them in the nicest language that I could muster the painful fact that no amount of nice language could make painless—that we are suspending our activities in Italy because of circumstances beyond our control, and that we will no longer be able to assist them. And of course they all wrote back the most heart-rending letters asking what they could do now, and to whom they might turn for help, and we have no answer to that. All immigration to the U.S. stopped on June 30,[35] thereby robbing many people of their hopes. Most of these people would never have gotten visas in all probability, but they all had hopes, and are now plunged in despair. It was particularly tragic for a number of cases who were actually just on the point of getting their visas—especially for about ten cases who had been told that on July 1, when the new month's quota numbers came due they would be given the visas. They could not understand what difference one day should make, and are naturally unable

35. On July 1, 1941, all US consulates in Nazi-occupied and controlled territory shut down, making it nearly impossible for Jews and others in those areas to secure US immigration visas.

to reconcile themselves to the arbitrariness of laws that affect their whole futures so disastrously. Our office has served as a sort of mourning ground for these people. We can't do a thing in the world to change the situation, we can only give them sympathy, but of course they want to talk and talk about it, and the least we can do is talk with them, although the talk is futile from a practical viewpoint and leads nowhere, and almost breaks your heart. [. . .] Naturally it is difficult to keep ourselves from brooding considerably about this situation, especially after having known the people. It seems very different when you actually know the people involved, than it seems when you just read about the refugee situation, or think of them as a certain number of cases. We comfort ourselves by thinking of the 108 people that we have helped to emigrate since we set up shop in October, but we wish that the number could have been larger.

Another thing that discourages us somewhat is the general attitude of Americans toward the problems with which we have been working. I imagine that it is even worse at home than it is here, but I am horrified with the misconception that is entertained in the minds of a number of our fellow-citizens with regard to our work. Some few of them regard us as actually instruments of harm: a) we are working for a wholesale importation of a lot of worthless Jews into America who will take the bread out of the mouths of the honest citizens, b) we are proving again what suckers Americans are by giving money away, thereby forfeiting the respect of the Europeans who wouldn't dream of doing such a thing and look down on Americans for doing it. Really I am so tired of having well-meaning and opinionated people tell me about the Jews, and sounding off to the effect of why don't we use all this splendid zeal and energy for some really *American* activity. Who should know about the Jews if not Ross and I after this year? I don't mean to imply that all the American community adopts these views; there are a number of them who are most interested, sympathetic, and appreciative of our work. The ones who are not in sympathy have for the most part never troubled themselves to take the time to hear the information about its actual nature, which we are only too glad to impart if given half a chance. These people all seem to like us personally, but regard our activities as a little misguided. [. . .]

Much, much love to each of you,
Marjorie and Ross

—Letter, July 15, 1941, Roswell and Marjorie McClelland
Papers, USHMM Collection, Gift of Kirk McClelland.

America First Committee, "War's First Casualty," 1941, Division of Political and Military History, National Museum of American History, Smithsonian Institution.

CHAPTER 3

Storm Clouds Gather, 1939–1941

World War II began on September 1, 1939, when Nazi Germany invaded Poland. Two days later, Poland's allies, the United Kingdom and France, declared war on Germany. For Americans, the onset of war raised the immediate and uppermost question: *What should the United States do?* President Roosevelt took to the radio airwaves to tell Americans that the United States would remain neutral in Europe's conflict, assurances that matched the sentiments of the vast majority of Americans against participating in the war. Even if the American people had been eager to go to war, the US Army would not have been ready; in 1938, the War Department had reported that the US Army ranked eighteenth in size among standing armies in the world.[1]

During the next two years, as Americans vigorously debated whether to get involved, Roosevelt gradually urged the US government toward measures of war preparedness. In September 1940, Congress instituted the first peacetime draft of men for military service in US history. And in March 1941, in a major change from the Neutrality Acts of the 1930s, the "Lend-Lease Bill" expanded the US government's ability to provide arms, food, and oil to nations fighting against Nazi Germany in return for leases on army and naval bases in their territories. These important steps laid some groundwork for US intervention and helped spur the economy by employing millions of Americans in war production.

With Europe at war, defense and national security became ever-present concerns in the United States. Profound fears of infiltration by Nazi spies and unease about internal enemies continued throughout the war. The vast majority of Americans believed that Nazi spies threatened the United States through organized activities. Like the fear of Communist radicals entering the United States after World War I, the fear of German spies contributed to putting up new barriers to immigration.

As Nazi Germany rapidly rolled across Europe, consideration for civilians trapped in the war zones was largely absent from the public debates in the United States. The 1939 Nazi invasion of eastern Europe posed a dire threat to 3.3 million Polish Jews; hundreds of thousands of them would be forced into closed-off, overcrowded urban

---

1. *Annual Report of the Secretary of War to the President* (Washington, DC: USGPO, 1938), 29.

ghettos inside. In spring 1940, the Nazi regime overran and took control of Denmark, Norway, the Netherlands, Belgium, Luxembourg, and France,[2] bringing more than 500,000 additional Jews under its rule. The June 1941 invasion of the Soviet Union engulfed an additional 2.2 million Jews, and the rate of ghettoization vastly increased. Occasional reports in American news outlets of ongoing, intensifying Nazi persecution of Jews during this period were always overshadowed by lingering domestic economic concerns; the shocking, rapid German military successes across Europe; and the question of whether the United States would be forced to defend itself.

Two days after war broke out in Europe, President Roosevelt delivered a "fireside chat"[3] on the radio to reassure Americans that the United States would "remain a neutral nation." He did not, however, expect them to be "neutral in thought as well." Roosevelt emphasized that he hated war and hoped the country would "keep out of this war."

The president also reminded his listeners of cherished American values as he framed their understanding of war, focusing specifically on freedom of the press and the free flow of uncensored news. This expression of democratic ideals stood in stark contrast to the authoritarian rule characteristic of fascism.

1.

War in Europe

My countrymen and my friends:

Tonight my single duty is to speak to the whole of America.

Until four-thirty o'clock this morning I had hoped against hope that some miracle would prevent a devastating war in Europe and bring to an end the invasion of Poland by Germany.

For four long years a succession of actual wars and constant crises have shaken the entire world and have threatened in each case to bring on the gigantic conflict which is today unhappily a fact.

It is right that I should recall to your minds the consistent and at times successful efforts of your Government in these crises to throw the full weight of the United States into the cause of peace. [. . .]

2. Nazi Germany occupied the northern and western provinces of France, including Paris. The remainder of the nation became the French State (État français), commonly called "Vichy France" after its new capital city. It was ruled by Nazi collaborator Marshal Philippe Pétain (1856–1951).

3. The phrase comes from the CBS Radio announcer's introduction for Roosevelt's first national radio broadcast in March 1933: "The President wants to come into your home and sit at your fireside for a little fireside chat." Margaret Biser, "The Fireside Chats: Roosevelt's Radio talks," White House Historical Association, https://www.whitehousehistory.org/the-fireside-chats-roosevelts-radio-talks.

It is right, too, to point out that the unfortunate events of these recent years have, without question, been based on the use of force or the threat of force. And it seems to me clear, even at the outbreak of this great war, that the influence of America should be consistent in seeking for humanity a final peace which will eliminate, as far as it is possible to do so, the continued use of force between nations.

It is, of course, impossible to predict the future. I have my constant stream of information from American representatives and other sources throughout the world. You, the people of this country, are receiving news through your radios and your newspapers at every hour of the day. [. . .]

You must master at the outset a simple but unalterable fact in modern relations between nations. When peace has been broken anywhere, the peace of all countries everywhere is in danger.

It is easy for you and for me to shrug our shoulders and to say that conflicts taking place thousands of miles from the continental United States, and, indeed, thousands of miles from the whole American Hemisphere, do not seriously affect the Americas—and that all the United States has to do is to ignore them and go about its own business. Passionately though we may desire detachment, we are forced to realize that every word that comes through the air, every ship that sails the sea, every battle that is fought does affect the American future.

Let no man or woman thoughtlessly or falsely talk of America sending its armies to European fields. At this moment there is being prepared a proclamation of American neutrality. This would have been done even if there had been no neutrality statute on the books, for this proclamation is in accordance with international law and in accordance with American policy.

This will be followed by a Proclamation required by the existing Neutrality Act. And I trust that in the days to come our neutrality can be made a true neutrality. [. . .]

I myself cannot and do not prophesy the course of events abroad—and the reason is that because I have of necessity such a complete picture of what is going on in every part of the world, that I do not dare to do so. And the other reason is that I think it is honest for me to be honest with the people of the United States. [. . .]

Some things we do know. Most of us in the United States believe in spiritual values. Most of us, regardless of what church we belong to, believe in the spirit of the New Testament—a great teaching which opposes itself to the use of force, of armed force, of marching armies and falling bombs. The overwhelming masses of our people seek peace—peace at home, and the kind of peace in other lands which will not jeopardize our peace at home.

We have certain ideas and certain ideals of national safety and we must act to preserve that safety today and to preserve the safety of our children in future years.

That safety is and will be bound up with the safety of the Western Hemisphere and of the seas adjacent thereto. We seek to keep war from our own firesides by keeping war from coming to the Americas. For that we have historic precedent that goes back to the days of the Administration of President George Washington. It is serious enough and tragic enough to every American family in every state in the Union to live in a world that is torn by wars on other Continents. And those wars today affect every American home. It is our national duty to use every effort to keep those wars out of the Americas.

And at this time let me make the simple plea that partisanship and selfishness be adjourned; and that national unity be the thought that underlies all others.

This nation will remain a neutral nation, but I cannot ask that every American remain neutral in thought as well. Even a neutral has a right to take account of facts. Even a neutral cannot be asked to close his mind or close his conscience.

I have said not once but many times that I have seen war and that I hate war. I say that again and again.

I hope the United States will keep out of this war. I believe that it will. And I give you assurance and reassurance that every effort of your Government will be directed toward that end.

As long as it remains within my power to prevent, there will be no blackout of peace in the United States.

—Transcript of broadcast audio, based on Fireside Chat 14—"War in Europe," September 3, 1939, box 47, Master Speech File, 1898–1945, FDRL. Audio at https://www.fdrlibrary.org/utterancesfdr#afdr149.

The Foreign War and the National Defense

Warnings about spies and pro-Nazi agents in the United States, sometimes referred to as a "fifth column," increasingly dominated American popular and political culture by the time that the war in Europe began. The 1939 film *Confessions of a Nazi Spy*—one of the first Hollywood studio movies to address Nazism directly—was based on the true story of a New York-based German espionage ring discovered by federal authorities in 1938. Rather than focusing on the danger that Nazism posed to Europe's Jews, or the threat to peace in Europe generally, the movie warned Americans to be vigilant against sabotage by Nazis on their own shores.

FBI director J. Edgar Hoover[4] published cautionary articles in popular magazines about spies and saboteurs infiltrating the United States. Hoover and Courtney Ryley Cooper, the author of numerous books about crime, explained in the popular *American Magazine* that the FBI was regularly investigating nearly twenty times the number of alleged Nazi spy activities than it had before 1938. Even as he warned Americans to be conscientious of the threat of spies, Hoover insisted that the United States "was never so well prepared to combat espionage activities."

4. J. Edgar Hoover (1895–1972): director of the national Bureau of Investigation beginning in 1924 and of the successor Federal Bureau of Investigation from 1935 until his death in 1972.

2.

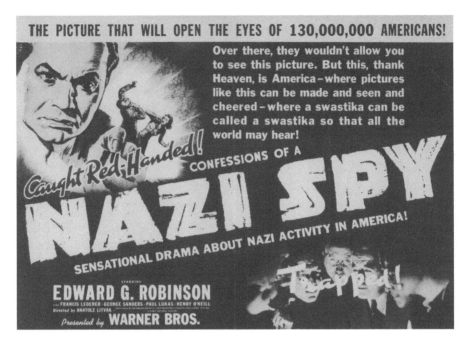

Advertisement for Warner Bros. film *Confessions of a Nazi Spy*, 1939, USHMM Collection, Gift of Ken Sutak.

3.

Stamping Out the Spies

By J. Edgar Hoover with Courtney Ryley Cooper

In a little Midwest town is a fellow of decided opinions who inflicts his views concerning the current European troubles on anyone who will listen. Since he criticizes many of this country's institutions, he has been reported as a possible spy.

In that same town the municipal meal ticket, a factory which makes gadgets, shirt and underwear buttons, metal clips, snap fasteners, and the like, is working overtime on a huge military order. Anyone who is curious can learn all about it. Enthusiastic over their upswing in business, the owners volunteer detailed information on the scope of the order, the method of delivery, when the goods must be on the New York docks. They have hired new workers with practically no inquiry into backgrounds. At night only an aged watchman, deaf and of uncertain vision, guards the factory.

Yet that factory is of vital interest to at least two foreign countries: the one which urgently needs the order, and the one which desperately desires that the goods never be delivered, since they form essential parts of military uniform equipment. Beyond this, other products of this factory would be of vital importance to the United States in time of grave emergency.

Now, suppose acid should be introduced into shipments, factory machinery wrecked, the plant destroyed by fire or explosion. The little Midwest town probably would blame its "official spy." But it would place no responsibility whatever upon those otherwise honorable Americans who had made espionage possible—the factory owners, workers, and others, whose enthusiasm played directly into the hands of an enemy. Their loose talk could have furnished the very information needed for the plot. The inefficient guarding of the plant could have permitted saboteurs to enter. Lax working conditions and inspection could have been an actual aid to arson.

Magnify this little town to include much of the nation and you see why I believe it necessary to discuss espionage, sabotage, and other subversive forces which seek to undermine our national defense. There is no denying that we have a distinct spy menace, that hundreds upon hundreds of foreign agents are busily engaged upon a program of peering, peeking, eavesdropping, propaganda, subversiveness, and actual sabotage.

On an average of once every 6 minutes of a 24-hour day, someone, somewhere, reports suspected spy activities to the Federal Bureau of Investigation. So great has the burden of espionage cases become that they outnumber all other complaints of infractions within the scope of the FBI.

A clear picture of the progress of the European conflict can be gained by the spy records of the FBI. In the 5-year period prior to 1938 this Bureau investigated an average of about 35 espionage cases a year. The number then jumped to 637, and it has climbed steadily, until now complaints are flooding in by the multiple thousands.

This does not mean that spies are leaping over our frontiers and through our ports in constantly increasing armies. But the European conflict has brought more alertness in the interest of self-protection, more requests for investigation of activities that might pass unnoticed in more peaceful times.

Never before has America occupied such an important position in world affairs, and other nations naturally focus their attention upon what this nation is thinking, doing, planning. We form a field for spy activities far more important than that which existed during the comparable period before we entered the World War.

Certainly we should look as much askance at the goose-stepping Bund, with its self-appointed Fuehrer and his un-American credos, as at the Communist termites, whether they be in the field of politics or labor. America is no place for transplanted dictators. [. . .]

Let me hastily add that while there are more spies at work in America than at any time since the World War, this country was never so well prepared to combat espionage activities. There are laws which did not exist in the troubled days before our entrance into the previous conflict, such as the Espionage Act of 1917,[5] the Federal

---

5. The 1917 Espionage Act criminalized any effort to obtain, possess, or share information about US national defenses with the intent to injure the United States or to give advantage to a foreign nation.

Sabotage Law,[6] and the 1938 enactment which requires that all individuals and associations agitating for a foreign principle must register with the State Department. [. . .]

The FBI has received thousands of letters from earnest citizens, asking how they may aid in the battle against spydom. I shall attempt to point out certain definite rules.

Remember that suspicion does not make fact. The real job is to establish the guilt of a person suspected as a foreign agent before invoking the law. This is a job for skilled investigators. The citizen should consider his particular task fulfilled when he reports his suspicions to the nearest FBI office. After that they should not become gossip. Idle talk can hamper proper investigation.

In the wave of patriotism which, fortunately, is rising throughout the nation, are dangers of overzealousness. We must not stoop to un-American methods, no matter how great the provocation or how patriotic the aim. We should regard vigilantes or vigilante methods as abhorrent. We should all think clearly, sanely. [. . .]

[Hoover and Cooper discuss several case histories of FBI sabotage investigations.]

Above all, be on guard, but remain calm. The nation is better today than in years gone by. An offensive has started. The combined attack by federal and state forces should be sufficient so far as investigation and prosecution are concerned. Beyond the efforts of these forces there is a need, of course, for the individual co-operation of all sincere and earnest Americans. But this co-operation should be limited to passing on to the proper officials all questionable facts or rumors which may come one's way. An alert, intelligent public is the best defense against traitorous activities.

—*American Magazine*, January 1940, 20–21, 83–84.

4.

Fortune/Roper Organization survey, June 1940

"Do you believe that Germany has already started to organize a "Fifth Column" in this country?"

71% Yes
 7% No
22% Don't know

—Survey sponsored by *Fortune Magazine*. Roper Fortune # 18: War Attitudes 3. Question 25: USROPER.40-018.R10. Cornell University, Ithaca, NY: Roper Center for Public Opinion Research. https://doi.org/10.25940/ROPER-31097168.

6. In April 1918, Congress passed an act "to punish the willful injury or destruction of war material, or of war premises or utilities used in connection with war material" when the United States is at war. It was amended in late 1940 to update the definition of "war material," and repealed in 1948.

As Nazi Germany invaded and took over European countries to its north and west in May 1940, the president broadcast a fireside chat on the nation's military preparedness. He warned Americans to remain vigilant against both spies and internal "discord." Even as he cited these significant threats to national security, Roosevelt told his listeners that he would continue to "pray for the restoration of peace in this mad world of ours."

5.

National Defense

My friends:

At this moment of sadness throughout most of the world, I want to talk with you about a number of subjects that directly affect the future of the United States. We are shocked by the almost incredible eyewitness stories that come to us, stories of what is happening at this moment to the civilian populations of Norway and Holland and Belgium and Luxembourg and France.

I think it is right on this Sabbath evening that I should say a word in behalf of women and children and old men who need help—immediate help in their present distress—help from us across the seas, help from us who are still free to give it.

Tonight over the once peaceful roads of Belgium and France millions are now moving, running from their homes to escape bombs and shells and fire and machine gunning, without shelter, and almost wholly without food. They stumble on, knowing not where the end of the road will be. I speak to you of these people because each one of you that is listening to me tonight has a way of helping them. The American Red Cross that represents each of us, is rushing food and clothing and medical supplies to these destitute civilian millions. Please—I beg you—please give according to your means to your nearest Red Cross chapter, give as generously as you can. I ask this in the name of our common humanity.

Let us sit down together again, you and I, to consider our own pressing problems that confront us.

There are many among us who in the past closed their eyes to events abroad—because they believed in utter good faith what some of their fellow Americans told them—that what was taking place in Europe was none of our business; that no matter what happened over there, the United States could always pursue its peaceful and unique course in the world.

There are many among us who closed their eyes, from lack of interest or lack of knowledge; honestly and sincerely thinking that many hundreds of miles of salt water made the American Hemisphere so remote that the people of North and Central and South America could go on living in the midst of their vast resources without reference to, or danger from, the other Continents of the world.

There are some among us who were persuaded by minority [political] groups that we could maintain our physical safety by retiring within our continental boundaries—the Atlantic on the east, the Pacific on the west, Canada on the north and Mexico on the south. I illustrated the futility—the impossibility—of that idea in my Message to the Congress last week.[7] Obviously, a defense policy based on that is merely to invite future attack.

And, finally, there are a few among us who have deliberately and consciously closed their eyes because they were determined to be opposed to their government, its foreign policy and every other policy, to be partisan, and to believe that anything that the Government did was wholly wrong.

To those who have closed their eyes for any of these many reasons, to those who would not admit the possibility of the approaching storm—to all of them the past two weeks have meant the shattering of many illusions.

They have lost the illusion that we are remote and isolated and, therefore, secure against the dangers from which no other land is free.

In some quarters, with this rude awakening has come fear, fear bordering on panic. It is said that we are defenseless. It is whispered by some that, only by abandoning our freedom, our ideals, our way of life, can we build our defenses adequately, can we match the strength of the aggressors.

I did not share those illusions. I do not share these fears.

Today we are more realistic. But let us not be calamity-howlers and discount our strength. Let us have done with both fears and illusions. On this Sabbath evening, in our homes in the midst of our American families, let us calmly consider what we have done and what we must do.

In the past two or three weeks all kinds of stories have been handed out to the American public about our lack of preparedness. It has even been charged that the money we have spent on our military and naval forces during the last few years has gone down the rat-hole. I think that it is a matter of fairness to the nation that you hear the facts.

Yes, we have spent large sums of money on the national defense. This money has been used to make our Army and Navy today the largest, the best equipped, and the best trained peace-time military establishment in the whole history of this country.

[At this point in his broadcast, Roosevelt recounted with much statistical detail the increased capacity of the US military in 1940 since he took office in 1933. These changes had come at great expense to the United States, yet he thought them still "inadequate" for the needs of the nation's defense in a time of war.]

7. In his message to Congress about defense appropriations on May 16, 1940, the president emphasized how modern aircraft had drastically reduced enemy attack time from days by sea to hours by air. (Message to Congress, May 16, 1940, box 51, Master Speech File 1898–1945, FDRL.)

The Government of the United States stands ready to advance the necessary money to help provide for the enlargement of factories, the establishment of new plants, the employment of thousands of necessary workers, the development of new sources of supply for the hundreds of raw materials required, the development of quick mass transportation of supplies. And the details of all of this are now being worked out in Washington, day and night. [. . .]

Today's threat to our national security is not a matter of military weapons alone. We know of other methods, new methods of attack.

The Trojan Horse. The Fifth Column that betrays a nation unprepared for treachery. Spies, saboteurs and traitors are the actors in this new strategy. With all of these we must and will deal vigorously.

But there is an added technique for weakening a nation at its very roots, for disrupting the entire pattern of life of a people. And it is important that we understand it.

The method is simple. First, discord, the dissemination of discord. A group—not too large—a group that may be sectional or racial or political—is encouraged to exploit its prejudices through false slogans and emotional appeals. The aim of those who deliberately egg on these groups is to create confusion of counsel, public indecision, political paralysis and eventually, a state of panic.

Sound national policies come to be viewed with a new and unreasoning skepticism, not through the wholesome debates of honest and free men, but through the clever schemes of foreign agents.

As a result of these new techniques, armament programs may be dangerously delayed. Singleness of national purpose may be undermined. Men can lose confidence in each other, and therefore lose confidence in the efficacy of their own united action. Faith and courage can yield to doubt and fear. The unity of the state can be so sapped that its strength is destroyed.

All this is no idle dream. It has happened time after time, in nation after nation, during the last two years. Fortunately, American men and women are not yet easy dupes. Campaigns of group hatred or class struggle have never made much headway among us, and are not making headway now. But new forces are being unleashed, deliberately planned propaganda to divide and weaken us in the face of danger as other nations have been weakened before.

These dividing forces I do not hesitate to call undiluted poison. They must not be allowed to spread in the New World as they have in the Old. Our moral, our mental defenses must be raised up as never before against those who would cast a smoke-screen across our vision.

The development of our defense program makes it essential that each and every one of us, men and women, feel that we have some contribution to make toward the security of our nation.

At this time, when the world—and the world includes our own American Hemisphere—when the world is threatened by forces of destruction, it is my resolve and yours to build up our armed defenses.

We shall build them to whatever heights the future may require.

We shall rebuild them swiftly, as the methods of warfare swiftly change. [. . .]

We build and defend not for our generation alone. We defend the foundations laid down by our fathers. We build a life for generations yet unborn. We defend and we build a way of life, not for America alone, but for all mankind. Ours is a high duty, a noble task.

Day and night I pray for the restoration of peace in this mad world of ours. It is not necessary that I, the President, ask the American people to pray in behalf of such a cause—for I know you are praying with me.

I am certain that out of the hearts of every man, woman and child in this land, in every waking minute, a supplication goes up to Almighty God; that all of us beg that suffering and starving, that death and destruction may end—and that peace may return to the world. In common affection for all mankind, your prayers join with mine—that God will heal the wounds and the hearts of humanity.

> —Transcript of broadcast audio, based on Fireside Chat #15—"National Defense," May 26, 1940, box 51, Master Speech File, 1898–1945, FDRL. Audio at https://www.fdrlibrary.org/utterancesfdr#afdr169.

Gallup asked Americans a variation of the question below at least once every month between the outbreak of war in Europe (September 1939) and the US entrance into the war (December 1941). After this May 1940 poll, the percentage of Americans who favored intervention gradually increased.

6.

Gallup Poll, May 1940

"Do you think the United States should declare war on Germany and send our army and navy abroad to fight?"

7% Yes
93% No

> —Gallup Organization. 1940. Gallup Poll # 1940-0195: CCC Camps/ War in Europe/Labor Unions/1940 Presidential Election. Question 3: USGALLUP.052940.RK05. Cornell University, Ithaca, NY: Roper Center for Public Opinion Research. https://doi.org/10.25940/ROPER-31087179.

"A Wall of Bureaucratic Measures"

Apprehensions in the US State Department that refugees from Nazi-occupied Western Europe would threaten national security if they were admitted to the United States led to new practices that restricted immigration in 1940 and 1941. Assistant Secretary of State Breckinridge Long[8] oversaw the State Department's Visa Division, which controlled the issuance of visas to enter the United States. His directives stressed national security concerns and slowed the immigration process for applicants from Nazi-controlled territories. Critics of Long accused him of intentionally blocking refugees, and many believed he held antisemitic views that influenced his decision making.

In this 1940 memo to colleagues in the State Department, Long proposes a number of ways that, in a time of national emergency, consular officials could use bureaucratic obstacles to limit the flow of immigrants into the United States while awaiting congressional action. Three days after Long wrote this memo, US Secretary of State Cordell Hull ordered all diplomatic and consular officers to exercise "extreme care" in examining all applications for visas during the present period of "emergency."

7.

DEPARTMENT OF STATE
ASSISTANT SECRETARY

June 26, 1940.

Attached is a memorandum [that spells out the legal restrictions on limiting immigration]. There are two possibilities and I will discuss each category briefly.

Nonimmigrants

Their entry into the United States can be made to depend upon prior authorization by the [State] Department. This would mean that the consuls would be divested of discretion and that all requests for nonimmigrant visas (temporary visitor and transit visas) be passed upon here [in Washington, DC]. It is quite feasible and can be done instantly. It will permit the Department to effectively control the immigration of persons in this category and private instructions can be given the Visa Division as to nationalities which should not be admitted as well as to individuals who are to be excluded.

This must be done for universal application and could not be done as regards Germany, for instance, or Russia, for instance, or any other one government because it would first, invite retaliation and second, would probably be a violation of some of our treaty arrangements. [. . .]

Immigrants

We can delay and effectively stop for a temporary period of indefinite length the number of immigrants coming into the United States. We could do this by simply

8. Samuel Breckinridge Long (1881–1958): a personal friend of Roosevelt, ambassador to Italy (1933–36), special assistant secretary of state for matters related to the war (1939–40), and assistant secretary of state (1940–44). In November 1943, he gave misleading testimony to Congress about the number of European refugees admitted to the United States. He resigned a year later.

advising our consuls to put every obstacle in the way and to require additional evidence and to resort to various administrative advices which would postpone and postpone and postpone the granting of the visas. However, this could only be temporary. In order to make it more definite it would have to be done by suspension of the rules under the law by the issuance of a proclamation of emergency—which I take it we are not yet ready to proclaim.

Summing up

We can effectively control nonimmigrants by prohibiting the issuance of visas unless the consent of the Department is obtained in advance, for universal application.

We can temporarily prevent the number of immigrants from certain localities such as Cuba, Mexico and other places of origin of German intending immigrants[9] by simply raising administrative obstacles.

The Department will be prepared to take these two steps immediately upon the decision but emphasis must be placed on the fact that discrimination must not be practiced and with the additional thought that in case a suspension of the regulations should be proclaimed under the need of an emergency, it would be universally applicable. [. . .]

[Initials]
B[reckinridge]. L[ong].

—Memorandum, June 26, 1940, box 220, General Visa Correspondence, 1940–1944, 811.111 W.R./107, Records of the Department of State, Record Group 59, NACP.

8.

TELEGRAM SENT
Department of State

Washington,
June 29, 1940

DIPLOMATIC TELEGRAM TO
ALL DIPLOMATIC AND CONSULAR OFFICES.

Nonimmigrant visas issued prior to June 6, 1940 must be revalidated by an American consular officer unless the holders are on the high seas enroute to the United States. [. . .] In revalidating each visa a most careful examination will be given to ascertain that the alien's entry would not be contrary to the public safety and to ascertain that the entry involves a reasonable need or legitimate purpose.

---

9. By "German intending immigrants," Long means German-born people who intend to immigrate to the United States.

All applications for immigration visas must be examined with extreme care and during the present period of emergency no such visa should be issued if there is any doubt whatsoever concerning the alien. Although a drastic reduction in the number of quota and nonquota immigration visas issued will result therefrom and quotas against which there is a heavy demand will be under issued, it is essential to take every precaution at this time to safeguard the best interests of the United States.

[*signed*] Hull
[*initialed*] S[umner]. W[ells].[10]

—Circular telegram, June 29, 1940, box 220, General Visa Correspondence, 1940–1944, 811.111 W.R./108, Records of the Department of State, Record Group 59, NACP.

Internationally renowned theoretical physicist Albert Einstein, himself a refugee from Nazi Germany, wrote to First Lady Eleanor Roosevelt in 1941 about the policies in the State Department that made it nearly impossible for immigrants to find refuge in the United States, lamenting that a "wall of bureaucratic measures" had been put in place.

9.

A. EINSTEIN
July 26, 1941

Mrs. Franklin D. Roosevelt
The White House
Washington D.C.

Dear Mrs. Roosevelt:

I have noted with great satisfaction that you always stand for the right and humaneness even when it is hard. Therefore in my deep concern, I know of no one else to whom to turn for help.

A policy is now being pursued in the State Department which makes it all but impossible to give refuge in America to many worthy persons who are the victims of Fascist cruelty in Europe. Of course, this is not openly avowed by those responsible for it. The method which is being used, however, is to make immigration impossible by erecting a wall of bureaucratic measures alleged to be necessary to protect America against subversive, dangerous elements. I would suggest that you talk about this question to some well-informed and right-minded person such as Mr. Hamilton

---

10. Sumner Welles (1892–1961): a major foreign policy adviser to Roosevelt who served from 1937 to 1943 as under secretary of state, the second-highest position in the department.

Fish Armstrong.[11] If then you become convinced that a truly grave injustice is under way, I know that you will find it possible to bring the matter to the attention of your heavily burdened husband in order that it may be remedied.

Very sincerely yours,
[*signature*]
Professor Albert Einstein.

[*Eleanor Roosevelt's handwriting*]   FDR

Tell Mr. Einstein I will bring his
letter at once to the President.

—Letter, July 26, 1941, file 7177, "Einstein, Albert,"
President's Personal File, FDRL.

The Nazi War on Europe's Jews

Although the war dominated American news coverage from Europe, newspapers throughout the United States also printed what limited information was available on the Nazi regime's persecution of Europe's Jews. In general, the Western press was banned from Nazi-occupied territories, particularly after 1941, so dispatches from within these territories were rare. The three articles below, written by wire service reporters, appeared between autumn 1940 and autumn 1941 (after the German invasion of the Soviet Union but before the United States entered the war). They provided readers with some details about the Nazi regime's forced isolation of eastern European Jews into overcrowded ghettos, its mandate that Jews wear Stars of David to publicly mark them, and its imposition of Nazi anti-Jewish laws in western Europe after spring 1940.

10.

A Walled Ghetto, Ruin Everywhere, Is What Writer Finds in Warsaw

___

District for Jews May Be Closed by 18 Police

___

Germans Insist It's for Protection Against Typhus

[Newspaper] Editor's note—Alvin J. Steinkopf of Milwaukee, member of the Associated Press staff in Berlin, visited Warsaw as the first and only non-German correspondent permitted to make an exhaustive inspection of the little surrounding state which, since the German

___

11. Hamilton Fish Armstrong (1893–1973): a journalist, the long-time editor of the influential journal *Foreign Affairs,* and an occasional adviser to the US State Department.

conquest, is called the "general government of Poland"—as distinguished from the parts of the country actually annexed by Germany and Russia.[12]

by ALVIN J. STEINKOPF

WARSAW, OCT. 12.—(AP)—A year after the German conquest, Warsaw still looks like an untidy brickyard.

Building stones lie helter skelter in the great city which was once the capital of independent Poland.

Great open spaces yawn where once stood apartment houses, shops and stately government buildings.

There is ruin everywhere; houses without roofs, houses without windows, houses that now are but a few blackened walls.

Warsaw had 22,000 buildings. Two thousand were destroyed, 8,000 extensively damaged.

Railway Station Gone

The old central railway station is gone. German Stukas[13] hammered it to pieces. The debris has been hauled away, and where the station stood there is a vast vacant space, without even a pebble on its smooth surface.

To the rear is what is left of the new central station, which burned shortly before the war. Improvised boarding makes a sort of a barn where Polish trains, under German management, come in exactly on time. [. . .]

Post Office Barely Scratched

The ministry of post and communications is gone—again, Stukas. Beside it, the post office stands, barely scratched, and a block-long line of people waits before it, trying to mail letters abroad. Foreign mail must be handed in personally.

The Opera House is as good as gone; a bomb smashed the roof and fire gutted the interior.

The Jews walk down the streets in white and blue arm bands.[14]

These are their tags of identification, and every one of them must wear them on their right sleeves.

There are many Jews.

---

12. In September 1939, under secret terms of a bilateral nonaggression pact, Germany (on the west) and the Soviet Union (on the east) partitioned and annexed much of Poland. A third portion between, later called the General Government, was held under German occupation.

13. German dive-bomber aircraft that proved especially effective during military invasions.

14. In November 1939, Jews over the age of ten living in the General Government portion of Nazi-occupied Poland, which included Warsaw, were ordered to wear white armbands with a blue Star of David over their outer garments.

Wall Around Ghetto

There is a new concrete wall around the ghetto which lies in the central district.[15]

The Germans say the wall, which is unique in modern times, is not anti-Semitic, but simply a desperate health measure necessary to protect Pole and Jew alike from the pestilences which are likely to follow in the wake of total war.

Jews can and do use any other street in Warsaw.

The wall is eight feet high and so tight a cat couldn't get through it.

It surrounds the central district ghetto comprising a hundred or more city blocks into which the population is crowded with astonishing density, and closes off 200 streets and even street car lines—it is built right over their rails.

Wall Built by Germans

The wall was built by German occupation authorities but conditions in the ghetto which the German officials are trying to cut off from the rest of the population are declared to have existed long before the German army marched in a year ago.

Eighteen streets, the most important traffic lanes, remain unobstructed. Hence one may enter and leave the ghetto at 18 points and it is possible on through streets to traverse the whole region without being aware of confinement on either side.

18 May Close District

The restraining walls are of comparative little hindrance in normal times. But at a moment's notice the authorities, by posting 18 policemen at the points of entry, can close off the entire district. It is also possible to cut off access to two or three streets, or to a larger part of the ghetto, by stationing guards at house doors and street corners inside the district.

Inside this walled area live half a million Jews and Poles. Many have lived their whole lives in this sharply delimited region. Within are their homes, businesses, schools and synagogues.

'A Wall Against Typhus'

"It is not a wall against the Jews," I was told by Dr. Jost Walbaum, eminent Berlin physician who is health leader (minister of health in any other country) of the general government of Poland. "It's a wall against typhus."[16]

Several months ago, 30,000 of the district's population were quarantined by a part of the wall and by guards for 14 days.

15. The Nazi regime walled off the Warsaw ghetto between April and November 1940. Warsaw's was the largest of more than 1,000 ghettos that imprisoned Jews in occupied Poland. At one point, more than 400,000 people lived within the Warsaw ghetto's 1.3 square miles.

16. A highly infectious and often fatal bacterial disease that generally occurs in crowded living situations with poor sanitation.

Authorities said the 30,000 became infested with typhus-spreading lice and they were kept isolated until gas, brought from Germany, could be used to fumigate their homes.

58 Cases of Typhus

There are 58 cases of typhus in Warsaw today, a number which would cause alarm in any American city but which is not regarded as extraordinary in Warsaw under present conditions. Typhus is a disease which abounds in the winter months and the German authorities are concerned lest there be an upward trend through the autumn. If there is they won't hesitate a moment to wall the ghetto, and pen up half a million people while they fight the disease.

"And it won't be persecution of the Jews," Dr. Walbaum said. "It would be a national, even a European, catastrophe to let a situation like this get out of hand; and when it comes to communicable disease, I'll lock up any possible spreader of contagion be he Jew, Gentile, prince or pauper."

Facing Fate Bravely

The Poles are facing their fate courageously.

The Poles are not happy, of course desolation hangs over the town. Certainly, no great city in modern times had been brought so close to total destruction.

—Associated Press, *Minneapolis Tribune,* October 13, 1940, 6.

11.

NAZIS DECREE JEWS MUST WEAR BADGE

Large Yellow Star Ordered for All Over 6 Years of Age

BERLIN, Sept. 6 (U.P.).—All Jews over six years or age were ordered by the Gestapo, secret police, today to wear a large yellow "Star of David" with a black superscription: "Jew."

The order, issued by Secret Police Chief Reinhard Heydrich,[17] said that Jews would not be permitted to leave the area in which they reside without police permission.

Jews must not wear any orders or decorations, Heydrich said.

Covers Entire Reich

The order becomes effective on Sept. 15. As published in the official Gazette [*Reichsgesetzblatt,* Reich Law Book], it covers the entire Reich as well as the Protectorate of Bohemia and Moravia.

17. Reinhard Heydrich (1904–42): joined the Nazi Party in 1931 and became a leading figure in the SS and Nazi police and security services. He helped organize the Kristallnacht pogrom and, after the war began, the persecution and mass murder of eastern European Jews. He was assassinated in 1942.

It was regarded here as the sharpest official measure against Jews since those introduced following the anti-Semitic outbreaks of Nov. 9, 1938.[18]

"Jews who have completed their sixth year are forbidden to show themselves in public without the Jewish star," the order said.

Worn on Clothing

"The star consists of a six-pointed star, outlined in black on yellow cloth the size of the palm of one's hand, with a black superscription: Jew.

"It must be worn visibly and firmly sewed to the left breast of clothing."

The order provided a fine of 150 marks (about $60) or six weeks' imprisonment for violation of the new regulations.

The new regulations were similar to restrictions which have been in effect in such cities as Warsaw since the fall of Poland. Jews are confined largely to a Ghetto in Warsaw and must wear prominent identification marks.

—United Press, *Philadelphia Inquirer,* September 7, 1941, 3.

12.

Germans Crowding Millions of Eastern European Jews Into Ghettoes

PROPERTY AND MONEY SEIZED BY HITLERITES

Thousands of Russian Jews Get Same Treatment as Those in Other Occupied Nations

By JACK FLEISHER
(United Press Correspondent)

BERLIN, Nov. 7.— Eastern Europe's Jewish millions are being swept into ghettoes in the wake of German armies smashing their way toward the heart of Russia, and drastic anti-Semitic measures are being put into effect in German-dominated countries.

The segregation of Polish Jews already has been virtually completed and the process is being extended to western Russia as fast as Nazi civil authorities following close behind the advancing troops can complete the necessary organization.

Already thousands of Russian Jews have been evicted from German-occupied villages and herded to towns for isolation in sections set aside as ghettoes.

Travelers from Russia reported that in numerous places Jews were being dealt with summarily[19] and German propaganda company dispatches reported that local popula-

---

18. November 9, 1938, was the start of the November pogrom known as Kristallnacht.

19. The so-called mobile killing squads (*Einsatzgruppen*), accompanying the German army in the June 1941 invasion of the Soviet Union, rounded up Jews in towns and villages and shot them

tions in the Baltic countries for several days after German occupation "took revenge" on Jews.

In former Russian Poland, as in the area under the Polish general government, the Jews now must wear armbands inscribed "Jew" and are being put to work in gangs repairing roads, clearing war debris and exhuming dead bodies. [. . .]

Meantime, in German-occupied France, Jewish businesses have been taken over by German-appointed aryan "administrators." In Paris alone, with a population of 120,000 Jews, approximately 5,000 Jewish-owned stores were affected. Jews also were barred from the Paris bourse[20] and from public jobs.

All Registered

German authorities in Belgium and the Netherlands ordered the Jews to report all their property. In Belgium also, Jews were barred from serving as lawyers, teachers, managers, directors and editors. All Jewish business must be registered and display a sign in German, Flemish and French, "Jewish undertaking."

Netherlands Jews were dismissed from public services and barred from restaurants and theaters. [. . .]

—United Press, *San Bernardino (CA) Daily Sun,* November 8, 1941, 4.

Intervention or Isolation?

For the first two years of the war in Europe, while the United States officially remained neutral, Americans fiercely debated whether to intervene in the fight against Nazi Germany or remain isolated across the Atlantic Ocean.

"Interventionists" recognized the very real threat Hitler, his dictatorship, and Germany's armed forces posed to the United States. They argued that the best defense strategy would be backing President Roosevelt's efforts to provide the United Kingdom with weapons, planes, ships, and supplies to aid the war against Nazi Germany. Among many interventionist groups was the Fight for Freedom Committee, founded in April 1941 and composed of a number of prominent Americans.

"Isolationists" hoped the United States would stay out of the war. In 1940, a group of Yale University students founded the America First Committee to support the isolationist cause. They quickly mobilized antiwar students at many colleges nationwide to join the organization, which advocated defending US borders from attack but opposed sending US troops abroad to fight.

---

en masse. In the first six months of the Nazi occupation, at least 500,000 and as many as 900,000 Soviet Jews were murdered.

20. France's stock exchange.

13.

To the President of the United States,
Washington, D. C.

 I have pledged my belief in the following statetments of the Fight For
Freedom Committee:

 "The danger which faces America from Nazism is absolute. The time for
half measures is gone. We can win if we fight. We believe a national
emergency must be proclaimed at once. We urge a break in diplomatic
relations with our implacable foes. We urge the use of our mighty naval
force to hold the seas of the world against the enemies of the world.
Let's wait no longer."

 I pledge my support to you, Mr. President, in anything you may do
to implement this stand.

Signature

—Postcard, ca. 1941, Fight for Freedom, Inc. Records, MC025, Public Policy
   Papers, Department of Special Collections, Princeton University Library.

This pin and mock "Wanted" flyer (overleaf), produced and distributed by the interventionist Fight for Freedom Committee in 1941, explicitly presented Hitler as a murderer. Even anti-Nazi propaganda that directly mentioned murder or other crimes, however, failed to include any specific reference to Jewish victims.

Pin-back button for Fight for Freedom, Inc., ca.
1941, USHMM Collection, Gift of Forrest James
Robinson Jr.

14.

WANTED FOR MURDER
ADOLF SCHICKLGRUBER[21]

Alias Hitler

Wanted for MURDER; ARSON; GRAND LARCENY; POSSESSION OF FIREARMS; PIRACY; TREACHERY; RELIGIOUS PERSECUTION

DESCRIPTION—Age, 52 in 1941; height, five feet, seven inches; weight, 150–165; hair, black, shaggy lock hang over forehead; eyes, black, [half-]demented gaze; complexion, sallow; football mustache, eleven hairs on each side; foppish dresser,[22] but has marked devotion to brown shirts and an old trench-coat.

21. "Schicklgruber": Adolf Hitler's paternal grandmother's name. Adolf's father, born illegitimately, was named Alois Schicklgruber until adopting his stepfather's name *Hiedler* at age 39. In registering Alois's new name, a government official spelled it *Hitler*.

22. A fop: one who is excessively concerned with his clothing and appearance.

PARTICULARS—This man has tendency to become hysterical on slight provocation, has been known to throw himself on floor and gnaw rugs; guttural voice apt to rise to shrill tones when excited or thwarted. He has delusions, particularly about his place in history and his powers over vast numbers of people. He is sadistic, malicious, bombastic, vengeful, mystical, maniacal, addicted to public hysteria on "race purity;" suffers from dreams of persecution. He is a congenital liar. He has worked at only one known trade—house painting.

RECORD—He has served one term in prison, and has a police record of inciting to riot in various cities.

SHOOT ON SIGHT! This man is dangerous, will attack without warning; he is always surrounded by armed thugs and expert gunmen.

REWARD! If captured, dead or alive, the reward will be freedom for the entire world and peace for all nations.

> —Flyer for Fight for Freedom, Inc., 1941, Fight for Freedom, Inc. Records, MC025, Public Policy Papers, Department of Special Collections, Princeton University Library.

President Roosevelt took to the radio airwaves again in September 1941 to inform Americans about Germany's rising threat to the United States. In this fireside chat, the president provides details about an attack by a German submarine on an American destroyer. Though Roosevelt did not seek a declaration of war against Germany in response to this incident, he did use the opportunity to explain to the American people his increasingly interventionist position.

15.

Maintaining Freedom of the Seas

My fellow Americans:

The Navy Department of the United States has reported to me that on the morning of September fourth the United States destroyer *Greer*, proceeding in full daylight toward Iceland, had reached a point southeast of Greenland. She was carrying American mail to Iceland. She was flying the American flag. Her identity as an American ship was unmistakable.

She was then and there attacked by a submarine. Germany admits that it was a German submarine. The submarine deliberately fired a torpedo at the *Greer*, followed later by another torpedo attack. In spite of what Hitler's propaganda bureau has invented, and in spite of what any American obstructionist organization may prefer to believe, I tell you the blunt fact that the German submarine fired first upon this American destroyer without warning, and with deliberate design to sink her. [. . .][23]

This was piracy—piracy legally and morally. It was not the first nor the last act of piracy which the Nazi Government has committed against the American flag in this war. For attack has followed attack. [. . .]

[FDR adds three more examples of American ships attacked by German submarines in recent weeks.]

The important truth is that these acts of international lawlessness are a manifestation of a design—a design that has been made clear to the American people for a long time. It is the Nazi design to abolish the freedom of the seas, and to acquire absolute control and domination of these seas for themselves.

For with control of the seas in their own hands, the way can obviously become clear for their next step—domination of the United States, domination of the Western Hemisphere—by force of arms. Under Nazi control of the seas, no merchant ship of the United States or of any other American Republic would be free to carry on any peaceful commerce, except by the condescending grace of this foreign and tyrannical power. The Atlantic Ocean which has been, and which should always be, a free and friendly highway for us would then become a deadly menace to the commerce of the United States, to the coasts of the United States, and even to the inland cities of the United States.

The Hitler Government, in defiance of the laws of the sea, in defiance of the recognized rights of all other nations, has presumed to declare, on paper, that great areas of the seas—even including a vast expanse lying in the Western Hemisphere—are to be closed, and that no ships may enter them for any purpose, except at peril of being sunk. Actually they are sinking ships at will and without warning in widely separated areas both within and far outside of these far-flung pretended zones. [. . .]

This Nazi attempt to seize control of the oceans is but a counterpart of the Nazi plots now being carried on throughout the Western Hemisphere —all designed toward the same end. For Hitler's advance guards—not only his avowed agents but also his dupes among us—have sought to make ready for him footholds, bridgeheads in the New World, to be used as soon as he has gained control of the oceans. [. . .]

To be ultimately successful in world mastery, Hitler knows that he must get control of the seas. He must first destroy the bridge of ships which we are building across the Atlantic and over which we shall continue to roll the implements of war to help destroy him, to destroy all his works in the end. He must wipe out our patrol on sea and in the air if he is to do it. He must silence the British Navy.

23. Historians have cast doubts on Roosevelt's assertion that the German submarine was the aggressor in this confrontation.

I think it must be explained over and over again to people who like to think of the United States Navy as an invincible protection, that this can be true only if the British Navy survives. [. . .]

It is time for all Americans, Americans of all the Americas to stop being deluded by the romantic notion that the Americas can go on living happily and peacefully in a Nazi-dominated world. [. . .]

The Nazi danger to our Western world has long ceased to be a mere possibility. The danger is here now—not only from a military enemy but from an enemy of all law, all liberty, all morality, all religion. [. . .]

No act of violence, no act of intimidation will keep us from maintaining intact two bulwarks of American defense: First, our line of supply of materiel to the enemies of Hitler; and second, the freedom of our shipping on the high seas. [. . .]

It is clear to all Americans that the time has come when the Americas themselves must now be defended. A continuation of attacks in our own waters, or in waters that could be used for further and greater attacks on us, will inevitably weaken our American ability to repel Hitlerism.

My obligation as President is historic; it is clear. Yes, it is inescapable.

It is no act of war on our part when we decide to protect the seas that are vital to American defense. The aggression is not ours. Ours is solely defense.

But let this warning be clear. From now on, if German or Italian vessels of war enter the waters, the protection of which is necessary for American defense, they do so at their own peril.

The orders which I have given as Commander-in-Chief of the United States Army and Navy are to carry out that policy—at once.

The sole responsibility rests upon Germany. There will be no shooting unless Germany continues to seek it. [. . .]

I have no illusions about the gravity of this step. I have not taken it hurriedly or lightly. It is the result of months and months of constant thought and anxiety and prayer. In the protection of your nation and mine it cannot be avoided.

The American people have faced other grave crises in their history—with American courage, with American resolution. They will do no less today.

They know the actualities of the attacks upon us. They know the necessities of a bold defense against these attacks. They know that the times call for clear heads and fearless hearts.

And with that inner strength that comes to a free people conscious of their duty, conscious of the righteousness of what they do, they will—with Divine help and guidance—stand their ground against this latest assault upon their democracy, their sovereignty, and their freedom.

—Transcript of broadcast audio, based on Fireside Chat #17—"Maintaining Freedom of the Seas," September 11, 1941, box 62, Master Speech File, 1898–1945, FDRL. Audio at https://www.fdrlibrary.org/utterancesfdr#afdr238.

Within months of its founding, the America First Committee persuaded one of the nation's most outspoken isolationists, world-renowned aviator Charles Lindbergh, to support its cause. Lindbergh's enormous celebrity—dating to his 1927 solo, nonstop flight across the Atlantic Ocean—helped the America First Committee become a national organization with some 800,000 members.

The America First Committee's reputation changed significantly after Lindbergh accused Jews of being "war agitators" in a speech at Des Moines, Iowa, on September 11, 1941—the same evening that President Roosevelt delivered his fireside chat stating that the nation would defend itself against Nazi Germany's aggression. Newspapers and magazines across the country denounced Lindbergh and the committee itself for promoting antisemitism and intolerance. America First Committee leaders denied the accusation, but the criticism continued, and the organization's influence diminished rapidly. As soon as the United States was attacked at Pearl Harbor, Hawaii, and entered World War II in December 1941, the committee disbanded.

16.

WHO ARE THE WAR AGITATORS?

It is now two years since this latest European war began. From that day in September, 1939, until the present moment, there has been an ever-increasing effort to force the United States into the conflict. That effort has been carried on by foreign interests, and by a small minority of our own people; but it has been so successful that, today, our country stands on the verge of war.

At this time, as the war is about to enter its third winter, it seems appropriate to review the circumstances that have led us to our present position. Why are we on the verge of war? Was it necessary for us to become so deeply involved? Who is responsible for changing our national policy from one of neutrality and independence to one of entanglement in European affairs? [. . .]

The subterfuge and propaganda that exists in our country is obvious on every side. Tonight, I shall try to pierce through a portion of it, to the naked facts which lie beneath.

When this war started in Europe, it was clear that the American people were solidly opposed to entering it. Why shouldn't we be? We had the best defensive position in the world; we had a tradition of independence from Europe; and the one time we did take part in a European war left European problems unsolved, and debts to America unpaid. National polls showed that when England and France declared war on Germany, in 1939, less than ten percent of our population favored a similar course for America.

But there were various groups of people, here and abroad, whose interests and beliefs necessitated the involvement of the United States in the war. I shall point out some of these groups tonight, and outline their methods of procedure. In doing this, I must speak with the utmost frankness, for in order to counteract their efforts, we must know exactly who they are.

The three most important groups who have been pressing this country toward war are the British, the Jewish, and the Roosevelt administration. Behind these groups, but of lesser importance, are a number of capitalists, anglophiles, and intellectuals, who believe that their future, and the future of mankind, depend upon the domination of the British Empire. Add to these the Communistic groups who were opposed to intervention until a few weeks ago, and I believe I have named the major war agitators in this country. [. . .]

These war agitators comprise only a small minority of our people; but they control a tremendous influence. Against the determination of the American people to stay out of war, they have marshalled the power of their propaganda, their money, and their patronage.

Let us consider these groups, one at a time. First, the British: It is obvious, and perfectly understandable, that Great Britain wants the United States in the war on her side. England is now in a desperate position. Her population is not large enough, and her armies are not strong enough, to invade the continent of Europe and win the war she declared against Germany. Her geographical position is such that she cannot win the war by the use of aviation alone, regardless of how many planes we send her. Even if America entered the war, it is improbable that the Allied armies could invade Europe and overwhelm the Axis powers.

But one thing is certain. If England can draw this country into the war, she can shift to our shoulders a large portion of the responsibility for waging it, and for paying its cost. As you all know, we were left with the debts of the last European war; and unless we are more cautious in the future than we have been in the past, we will be left with the debts of the present one. If it were not for her hope that she can make us responsible for the war financially, as well as militarily, I believe England would have negotiated a peace in Europe many months ago, and be better off for doing so. [. . .]

The second major group I mentioned is the Jewish. It is not difficult to understand why Jewish people desire the overthrow of Nazi Germany. The persecution they suffered in Germany would be sufficient to make bitter enemies of any race. No person with a sense of the dignity of mankind can condone the persecution of the Jewish race in Germany. But no person of honesty and vision can look on their pro-war policy here today without seeing the dangers involved in such a policy, both for us and for them.

Instead of agitating for war, the Jewish groups in this country should be opposing it in every possible way, for they will be among the first to feel its consequences. Tolerance is a virtue that depends upon peace and strength. History shows that it cannot survive war and devastation. A few far-sighted Jewish people realize this, and stand opposed to intervention. But the majority still do not. Their greatest danger to this country lies in their large ownership and influence in our motion pictures, our press, our radio and our Government.[24]

I am not attacking either the Jewish or the British people. Both races, I admire. But I am saying that the leaders of both the British and the Jewish races, for reasons which are as understandable from their viewpoint as they are inadvisable from ours, for reasons which are not American, wish to involve us in the war. We cannot blame them for looking out for what they believe to be their own interests, but we also must look out for ours. We cannot allow the natural passions and prejudices of other peoples to lead our country to destruction.

The Roosevelt administration is the third powerful group which has been carrying this country toward war. Its members have used the war emergency to obtain a third presidential term for the first time in American history.[25] They have used the war to add unlimited billions to a debt which was already the highest we have ever known. And they have used the war to justify the restriction of congressional power, and the assumption of dictatorial procedures on the part of the President and his appointees.

The *power* of the Roosevelt administration depends upon the maintenance of a wartime emergency. The *prestige* of the Roosevelt administration depends upon the success of Great Britain to whom the President attached his political future at a time when most people thought that England and France would easily win the war. The *danger* of the Roosevelt Administration lies in its subterfuge. While its members have promised us peace, they have led us to war—heedless of the platform upon which they were elected.

In selecting these three groups as the major agitators for war, I have included only those whose support is essential to the War Party. If any of these groups—the British, the Jewish, or the Administration—stops agitating for war, I believe there will be little danger of our involvement. I do not believe that any two of them are powerful enough to carry this country to war without the support of the third. And to these three, as I have said, all other war groups are of secondary importance.

When hostilities commenced in Europe, in 1939, it was realized by these groups that the American people had no intention of entering the war. They knew it would be worse than useless to ask us for a declaration of war at that time. But they believed that this country could be enticed into the war in very much the same way that we were enticed into the last one. They planned; first, to prepare the United States for foreign war under the guise of American defense; second, to involve us in the war, step

24. Lindbergh's list of "dangers" echoes common antisemitic accusations against Jews. These accusations have no basis in fact.

25. Roosevelt's decision to seek a third term as president in 1940 broke the traditional limit of US presidents serving no more than two terms. The tradition became law with the 22nd Amendment to the US Constitution, ratified in 1951: "No person shall be elected to the office of the President more than twice."

by step, without our realization; third, to create a series of incidents which would force us into the actual conflict. These plans were, of course, to be covered and assisted by the full power of their propaganda.

Our theaters soon became filled with plays portraying the glory of war. Newsreels lost all semblance of objectivity. Newspapers and magazines began to lose advertising if they carried anti-war articles. A smear campaign was instituted against individuals who opposed intervention. The terms "Fifth Columnist," "Traitor," "Nazi," "Anti-semitic" were thrown ceaselessly at any one who dared to suggest that it was not to the best interests of the United States to enter war. Men lost their jobs if they were frankly anti-war. Many others dared no longer speak. Before long, lecture halls that were open to the advocates of war were closed to speakers who opposed it. A fear campaign was inaugurated. [. . .]

There was no difficulty in obtaining billions of dollars for arms under the guise of defending America. Our people stood united on a program of defense. Congress passed appropriation after appropriation for guns and planes and battleships, with the approval of the overwhelming majority of our citizens. That a large portion of these appropriations was to be used to build arms for Europe, we did not learn until later. [. . .] Ever since its inception, our arms program has been laid out for the purpose of carrying on the war in Europe, far more than for the purpose of building an adequate defense for America.

[. . .] The greatest armament program in our history is under way. We have become involved in the war from practically every standpoint except actual shooting. Only the creation of sufficient "incidents" yet remains; and you see the first of these already taking place, according to plan—a plan that was never laid before the American people for their approval.

Men and women of Iowa: only one thing holds this country from war today. That is the rising opposition of the American people. Our system of democracy and representative government is on test today as it has never been before. We are on the verge of a war in which the only victor would be chaos and prostration. We are on the verge of war for which we are still unprepared, and for which no one has offered a feasible plan of victory—a war which cannot be won without sending our soldiers across the ocean to force a landing on a hostile coast against armies stronger than our own.

We are on the verge of war, but it is not yet too late to stay out. It is not yet too late to show that no amount of money, or propaganda, or patronage, can force a free and independent people into war against its will. It is not yet too late to retrieve and to maintain the independent American destiny that our forefathers established in this New World.

The entire future of America rests upon our shoulders. It depends upon our action, our courage, and our intelligence. If you oppose our intervention in the war, now is the time to make your voice heard. Help us to organize these meetings; and write to your representatives in Washington. I tell you that the last stronghold of democracy and representative government in this country is in our House of Representatives and our Senate. There, we can still make our will known. And if we, the American people, do that, independence and freedom will continue to live among us, and there will be no foreign war.

—Speech, September 11, 1941, MS 325, Charles Augustus Lindbergh
Papers Manuscripts and Archives, Yale University Library.

Lindbergh often wrote in his diary about his public appearances for the America First Committee. In the days and months following his "war agitators" speech, Lindbergh took note of the negative reactions but continued to blame what he perceived as undue Jewish influence in the United States. Just days after the United States entered the war, Lindbergh wrote of his worry that the nation was "unprepared" in many ways to fight the war.

17.

Diaries of Charles A. Lindbergh

September 11, 1941: "When I mentioned the three major groups agitating for war—the British, the Jewish, and the Roosevelt Administration—the entire audience seemed to stand and cheer. At that moment whatever opposition existed was completely drowned out by our support."

September 13, 1941: "New York *Times* carries bitter attacks on my address from Jewish and other organizations and from the White House."

September 15, 1941: "My Des Moines address has caused so much controversy that General Wood[26] has decided to hold a meeting of the America First National Committee in Chicago. I must, of course, attend. I felt I had worded my Des Moines address carefully and moderately. It seems that almost anything can be discussed today in America except the Jewish problem."

October 4, 1941: "Our strength and influence is growing rapidly, but the power of our opposition is great. The amazing thing is not that we are so close to war but that we have been able to hold the war forces back as long as we have. Their ranks include the American government, the British government, the Jews, and the major portion of the press, radio, and motion-picture facilities of the country. We have on our side the mass

---

26. Gen. Robert E. Wood (1879–1969): promoted to US Army general at the end of World War I; president, then chairman of Sears, Roebuck & Co. from 1928 to 1954; named head of America First Committee soon after its founding in September 1940.

of the people, but it is a question of how long the people can withstand the flood of propaganda with which the country is being covered."

October 6, 1941: "Hoover[27] told me that he felt my Des Moines address was a mistake (the mention of the Jews in connection with the war agitating groups). I told him I felt my statements had been both moderate and true. He replied that when you had been in politics long enough you learned not to say things just because they are true. (But, after all, I am not a politician—and that is one of the reasons why I don't wish to be one. [. . .])"

December 11, 1941: "Germany and Italy have declared war on the United States. Now, all that I feared would happen has happened. We are at war all over the world, and we are unprepared for it from either a spiritual or a material standpoint."

—Charles A. Lindbergh, The Wartime Journals of Charles A. Lindbergh
(New York: Harcourt Brace Jovanovich, 1970), 538–47, 565, passim.

Soon after its founding in 1940, the America First Committee set up local chapters and recruited community leaders to promote its cause of staying out of war. These "Principles of the America First Committee," issued by the New York City chapter, helped leaders communicate the urgency of the organization's mission to members. The committee also promoted its cause by asking members to wear America First pins and place stickers in their car windshields with its slogans.

18.

America First Bulletin

Official Publication of the America First Committee,
New York Chapter, Inc.

vol. 1. No. 26   New York City   November 22, 1941

Principles of America First Committee

1. Our first duty is to keep America out of foreign wars. Our entry would only destroy democracy, not save it.

2. We must build a defense, for our own shores, so strong that no foreign power or combination of powers can invade our country, by sea, air or land.

3. Not by acts of war abroad but by preserving and extending democracy at home can we aid democracy and freedom in other lands.

4. In 1917 we sent our American ships into the war zone, and this led us to war. In 1941 we must keep our naval convoys and merchant vessels on this side of the Atlantic.

27. Herbert Hoover (1874–1964), US president from 1929 to 1933.

5. Humanitarian aid is the duty of a strong, free country at peace. With proper safeguard for the distribution of supplies, we should feed and clothe the suffering and needy of the people of the occupied countries.

6. We advocate an official advisory vote by the people of the United States on the question of war or peace, so that when Congress decides this question, as the Constitution provides, it may know the opinion of the people on this gravest of all issues.

7. The Constitution of the United States vests the sole power to declare war in Congress. Until Congress has exercised that power it is not only the privilege but the duty of every citizen to express to his Representatives his views on the question of peace or war—in order that this grave issue may be decided in accordance with the will of the people and the best traditions of American democracy.

—Reprinted from *American First Bulletin*, Gerald Prentice Nye Papers, America First Committee—Clippings and Articles, 1941, Herbert Hoover Presidential Library and Museum, West Branch, IA.

19.

Pin-back buttons for America First Committee, ca. 1941, USHMM Collection.

Car windshield stickers for the America First Committee, ca. 1941, America First Movement Collection, MS 10, Charles Deering McCormick Library of Special Collections, Northwestern University.

20.

Theodor Seuss Geisel (1904–91), far better known as "Dr. Seuss," was the chief editorial cartoonist for *PM* newspaper in New York before he became known for writing children's books. Geisel's cartoons mocked Hitler and frequently ridiculed the America First Committee. In this October 1941 editorial cartoon, Geisel harshly criticizes the committee—depicting it as a woman reading a scary bedtime story about "Adolf the Wolf"—for wanting to stay out of the war and ignore the brutality of the Nazi German regime.

Dr. Seuss, ". . . and the Wolf chewed up the children and spit out their bones," for *PM*, October 1, 1941, Dr. Seuss Collection, UC San Diego Library.

21.

A Madman's Dream

Arthur Szyk (1894–1951), a Polish-born Jewish artist, arrived in the United States in 1940 and consistently challenged Nazi tyranny in his work. His "A Madman's Dream" presents Hitler as the Statue of Liberty and "madman" Charles Lindbergh (center) as the Nazi-uniformed *Gauleiter*—regional governor—of America. Sitting beneath the statue, left to right, are a German soldier, SS leader Heinrich Himmler, and Hermann Göring, supreme commander of the German air force. The base of the statue has an arched entry to an "Aryans Only" restroom ("W. C.").

Arthur Szyk, "A Madman's Dream," for *American Mercury*, November 1941.

Hitler in American Popular Culture

Representations of Adolf Hitler appeared frequently in American popular culture during the Nazi period. After the war began, many Americans came to see him as synonymous with the German enemy as a whole. The depictions of Hitler varied. Most American portrayals showed him as a serious danger to the United States and its democratic ideals. But at times, American popular culture mocked or belittled him.

22.

In his cover for *Captain America No. 1* (March 1941), Jack Kirby showed the new superhero punching out Hitler.

23.

A 1941 pincushion figurine of Hitler, sold as "Hotzi Notzi," was accompanied by a tag that reads: "It is good luck to find a pin. Here's an 'Axis' to stick it in. He who seeks to stick others—himself gets stuck in the 'end.'"

Bassons Dummy Products, 1941, USHMM Collection, Gift of Forrest James Robinson Jr.

President Roosevelt had one of these pincushions on his desk among numerous other knickknacks. The president was said to have taken a special liking to this representation of Hitler.

Associated Press, May 16, 1942.

Hollywood studios made only a handful of motion pictures about Nazism during the 1930s. But when Europe went to war in 1939, the tone of Hollywood movies changed. Popular films such as *The Mortal Storm* (1940), *Foreign Correspondent* (1940), and *Sergeant York* (1941) emphasized fighting for democracy and reinforced the increasingly pronounced turn toward intervention in the war. Missing from these movies was any direct reference to Nazism's victims. *Casablanca* (1942), which won the Oscar® for Best Picture, did dramatize the plight of stranded refugees but without mentioning Europe's Jews explicitly.

One exception was Charlie Chaplin's *The Great Dictator* (1940), which he produced independently, outside of the Hollywood studio system. In this political satire about the fictional nation of Tomainia, Chaplin played two look-alike characters: a dictator modeled on Hitler and a Jewish barber. His movie showed Jews being assaulted by the fictional "Double Cross" Party, a stand-in for the Nazis. In the movie's final scene, the Jewish barber, mistaken for Tomainia's dictator, gives a speech before a massive crowd of stormtroopers (photo). Chaplin drops the veneer of comedic ridicule entirely and passionately pleads directly to the theater audience to fight against fascism "in the name of democracy."

24.

The Great Dictator: **Final Speech**

I'm sorry, but I don't want to be an emperor. That's not my business. I don't want to rule or conquer anyone. I should like to help everyone—if possible—Jew, Gentile— black man—white. We all want to help one another. Human beings are like that. We want to live by each other's happiness—not by each other's misery. We don't want to hate and despise one another. In this world there is room for everyone. And the good earth is rich and can provide for everyone. The way of life can be free and beautiful, but we have lost the way.

Greed has poisoned men's souls, has barricaded the world with hate, has goose-stepped us into misery and bloodshed. We have developed speed, but we have shut ourselves in. Machinery that gives abundance has left us in want. Our knowledge has made us cynical. Our cleverness, hard and unkind. We think too much and feel too little. More than machinery we need humanity. More than cleverness we need kindness and gentleness. Without these qualities, life will be violent and all will be lost. . . .

The airplane and the radio have brought us closer together. The very nature of these inventions cries out for the goodness in men—cries out for universal brotherhood—for the unity of us all. Even now my voice is reaching millions throughout the world—millions of despairing men, women, and little children—victims of a system that makes men torture and imprison innocent people.

To those who can hear me, I say—do not despair. The misery that is now upon us is but the passing of greed—the bitterness of men who fear the way of human progress. The hate of men will pass, and dictators die, and the power they took from the people will return to the people. And so long as men die, liberty will never perish. . . .

Soldiers! don't give yourselves to brutes—men who despise you—enslave you— who regiment your lives—tell you what to do—what to think and what to feel! Who drill you—diet you—treat you like cattle, use you as cannon fodder. Don't give yourselves to these unnatural men—machine men with machine minds and machine hearts! You are not machines! You are not cattle! You are men! You have the love of humanity in your hearts! You don't hate! Only the unloved hate—the unloved and the unnatural! Soldiers! Don't fight for slavery! Fight for liberty!

In the 17th Chapter of St. Luke it is written: "The Kingdom of God is within man"—not one man nor a group of men, but in all men! In you! You, the people have the power—the power to create machines. The power to create happiness! You, the people, have the power to make this life free and beautiful, to make this life a wonderful adventure.

Then—in the name of democracy—let us use that power—let us all unite. Let us fight for a new world—a decent world that will give men a chance to work—that will give youth a future and old age a security. By the promise of these things, brutes have risen to power. But they lie! They do not fulfil that promise. They never will!

Dictators free themselves but they enslave the people! Now let us fight to fulfill that promise! Let us fight to free the world—to do away with national barriers—to do away with greed, with hate and intolerance. Let us fight for a world of reason, a world where science and progress will lead to all men's happiness. Soldiers! in the name of democracy, let us all unite!

—Charlie Chaplin, script for *The Great Dictator,* Charlie Chaplin Productions, 1940.

Chester Raymond Miller, "We're fighting to prevent this!" Think American Institute poster no. 186, 1943, Prints and Photographs Division, Library of Congress.

CHAPTER FOUR

America at War, 1942–1945

Divisions among Americans about whether the United States should intervene in World War II disappeared from public debate immediately after Japan bombed the US naval base at Pearl Harbor, Hawaii, on December 7, 1941. The next day, the United States declared war on Japan; on December 11, Hitler's Germany declared war on the United States. President Roosevelt steeled the nation in a fireside chat. "We're now in this war," he said. "We are all in it—all the way. Every single man, woman, and child is a partner in the most tremendous undertaking of our American history."[1] The vast majority of Americans united in the fight against the Axis powers—Germany, Italy, and Japan. For almost four years, American soldiers and civilians alike would make enormous sacrifices to help free Europe and Asia from Nazi German and Imperial Japanese oppression, with some 16 million Americans serving and more than 400,000 dying in the conflict.

Unity at home, however, had significant limits. Pervasive racial prejudice and discrimination continued unchanged throughout the war. Thousands of African Americans rushed to enlist in the US Army, but were assigned to segregated, support service units. The War Department formed some segregated combat units as the war's need for manpower increased. Civil rights activists hoped that their contributions to victory over fascism abroad would help to overturn the fundamental domestic hypocrisy that had long denied African Americans both the guarantees of equality under the Constitution and the economic opportunities that the United States' legal system should have assured.

The attack by Japan renewed fears of internal enemies, spies, and saboteurs and intensified decades of local discrimination against people of Japanese descent in the western United States. Within hours of the bombing of Pearl Harbor, the US government began rounding up "enemy aliens"—mainly Japanese immigrants living on the Pacific coast who were not US citizens. By spring 1942, the government authorized relocation camps for US residents of Japanese ancestry regardless of their citizenship. Two-thirds of the more than 110,000 who were forcibly moved were American

---

1. Fireside Chat #18—War with Japan, December 9, 1941, box 63, Master Speech File, 1898, 1910–1945, FDRL, 4.

citizens. Proponents of the action argued its importance for national security; opponents charged it was blatant racism.

As US forces battled throughout the Pacific islands and progressed slowly across North Africa, Italy, and France between 1942 and 1945, news of the war dominated the American media. Yet from time to time, shocking facts about the cruel maltreatment and killing of Europe's Jews reached the American public—even though the Holocaust occurred well inside German-occupied territory, hidden from nearly all outside view. Although reports about mass murder reached the highest levels of government and eventually became public, many Americans had trouble believing that they could be true. Not until spring 1945, as American troops and reporters encountered the horrors of German concentration camps during the final days of the war, did photographs and newsreel footage dispel Americans' doubts.

The Double V Campaign

As the US government prepared to join the war against Nazism, it sought to unite all Americans in the fight to defend democratic values. These efforts, however, neglected to acknowledge pervasive racism and White supremacy in the United States. Public facilities, churches, schools, and the US Army remained racially segregated under "Jim Crow" laws.

A. Philip Randolph (1889–1979), a leader in the American labor movement, focused on the civil rights of African American workers. He promised to organize a march on Washington to protest their exclusion from defense industry jobs and New Deal programs. In response, President Roosevelt issued Executive Order 8802 in June 1941, banning discriminatory hiring practices in federal agencies and all unions and companies involved in defense production.[2] After Roosevelt issued the order, Randolph called off the march.

Some African Americans spoke out against the hypocrisies they saw in the American effort to fight fascism abroad without addressing discrimination at home. In February 1942, the *Pittsburgh Courier,* a popular African American newspaper, published a letter to the editor by 26-year-old James Thompson that proposed a "Double V" campaign, which insisted that African Americans should fight for two wartime goals: victory against fascism abroad and victory against racism at home. In the proponents' view, the willingness to sacrifice one's life by serving in the US Army required the guarantee in return that African Americans would no longer suffer the indignities of a racist American society. Although the Double V campaign was short-lived, it helped to

2. President, Executive Order 8802, "Reaffirming Policy of Full Participation in the Defense Program by All Persons, Regardless of Race, Creed, Color, or National Origin," *Federal Register* 6, no. 123 (Washington, DC: USGPO, June 27, 1941): 3109.

spark pride and unity among African Americans during wartime. It did little, however, to stop the pervasive discrimination across the United States. The US Army remained segregated until 1948, three years after the war ended.

1.

The Negro and The War

By A. PHILIP RANDOLPH

Japan has fired upon the United States, our country. We, all of us, black and white, Jew and Gentile, Protestant and Catholic, are at war, not only with Japan but also with Hitler and the Axis powers.

What shall the Negro do? There is only one answer. He must fight. He must give freely and fully of his blood, toil, tears and treasure to the cause of victory for the United States over Japan, Nazi Germany, and world Fascism.

There is no alternative to this decision. There should be no alternative to this decision. We are citizens of these United States and we must proudly and bravely assume the obligations, responsibilities and duties of American citizenship. We cannot escape this fact. We ought not to want to escape it. Happily, the Negro has never sought to escape it in the wars and crisis of the past of our country.

Democracy at Stake

Moreover, the Negro has a great stake in this war. It is the stake of democracy—at home and abroad. Without democracy in America, limited though it be, the Negro would not have even the right to fight for his rights. Under the rule of Japan, Nazi Germany or Fascist Italy minority groups like the Negro and organized labor are not only without rights, such as freedom of speech, the press, assembly, petition, trial by jury and habeas corpus and so forth, they don't have the right to exist. They are liquidated or put into concentration camps for non-conformity to the pattern of totalitarian regimentation.

If the democratic nations are swept under the sword and fire of Hitler and Japan, our America is not secure: and if the United States goes down, the Negro is through in the western world.

But the fight to stop and destroy totalitarian Japan, Nazi Germany and Italy and their Axis partners also involves the obligation, responsibility and task for the Negro people to fight with all their might for their constitutional, democratic rights and freedoms here in America—including equality of opportunity to work in all categories of skills upon a basis of ability and merit in the defense and non-defense industries; to full and equal integration and participation in the army, navy, air corps, and marines; in short, the right to the full stature of constitutional citizenship, free from discriminations, segregations and Jim-Crowisms of any and all kind.

Must Answer Call for Unity

Negroes cannot ask for anything more, nor can they accept anything less.

Yes, Negroes must fight. We must answer the call for national unity. We must see to it that the United States wins this war and the peace. For the interests, future and destiny of our country; and the interests, future and destiny of Great Britain and her allies.

We must fight to preserve democracy and liberty such as we now have in the world so that we may make it sounder and better. And Negroes must demand the right to fight and work alongside their fellow white Americans as full equal citizens, workers and soldiers, sailors, air and marine men.

If we fail to fight to make the democratic process work in America while we fight to beat down Japan and Hitler, we will be traitors to democracy and liberty and the liberation of the Negro people.

—*Norfolk (VA) Journal and Guide*, January 3, 1942, p. A8.

2.

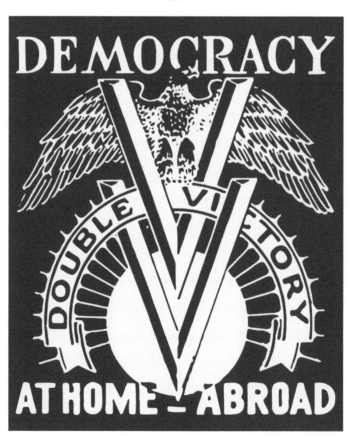

Wilbert L. Holloway of the *Pittsburgh Courier*, logo for the Double V campaign, February 7, 1942.

Should I Sacrifice To Live 'Half-American?'

_____

Suggest Double VV for Double Victory Against Axis Forces and Ugly Prejudices on the Home Front.

_____

(*[NEWSPAPER] EDITOR'S NOTE: A young man, confused and befuddled by all of this double talk about democracy and the defense of our way of life, is asking, like other young Negroes, some very pertinent questions. We reprint this in full because it is symbolic.*)

DEAR EDITOR:

Like all true Americans, my greatest desire at this time, this crucial point of our history, is a desire for a complete victory over the forces of evil, which threaten our existence today. Behind that desire is also a desire to serve, this, my country, in the most advantageous way.

Most of our leaders are suggesting that we sacrifice every other ambition to the paramount one, victory. With this I agree; but I also wonder if another victory could not be achieved at the same time. After all, the things that beset the world now are basically the same things which upset the equilibrium of nations internally, states, counties, cities, homes and even the individual.

Being an American of dark complexion and some 26 years, these questions flash through my mind: "Should I sacrifice my life to live half American?" "Will things be better for the next generation in the peace to follow?" "Would it be demanding too much to demand full citizenship rights in exchange for the sacrificing of my life? Is the kind of America I know worth defending? Will America be a true and pure democracy after this war? Will Colored [*sic*] Americans suffer still the indignities that have been heaped upon them in the past?" These and other questions need answering: I want to know, and I believe every colored American, who is thinking, wants to know.

This may be the wrong time to broach such subjects, but haven't all good things obtained by men been secured through sacrifice during just such times of strife.

I suggest that while we keep defense and victory in the forefront that we don't lose sight of our fight tor true democracy at home.

The V for victory sign is being displayed prominently in all so-called democratic countries which are fighting for victory over aggression, slavery and tyranny. If this V sign means that to those now engaged in this great conflict then let we colored Americans adopt the double VV for a double victory. The first V for victory over our enemies from without, the second V for victory over our enemies from within. For surely those who perpetrate these ugly prejudices here are seeking to destroy our democratic form of government just as surely as the Axis forces.

This should not and would not lessen our efforts to bring this conflict to a successful conclusion; but should and would make us stronger to resist these evil forces which threaten us. America could become united as never before and become truly the home of democracy.

In way of an answer to the foregoing questions in a preceding paragraph I might say that there is no doubt that this country is worth defending; things will be different for the next generation; colored Americans will come into their own, and America will eventually become the true democracy it was designed to be. These things will become a reality in time; but not through any relaxation of the efforts to secure them.

In conclusion let me say that though these questions often permeate my mind, I love America and am willing to die for the America I know will someday become a reality.

JAMES G. THOMPSON[3]

—Pittsburgh Courier, January 31, 1942, 3.

Relocating Japanese Americans

In the days after Japan's bombing of Pearl Harbor on December 7, 1941, President Roosevelt used a 1918 law to issue proclamations that people of Japanese, German, and Italian ancestry who were not US citizens "shall be liable to be apprehended, restrained, secured, and removed as alien enemies."[4] Before the war ended four years later, some 14,000 "enemy alien" German and Italian residents in the United States and their families were arrested and confined to detention camps operated by the Department of Justice.[5]

Two months after the attack, President Roosevelt signed an executive order permitting the government to take "every possible protection against espionage and against sabotage." Under that order, the US Secretary of War and his designated military commanders defined "military areas" from which to exclude any person for the purpose of defending the United States from these threats.[6] In practice, this order targeted Japanese Americans living in the west coast states. The government ultimately relocated more than 80,000 American citizens of Japanese ancestry and some 30,000 Japanese "enemy aliens" to ten War Relocation Authority camps across seven states.[7]

---

3. James Gratz Thompson (1915–99): a cafeteria worker at the Cessna Aircraft Corporation in Wichita, Kansas, when he wrote this letter, became the director of the *Pittsburgh Courier's* Double V campaign in June 1942. In February 1943, he was inducted into the US military.

4. President, Proclamation 2525 "[Alien Enemies—Japanese]," December 7, 1941; Proclamation 2526 "[Alien Enemies—German]," December 9, 1941; and Proclamation 2527 "[Alien Enemies—Italian]," December 9, 1941. *Federal Register* 6, no. 239 (Washington, DC: USGPO, December 10, 1941): 6321–6325.

5. David M. Kennedy, *Freedom from Fear: The American People in Depression and War, 1929–1945* (New York: Oxford University Press, 1999), 746.

6. President, Executive Order 9066, "Authorizing the Secretary of War to Prescribe Military Areas," *Federal Register* 7, no. 38 (Washington, DC: USGPO, February 25, 1942): 1407.

7. The relocation order remained in effect until December 17, 1944: War Department, "Persons of Japanese Ancestry Exemption from Exclusion Orders, [Public Proclamation 21]," *Federal Register* 10, no. 1 (Washington, DC: USGPO, January 2, 1945): 53–54.

A public opinion poll in 1942 revealed that more than 90 percent of Americans agreed with the policy of relocating Japanese "aliens" (noncitizens), and nearly 60 percent favored moving American citizens of Japanese ancestry.[8]

3.

EXECUTIVE ORDER 9102
ESTABLISHING THE WAR RELOCATION AUTHORITY
IN THE EXECUTIVE OFFICE OF THE PRESIDENT AND
DEFINING ITS FUNCTIONS AND DUTIES

By virtue of the authority vested in me by the Constitution and statutes of the United States as President of the United States and Commander in Chief of the Army and Navy, and in order to provide for the removal from designated areas of persons whose removal is necessary in the interests of national security, it is ordered as follows:

1. There is established in the Office for Emergency Management of the Executive Office of the President the War Relocation Authority, at the head of which shall be a Director appointed by and responsible to the President.

2. The Director of the War Relocation Authority is authorized and directed to formulate and effectuate a program for the removal, from the areas designated from time to time by the Secretary of War or appropriate military commander under the authority of Executive Order No. 9066 of February 19, 1942, of the persons or classes of persons designated under such Executive Order, and for their relocation, maintenance, and supervision.

3. In effectuating such program the Director shall have authority to:

   (a) Accomplish all necessary evacuation not undertaken by the Secretary of War or appropriate military commander, provide for the relocation of such persons in appropriate places, provide for their needs in such manner as may be appropriate, and supervise their activities.

   (b) Provide, insofar as feasible and desirable, for the employment of such persons at useful work in industry, commerce, agriculture, or public projects, prescribe the terms and conditions of such public employment, and safeguard the public interest in the private employment of such persons.

   (c) Secure the cooperation, assistance, or services of any governmental agency.

   (d) Prescribe regulations necessary or desirable to promote effective execution of such program, and, as a means of coordinating evacuation and relocation activities, consult with the Secretary of War with respect to regulations issued and measures taken by him. [. . .]

8. National Opinion Research Center, US Poll, March 28, 1942, questions 1 and 2, in *Public Opinion 1935–1946*, Hadley Cantril, ed. (Princeton, NJ: Princeton University Press, 1951), 380.

6. Departments and agencies of the United States are directed to cooperate with and assist the Director in his activities hereunder. The Departments of War and Justice, under the direction of the Secretary of War and the Attorney General, respectively, shall insofar as consistent with the national interest provide such protective, police and investigational services as the Director shall find necessary in connection with activities under the order. [. . .]

9. The Director shall keep the President informed with regard to the progress made in carrying out this order, and perform such related duties as the President may from time to time assign to him. [. . .]

FRANKLIN D. ROOSEVELT

THE WHITE HOUSE,

March 18, 1942

—President, Executive Order 9102, "Establishment of War Relocation
Authority to implement Order 9066," Federal Register 7, no. 55
(Washington, DC: USGPO, March 20, 1942): 2165–66.

The Crisis, the magazine of the National Association for the Advancement of Colored People (NAACP), published this denunciation of the forced relocation of people of Japanese ancestry shortly after it was completed. Author Harry Paxton Howard asserted: "Color seems to be the only reason why thousands of American citizens of Japanese ancestry are in concentration camps." He told readers that the plight of Japanese Americans should serve as a warning to African Americans and other minorities, including Jews, who continued to face discrimination in the United States. Howard claimed that where one group's rights are denied, other groups must beware. Anyone who values "democracy and human equality," he concluded, should be troubled by the forced relocation of Japanese and Japanese Americans.

4.

Americans in Concentration Camps

By Harry Paxton Howard

Over 70,000 native Americans,[9] citizens born, are now lodged in concentration camps in the American West, with no criminal charges of any kind against them. No court has found them guilty of any offence against American law; indeed, no formal indictment has ever been drawn up against them. It is acknowledged that the great

---

9. Paxton's phrase "native Americans" refers to Americans of Japanese ancestry born in the United States, and thereby citizens. It does not refer to the Indigenous peoples of North America.

majority of them are loyal, law-abiding Americans, true to the country of their birth. Some of them have given most useful assistance to the American government against enemy spies and other agents. Even in their present situation, most of them are trying bravely to make the best of things, and are willing to accept the government's explanation of "military necessity."

Why are they there? First of all, because the United States is at war, and the Army has secured tremendous power in national affairs. The hapless citizens who have been deprived of their constitutional rights and constitutional protection have the misfortune to include among their ancestors persons of a non-white country with which the United States is now at war. It is the "non-white" which must be emphasized.[10] American citizens of German, Italian, Hungarian, Bulgarian, or Romanian ancestry have not been legally discriminated against. It is only our citizens of Japanese ancestry who have been put in concentration camps. They are not "white." They are "not to be trusted."

There are also some 40,000 "enemy aliens" in the same camps. These aliens also are not "white." If they were "white," the great majority of them would not be aliens at all. Most of them have been in this country over thirty years; their average age is sixty-three years. But they have not been permitted to become American citizens, as they are "Asiatics." During the generation and more that they have been in this country, over a million Germans and Italians have entered the country and been naturalized as American citizens. German Nazis and Italian Fascists are "white"—whatever their politics. But American naturalization laws, as interpreted by the United States Supreme Court, deny the right of naturalization to Asiatics. So Asiatic immigrants remain "aliens." If we are at war with their homeland, they become "enemy aliens"— including hundreds who fought in the American armed forces in the first world war! They are "aliens" only because America has refused them citizenship. [. . .]

Our Concentration Camps

It was at the end of March—almost four months after Pearl Harbor—that the Army started the forcible removal of west coast Japanese and Japanese-Americans to concentration camps. It was not due to some urgent and pressing "present danger"; things were more fully under control along the Pacific Coast then they had ever been before—and far more than they had been during the previous December. It was not due to the sudden shock and hysteria occasioned by Pearl Harbor itself—that had long

10. US law allowed immigrants to seek citizenship through naturalization only if they were "free white persons" (Naturalization Act of 1790) or "persons of African nativity or persons of African descent" (Naturalization Act of 1870). Court rulings that immigrants of Japanese ancestry did not fit the "popularly known" definition of "white" were upheld by a unanimous US Supreme Court decision, *Ozawa v. United States,* in 1922. The racial restrictions were abolished in 1952.

passed. Neither was it due to any new revelations regarding Japanese espionage or sabotage in American territories; the wide rumors about widespread Japanese sabotage in Hawaii had been officially disproved. [. . .]

[. . .] Race prejudice is still a factor along the coast[. . . .] And there was widespread ignorance, as large number of persons had never come to know any of the Japanese-Americans, and were worked into actual fear and hysteria by the anti-Japanese blasts of the press and radio. Even among the Negroes along the coast, many failed to realize that the issue was basically *racial*, and directly concerned themselves. [. . .]

Filth and Squalor

If the Army's aim was the protection of Japanese-Americans, this aim seems to have been forgotten as soon as the evacuees were got into the pleasantly-named "reception centers" and "assembly centers." They were treated as dangerous aliens, and their accommodation was of the worst. The Army was in charge, and it was almost impossible to obtain permits to leave; the Army accused evacuees of "trying to escape" (from "protection!"). Ten thousand or more persons would be confined to an area of less than a square mile, sometimes surrounded by barbed wire and always by armed guards. At Manzanar [in east-central California] and some other centers the guards would not permit parcels—soap, clothing, shoes, baby things—to be brought into the camp. For a long time such urgent necessities as goggles—to keep dust from the eyes in windy and semi-desert centers—could not be brought in.

There was no direct torture. It was an American, not a Nazi, concentration camp. Some of the older inhabitants—most of the Japanese-born were over sixty—suffered from insufficiency of their customary rice. Persons accustomed to daily bathing and the most scrupulous cleanliness found it "troublesome" to live in filth, lacking tubs, buckets, washing machines, or sufficient soap. Perpetually dusty and dirty eyes were painful and "troublesome." Babies found unwashed diapers painful as well as odorous. Parents suffered as their children sickened and died, living in a filth and squalor such as neither they nor their ancestors had known with their long memories. But there was no "torture."

Not all the evacuees were yellow. There were some white and other non-Japanese—mostly women married to Japanese-Americans. And some of the Japanese-Americans were not more than one-eighth Japanese, owing to intermarriage. But a "Jap" was anyone with traceable Japanese blood—just as Hitler's "Jew" means anyone with traceable Jewish blood. A Japanese grandfather is as valuable to an American in California as a Jewish grandfather to a German in Berlin—or a Negro grandfather in Atlanta. Some of the women—Americans of Japanese descent—were separated from non-Japanese husbands who could not or would not make the sacrifice of following them into bondage.

Housing conditions vary in the different camps. Usually the houses are long barracks, with a single community toilet and laundry for a block of houses with hundreds of persons. At Manzanar and some other centers, the houses are built of rough lumber; dust seeps in continuously. At Manzanar there are two to three families, or eight to ten persons, to a room—assigned regardless of age or sex. The population density of Manzanar is about 30,000 persons per square mile—equal to that in Metropolitan New York.

There is no running water in houses in most of the camps. At Manzanar only two of the twelve blocks of houses have hot showers in the community toilet, and hot water for dishwashing. For weeks, there were almost no laundry and washing facilities—in a dusty and windy area, for a people accustomed to daily bathing at all times. At Puyallup, [Washington,] to the north, there was one small washroom for every 250 persons; an endless line was standing and waiting at all times—in a broiling sun most of the day, and with no shade. [. . .]

Food is adequate. Anyway, no one has died of starvation. But some old persons, accustomed to rice and vegetables, cannot digest stale bread and canned wieners and beans. Tea is their great solace—but some of them cannot drink it when it is dosed with saltpeter,[11] as is done at Camp Harmony[12] and some other "resorts." [. . .]

It Concerns the Negro

What has happened to these Americans in recent months is of direct concern to the American Negro. For the barbarous treatment of these Americans is the result of the color line. This cannot be too often repeated or too clearly understood. These men, women, and children have been taken from their pleasant homes and long-cultivated farms and businesses because their skins are yellow and their eyes have the tell-tale Mongolian eyefold. Americans of German or Italian descent are not being discriminated against. [. . .] Old Germans and Italians who have lived in the United States for a generation are not being discriminated against; they are white, and most of them are citizens. Even the Germans and Italians who have reached these shores during the past twenty years are not treated as "enemies." Many of them, in fact, are giving loyal service to their adopted country; these services are welcomed. They are white.

Negroes have been told again and again: "Work quietly, be industrious, mind your own business, and you will get justice even in America." That is what these yellow-skinned American believed. They worked, cheerfully and industriously. They turned deserts into beautiful and fertile farm-lands, grew vegetables and fruits for themselves and for others. They distinguished themselves at school, abstained from politics, had the lowest crime-rate of any group in the entire country. They earned the respect of all decent white persons who came in contact with them, overcoming racial prejudice

11. Saltpeter: a preservative once added to food in the erroneous belief it suppressed sexual drive.

12. The unofficial nickname for the Puyallup Assembly Center in Washington State.

among tens of thousands; many of these tried ineffectively to help them during recent months; most significant is the fact that there have actually been no lynchings, and that Japanese-Americans felt safe in their own American communities where they were known. They did not ask for the Army's "protection;" it was thrust upon them. [. . .]

If native-born Americans, of Asiatic descent, can be denied all civil rights and civil liberties, what about Americans of African descent? [. . .]

It is significant that southern senators and congressmen are among the most rabidly anti-Japanese. For if Asiatic-Americans can be reduced to bondage, deprived of citizenship and of property, the same thing can be done to Afro-Americans—and to Jews.

This is an integral part of the struggle for human and racial equality. It concerns every Negro. It concerns every believer in democracy and human equality, regardless of color. "For even as ye have done it unto the least of these my brethren, ye have done it unto me."

—*The Crisis*, September 1942, 281–84, 301.

Japanese Americans challenged curfew, evacuation, and detention orders in US courts at least twelve times during the war. Four cases reached the US Supreme Court. In each, the court concluded that the war powers of Congress and the president justified forcibly detaining Japanese American citizens in camps.

The best-known of the four cases, *Korematsu v. United States*, came before the US Supreme Court in 1944. Fred Korematsu had been picked up by San Leandro, California, police while walking with his White girlfriend on May 30, 1942. Though he tried to convince the police he was of Spanish-Hawaiian origin, Korematsu's effort to hide his Japanese ancestry failed. He was arrested and convicted of violating the zone's exclusion order. In response, Korematsu challenged the legality of these orders on the grounds that they violated his right to due process. The court ruled 6 to 3 in favor of the US government, arguing the relocation was in the interest of national security.

Associate Justice Frank Murphy dissented from the majority in *Korematsu*, arguing that the government had overstepped its war powers by, in effect, legalizing racism.

(All internal legal citations in this opinion have been deleted for ease of reading.)

5.

Korematsu v. United States (1944)

MR. JUSTICE MURPHY, dissenting.

This exclusion of "all persons of Japanese ancestry, both alien and non-alien," from the Pacific Coast area on a plea of military necessity in the absence of martial law ought not to be approved. Such exclusion goes over "the very brink of constitutional power," and falls into the ugly abyss of racism.

In dealing with matters relating to the prosecution and progress of a war, we must accord great respect and consideration to the judgments of the military authorities who are on the scene and who have full knowledge of the military facts. The scope of their discretion must, as a matter of necessity and common sense, be wide. And their judgments ought not to be overruled lightly by those whose training and duties ill-equip them to deal intelligently with matters so vital to the physical security of the nation.

At the same time, however, it is essential that there be definite limits to military discretion, especially where martial law has not been declared. Individuals must not be left impoverished of their constitutional rights on a plea of military necessity that has neither substance nor support. Thus, like other claims conflicting with the asserted constitutional rights of the individual, the military claim must subject itself to the judicial process of having its reasonableness determined and its conflicts with other interests reconciled. [. . .]

The judicial test of whether the Government, on a plea of military necessity, can validly deprive an individual of any of his constitutional rights is whether the deprivation is reasonably related to a public danger that is so "immediate, imminent, and impending" as not to admit or delay and not to permit the intervention of ordinary constitutional processes to alleviate the danger. Civilian Exclusion Order No. 34, banishing from a prescribed area of the Pacific Coast [along the southeast shore of San Francisco Bay] "all persons of Japanese ancestry, both alien and non-alien," clearly does not meet that test. Being an obvious racial discrimination, the order deprives all those within its scope of the equal protection of the laws as guaranteed by the Fifth Amendment. It further deprives these individuals of their constitutional rights to live and work where they will, to establish a home where they choose and to move about freely. In excommunicating them without benefit of hearings, this order also deprives them of all their constitutional rights to procedural due process. Yet no reasonable relation to an "immediate, imminent, and impending" public danger is evident to support this racial restriction, which is one of the most sweeping and complete deprivations of constitutional rights in the history of this nation in the absence of martial law.

[. . .] In adjudging the military action taken in light of the then apparent dangers, we must not erect too high or too meticulous standards; it is necessary only that the action have some reasonable relation to the removal of the dangers of invasion, sabotage and espionage. But the exclusion, either temporarily or permanently, of all persons with Japanese blood in their veins has no such reasonable relation. And that relation is lacking because the exclusion order necessarily must rely for its reasonableness upon the assumption that all persons of Japanese ancestry may have a dangerous tendency to commit sabotage and espionage and to aid our Japanese enemy in other ways. It is difficult to believe that reason, logic, or experience could be marshalled in support of such an assumption. [. . .]

The main reasons relied upon by those responsible for the forced evacuation [. . .] do not prove a reasonable relation between the group characteristics of Japanese Americans and the dangers of invasion, sabotage and espionage. The reasons appear, instead, to be largely an accumulation of much of the misinformation, half-truths and insinuations that for years have been directed against Japanese Americans by people with racial and economic prejudices—the same people who have been among the foremost advocates of the evacuation. A military judgment based upon such racial and sociological considerations is not entitled to the great weight ordinarily given the judgments based upon strictly military considerations. Especially is this so when every charge relative to race, religion, culture, geographical location, and legal and economic status has been substantially discredited by independent studies made by experts in these matters.

The military necessity which is essential to the validity of the evacuation order thus resolves itself into a few intimations that certain individuals actively aided the enemy, from which it is inferred that the entire group of Japanese Americans could not be trusted to be or remain loyal to the United States. No one denies, of course, that there were some disloyal persons of Japanese descent on the Pacific Coast who did all in their power to aid their ancestral land. Similar disloyal activities have been engaged in by many persons of German, Italian and even more pioneer stock in our country. But to infer that examples of individual disloyalty prove group disloyalty and justify discriminatory action against the entire group is to deny that, under our system of law individual guilt is the sole basis for deprivation of rights. [. . .] To give constitutional sanction to that inference in this case, however well-intentioned may have been the military command on the Pacific Coast, is to adopt one of the cruelest of the rationales used by our enemies to destroy the dignity of the individual and to encourage and open the door to discriminatory actions against other minority groups in the passions of tomorrow. [. . .]

I dissent, therefore, from this legalization of racism. Racial discrimination in any form and in any degree has no justifiable part whatever in our democratic way of life. It is unattractive in any setting, but it is utterly revolting among a free people who have embraced the principles set forth in the Constitution of the United States. All residents of this nation are kin in some way by blood or culture to a foreign land. Yet they are primarily and necessarily a part of the new and distinct civilization of the United States. They must, accordingly, be treated at all times as the heirs of the American experiment, and as entitled to all the rights and freedoms guaranteed by the Constitution.

—Black, Hugo Lafayette, and Supreme Court Of The United States,
U.S. Reports: Korematsu v. United States, 323 U.S. 214, (1944), 233–42.

"United We Win"

Wartime propaganda produced and circulated by the Office of War Information[13] and other government agencies helped shape the way Americans understood Nazism to be a direct threat to their own safety and to the security of the United States. Posters both portrayed Nazism as the enemy and promoted citizens' support for the war. They did not, however, focus attention on the danger that the Nazi regime posed to civilians in Europe, nor did they refer explicitly to the Nazis' ongoing persecution of Europe's Jews.

6.

Henry Koerner, "This Is the Enemy," US Office of War Information, poster no. 76 (Washington, DC: USGPO, 1943), USHMM Collection.

13. The Office of War Information, established by President Roosevelt in June 1942, produced a wide range of media (films, radio broadcasts, posters, photographs, etc.) to help keep the American public informed about the war's progress and the government's wartime policies.

In December 1941, the Roosevelt administration began to sell government-backed war bonds often using images in the campaign that reiterated the threat of Nazism. The bond sales provided significant funding for the US war effort. By the end of the war, some 85 million Americans had purchased nearly $186 billion in bonds—equivalent to $2.65 trillion in value in 2020.[14]

7.

Lawrence Beall Smith, "Don't Let That Shadow Touch Them— Buy War Bonds," US Department of the Treasury, War Savings Staff, poster no. 451 (Washington, DC: USGPO, 1942), USHMM Collection.

14. US Department of the Treasury, *A History of the United States Savings Bonds Program* (Washington, DC: US Savings Bond Division, Department of the Treasury, 1991), 28.

The United States experienced a labor shortage after 1941 as war production dramatically increased and millions of working men enlisted in the military. The War Manpower Commission, formed in 1942, mobilized workers from previously underrepresented groups to meet the nation's huge demands. It distributed these posters to spotlight the hiring of African Americans and women for the arms and ammunition industries, even as racism and gender discrimination remained prevalent within individual workplaces and across the labor market.

8.

Howard Liberman, photographer, "United We Win," US War Manpower Commission (Washington, DC: USGPO, 1943), USHMM Collection.

Two million American women had entered the workforce by 1942. Many held down war industry jobs that previously were filled by men.

9.

R. G. Harris, "Do the job HE left behind," US Employment Service, War Manpower Commission (Washington, DC: USGPO, 1943), Women at work World War II posters (1994.263.1), Hagley Museum and Library.

American artist Norman Rockwell (1894–1978) created multiple covers for *The Saturday Evening Post* that shaped how many Americans understood the fight against Nazism. Rockwell's depiction of "Rosie the Riveter" in May 1943 championed women's labor that supported the American war effort. Rockwell represented Nazism by including Hitler's autobiography, *Mein Kampf,* beneath Rosie's feet.

10.

Norman Rockwell, "Rosie the Riveter," for *Saturday Evening Post*, May 29, 1943.

President Roosevelt made numerous references to the United States' responsibility to defend all the republics in North, Central, and South America.[15] This poster for war support was part of the Office of War Information's outreach to the Spanish-speaking communities in the United States and to its Latin American allies.

11.

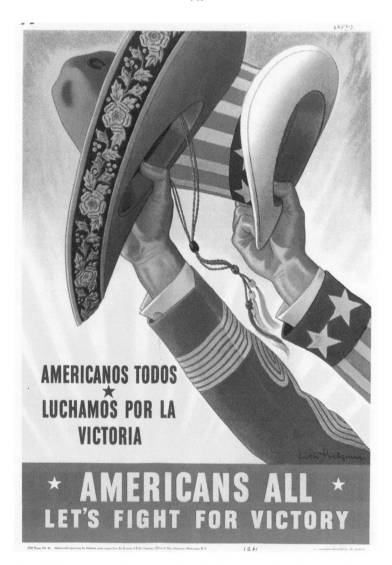

Leon Helguera, "Americanos Todos—Luchamos por la Victoria / Americans All—Let's Fight for Victory," US Office of War Information, poster no. 65 (Washington, DC: USGPO, 1943), USHMM Collection.

15. See, for example, his September 11, 1941, fireside chat "Maintaining Freedom of the Seas."

Nazi Germany's "Final Solution to the Jewish Question"

The mass murder of Jews by Germany's so-called mobile killing squads (*Einsatzgruppen*) began in the summer of 1941 as part of Germany's invasion of the Soviet Union. By the end of the year, German forces and their local collaborators had shot to death perhaps as many as 900,000 Jews in the Soviet territories of Lithuania, Latvia, Estonia, Belorussia, and Ukraine. During those same months, Nazi Germany began constructing in occupied Poland three killing centers—Bełżec, Auschwitz-Birkenau, and Chełmno—with gas chambers and crematoria.

In January 1942, high-ranking Nazi officials met at a villa in the Berlin suburb of Wannsee and secretly confirmed their plan for the "Final Solution to the Jewish Question," the effort to systematically annihilate all of Europe's Jews. To that end, the German regime built two more killing centers—Sobibór and Treblinka—and added gas chambers and crematoria at the Majdanek concentration camp, all located in occupied Poland.

In August 1942, news about the Nazis' "Final Solution" reached Gerhart Riegner, the secretary of the World Jewish Congress[16] in Switzerland. Riegner attempted to alert Rabbi Stephen Wise, the head of the congress, via the US State Department. Paul Culbertson of the State Department's Division of European Affairs drafted a letter to Rabbi Wise including Riegner's information, but added that State Department officials in Switzerland believed that the murder of Jews was "one of the many unreliable war rumors circulating in Europe today." Someone in the State Department, however, crossed out the text of the letter with the handwritten instruction "Do not send."

12.

16. The World Jewish Congress: founded in Geneva, Switzerland, in August 1936 by delegates from thirty-two countries to represent Jewish communities across the globe and to "mobilize the Jewish people and the democratic force against the Nazi onslaught." (https://www.worldjewishcongress.org/en/about/history).

DEPARTMENT OF STATE
WASHINGTON

My dear Dr. Wise:

The following message, in paraphrase, has been received from the American Legation at Bern. It was sent at the request of Mr. Gerhardt K. Riegner, Secretary of the World Jewish Congress at Geneva.

In Hitler's headquarters a plan is being considered to wipe out at one blow from 3,500,000 to 4,000,000 Jews this autumn, following their expulsion from countries controlled or occupied by Germany and their concentration in the East, according to a report from a person whose previous reports have been generally reliable and who is alleged to have intimate connections among the highest German officials. Prussic acid[17] has been contemplated but the manner of extermination has not yet been determined. The correctness of the report cannot be confirmed and the information is therefore sent with reservation.

The Legation at Bern has no information which would confirm this rumor and believes it is one of the many unreliable war rumors circulating in Europe today.

Sincerely yours,
For the Secretary of State:
[*signature*] Paul. T. Culbertson
Assistant Chief, Division of
European Affairs.

—Draft letter, August 13, 1942, box 5598, Central Decimal File, 1940–1944,
862.4016/2233, Records of the Department of State, Record Group 59, NACP.

In addition to trying to contact Rabbi Wise through the State Department, Riegner also informed the World Jewish Congress representative in the United Kingdom, Samuel Sydney Silverman, a member of the UK Parliament. Silverman then telegrammed Rabbi Wise directly. This in effect circumvented the State Department's decision to not pass along the information. Wise then asked Under Secretary of State Sumner Welles to confirm the report, a process that took three months.

17. Prussic acid: a common name for the highly poisonous chemical hydrogen cyanide. In Germany, it was produced by the Degesch chemical company and marketed under the name Zyklon B. The first experimental use of the gas occurred at the Auschwitz concentration camp in September 1941 to murder 850 Soviet POWs and "sick" Polish prisoners. It became the primary killing agent in the main gas chambers built at Auschwitz-Birkenau after spring 1942.

13.

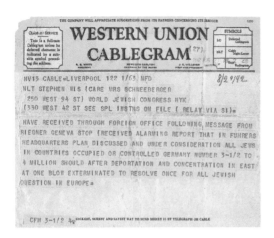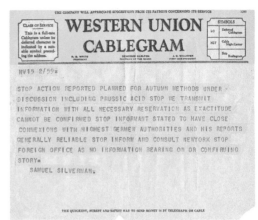

WESTERN UNION
CABLEGRAM

8/29/42

CABLE=LIVERPOOL
STEPHEN WISE (CARE MRS. SCHNEEBERGER)
(250 WEST 94 ST) WORLD JEWISH CONGRESS NYK
[...]
HAVE RECEIVED THROUGH FOREIGN OFFICE FOLLOWING MESSAGE FROM
RIEGNER GENEVA STOP (RECEIVED ALARMING REPORT THAT IN FUHRERS
HEADQUARTERS PLAN DISCUSSED AND UNDER CONSIDERATION ALL
JEWS IN COUNTRIES OCCUPIED OR CONTROLLED GERMANY NUMBER
3-1/2 TO 4 MILLION SHOULD AFTER DEPORTATION AND CONCENTRA-
TION IN EAST AT ONE BLOW EXTERMINATED TO RESOLVE ONCE FOR ALL
JEWISH QUESTION IN EUROPE STOP ACTION REPORTED PLANNED FOR
AUTUMN METHODS UNDER DISCUSSION INCLUDING PRUSSIC ACID STOP
WE TRANSMIT INFORMATION WITH ALL NECESSARY RESERVATION AS EX-
ACTITUDE CANNOT BE CONFIRMED STOP INFORMANT STATED TO HAVE
CLOSE CONNEXIONS WITH HIGHEST GERMAN AUTHORITIES AND HIS
REPORTS GENERALLY RELIABLE STOP INFORM AND CONSULT NEWYORK
STOP FOREIGN OFFICE HAS NO INFORMATION BEARING ON OR CONFIRM-
ING STORY=
SAMUEL SILVERMAN.

—Cable, August 29, 1942, SC-5027, MS-361, World Jewish
Congress records, 1918–1982, Jacob Rader Marcus Center
of the American Jewish Archives, Cincinnati, OH.

In late November 1942, just weeks after American and British troops began to battle the Germans and their Axis partners in the western part of North Africa, Rabbi Wise received the State Department's confirmation of the Nazi regime's plan, and he decided to tell the press. Newspapers across the country published the Associated Press report on Wise's shocking announcement.

Although these reports estimated that two million Jews had been killed, in fact some four million Jews were already dead. Wise's estimate of two million victims most likely resulted from his focus on events in annexed and occupied Poland. He may not yet have known about the mass shootings of Jews in the Nazi-occupied Soviet Union by German mobile killing squads and their local collaborators.

14.

Plan To Kill All Jews Is Revealed
Utter Extermination Before Close Of 1942 Said Hitler Purpose

WASHINGTON, Nov. 25 (AP)—Details of a campaign which Dr. Stephen S. Wise said was planned to exterminate all Jews in Nazi-occupied Europe by the end of the year, are to be laid before a committee of leading Jewish organizations today in New York.

THE STORY—reportedly confirmed by the State department and a personal representative of President Roosevelt—deals with how more than 2,000,000 Jews already have been slaughtered in accordance with a race extinction order by Adolf Hitler.

Before leaving for New York to address the committee this afternoon, Dr, Stephen S. Wise, chairman of the World Jewish Congress and president of the American Jewish Congress, said he carried official documentary proof that "Hitler has ordered the extermination of all Jews in Nazi-ruled Europe in 1942." [. . .]

To speed the slaughter of the other half during the remaining month before the edict's deadline, Wise said the Nazis were moving some four-fifths of the Jews in Hitler-ruled European countries to Poland. [. . .]

Dr. Wise, who heads the committee, asserted that already the Jewish population of Warsaw had been reduced from 500,000 to about 100,000.

—Associated Press, *Huntsville (AL) Times*, November 25, 1942, 1.

In response to the news that millions of Jews in Europe had been murdered, Jewish communities in many Allied nations held rallies and vigils and declared Wednesday, December 2, 1942, to be an international day of mourning. Some Hebrew-language newspapers added black borders to their covers. Jewish communities in Palestine, Egypt, Australia, Nicaragua, and other countries fasted, closing their businesses for the day. Thousands of workers in Ecuador paused for fifteen minutes as a gesture of protest. Services were held in over 1,500 synagogues in the United States, and thousands of Jews joined a somber parade down the streets of New York City.

From Brooklyn, New York, a ten-year-old boy named William Levine sent this letter to President Roosevelt, pleading with him to "stop all this manslaughter throughout Europe."

(The transcription includes William's youthful misspellings.)

15.

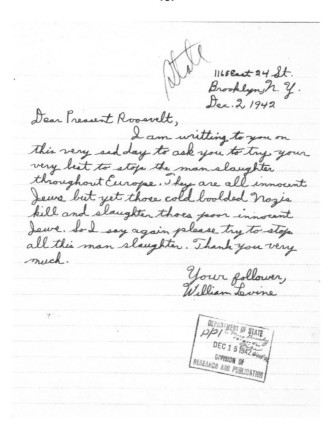

1165 East 24 St.
Brooklyn, N. Y.
Dec. 2, 1942

Dear Preasent Roosevelt,

    I am writting to you on this very sad day to ask you to try your very best to stop the manslaughter throughout Europe. They are all innocent Jews but yet those cold boolded [blooded] Nazis kill and slaughter those poor innocent Jews. So I say again please try to stop all this man slaughter. Thank you very much.

Your follower,
William Levine

—Letter, December 2, 1942, Central Decimal File 1940–1944, 840.4016/49A.
Records of the Department of State, Record Group 59, NACP.

On August 21, 1942, President Roosevelt released a statement that said, "The Government of the United States has been aware for some time" of "barbaric crimes against civilian populations" in Nazi-occupied Europe. He issued a warning of "fearful retribution," promising that, "when victory has been achieved," the perpetrators of these crimes "shall have to stand in courts of law."[18]

Four months later, on December 17, 1942, the United States, Great Britain, and ten other Allied governments issued a joint declaration denouncing Nazi Germany's implementation of "Hitler's oft-repeated intention to exterminate the Jewish people in Europe." The declaration warned that "those responsible for these crimes shall not escape retribution." It made no commitment to rescuing Jews still living under Nazi rule.

16.

DEPARTMENT OF STATE

FOR THE PRESS   DECEMBER 16, 1942
                                                   No. 589

[. . .]

The attention of the Belgian, Czechoslovak, Greek, Luxemburg, Netherlands, Norwegian, Polish, Soviet, United Kingdom, United States and Yugoslav Governments and also of the French National Committee[19] has been drawn to numerous reports from Europe that the German authorities, not content with denying to persons of Jewish race in all the territories over which their barbarous rule has been extended, the most elementary human rights, are now carrying into effect Hitler's oft repeated intention to exterminate the Jewish people in Europe. From all the occupied countries Jews are being transported in conditions of appalling horror and brutality to Eastern Europe. In [Nazi-occupied] Poland, which has been made the principal Nazi slaughter house, the Ghettos established by the German invader are being systematically emptied of all Jews except a few highly skilled workers required for war industries. None of those taken away are ever heard of again. The able-bodied

18. Press Conference #842, August 21, 1942, Press Conference Transcripts, Press Conferences of President Franklin D. Roosevelt, 1933–1945, FDRL, 052–55. The president repeated this goal in a statement released on October 6, 1942.

19. A French resistance movement organized by General Charles de Gaulle (1890–1970), leader of the Free France government-in-exile (1940–44) and based in London, to continue fighting Nazi Germany after the fall of France in June 1940.

are slowly worked to death in labor camps. The infirm are left to die of exposure and starvation or are deliberately massacred in mass executions. The number of victims of these bloody cruelties is reckoned in many hundreds of thousands[20] of entirely innocent men, women and children.

The above-mentioned Governments and the French National Committee condemn in the strongest possible terms this bestial policy of cold-blooded extermination. They declare that such events can only strengthen the resolve of all freedom loving peoples to overthrow the barbarous Hitlerite tyranny. They re-affirm their solemn resolution to ensure that those responsible for these crimes shall not escape retribution and to press on with the necessary practical measures to this end.

—Press release, December 16, 1942, box 2917, Central Decimal File, 740.00116/European War 1939/749, Records of the Department of State, Record Group 59, NACP.

Many Americans may have doubted that Rabbi Wise's report about the mass murder of Jews could be true, perhaps because it simply seemed too horrific to believe, or perhaps because some remembered that stories of German atrocities during World War I were later reported to be false.

17.

Gallup Poll, January 1943

"It is said that two million Jews have been killed in Europe since the war began. Do you think this is true or just a rumor?"

48% True
28% Rumor
24% No opinion

—Gallup Organization. 1943. Gallup Poll # 1943-0287: Wartime Employment/ Food Consumption and Shortages/Taxes/Lend-Lease Laws. Question 22: USGALLUP.43-287.QKT12. Cornell University, Ithaca, NY: Roper Center for Public Opinion Research. https://doi.org/10.25940/ROPER-31087270.

20. This estimate, added by Soviet authorities when the declaration was drafted, is far lower than the already circulating estimate of two million Jewish victims.

18.

Propaganda Front

by WILLIAM L. SHIRER[21]

Americans Yet to Grasp Truth of Nazi Terror

The other day, in the fourth year of the Nazi war against the world, the inquiring reporter of "The Detroit Free Press" stood on a street corner in that great city and put to the passers-by a simple question. He asked: "Do you believe that stories of Nazi atrocities will be proved false, as were many stories of German atrocities in the last world war?"

The answers of four typical American citizens, including an officer of the Navy, were given in "The Free Press" the next day. To this correspondent they were startling, to say the least. For if these answers are representative of the nation—and I suspect they are—they demonstrate the failure of the American people to grasp the very nature of this war and of the enemy who has been waging it since Sept. 1, 1939, on the lines of Adolf Hitler's strategy of terror.

Two of the citizens questioned, the naval officer and a pretty and intelligent young secretary (judging by her photograph), said they did not believe any of the stories about Nazi atrocities. A third, identified as a civilian expediter for the Navy Department, replied that he thought at least half of such stories were false, but "sort of necessary" for our propaganda purposes. The fourth citizen, a housewife, thought that the current accounts of the Nazi doings were "definitely not all true."

Three of the four—the naval officer, the secretary and the housewife—were dead sure that the present reports about Nazi atrocities were similar to those we heard about the Germans in the first war, and therefore no more true. [. . .]

Those who have seen the Nazi slaughter on the continent of Europe probably would desire frantically that the tales of the carnage could somehow turn out to have been merely "manufactured," for that would mean that the two or three million civilian victims of the Nazis were not really dead and buried. But that is another story. What concerns us here is why many of our citizens have remained highly skeptical about the Nazi killings and the whole terror which the present Germans have unloosed upon the conquered.

People Just Skeptical

I do not believe for one second that the good folk interviewed on the street corner in Detroit have been affected in the least by Nazi propaganda on the subject. [. . .]

21. William L. Shirer (1904–93): American journalist and war correspondent in Nazi Germany from 1934 to 1941, first with wire service agencies and after 1937 with the Columbia Broadcasting System (CBS). His bestselling *Berlin Diary* (1941) included information about the persecution of the Jews.

Still they are skeptical about Nazi atrocities. I suggest the explanation for this can be found in the peculiar turn the national mind took in the two decades that followed the World War Armistice. Our vast disillusionment over the peace degenerated into a silly sort of super-cynicism and super-skepticism. We would believe nothing. There was undoubtedly much in history to debunk, but we thought we were right (and righteous) in debunking everything, which we proceeded to do. In the weird process we lost track of the true currents of contemporary history. The result was a terrible and costly confusion.

For one of the main currents of contemporary history was the rise of Hitlerism, and if the good people on the street corner in Detroit are any criterion, we have not yet come—as a people—to understand its true significance.

From the first we mistook our false skepticism for wise judgment. Most of the Americans who visited Germany in the early Nazi days used to say: "The Nazis can't really be as bad as you correspondents paint them." They were skeptical of the facts we had reported. They could not believe that a great people like the Germans could go berserk. They could not believe that the Nazis would go to war.

Today the same people cannot believe that the Nazis are slaughtering the civilians of the conquered lands. [. . .] This is all the more strange because the Nazis themselves have told them part of the story.

Lidice—Nazis' Own Story

It was the Gestapo which first told us of the mass murder at Lidice.[22] Heinrich Himmler's men were not hesitant about giving the details of that cold-blooded Nazi atrocity. Indeed, they fairly boasted of how the entire male population of the village was executed, the houses burned to the ground, the women and children carried off into captivity. [. . .] There is nothing secret about the Nazi murder of Jews. Hitler publicly boasts of his intention to exterminate them all.

Were the people interviewed by the inquiring reporter in Detroit not aware of what the Nazis themselves have admitted, that atrocities had no parallel in the World War?

And have the American press and radio, and indeed the American government, labored in vain to bring home to the people the brutal truths of this war? Were the foreign correspondents who saw some of the Nazi slaughter merely fooling their fellow countrymen in their reports? Were President Roosevelt and Prime Minister Churchill[23]

22. In June 1942, Adolf Hitler and Heinrich Himmler ordered the destruction of the town of Lidice in Nazi-occupied Bohemia and Moravia (now the Czech Republic) in reprisal for the assassination of the Nazi leader of the region, Reinhard Heydrich. On June 10, all 173 males over the age of fifteen were shot, and all 184 women and 88 children were deported to concentration camps.

23. Winston S. Churchill (1874–1965): prime minister of the United Kingdom during the war years 1940–45. His close personal friendship with President Roosevelt was a major factor in the Allies' victory in Europe.

merely "manufacturing atrocity tales" when they spoke solemnly and officially of the "organized (Nazi) murder of thousands of innocent persons and the committing of atrocities which have violated every tenet of the Christian faith"?

Truth Must Be Brought Home

Of course they weren't. They were, if anything, understanding the truth, at least in regard to the number slain. [. . .]

These things, unfortunately, are the truth, and yet it is evident that many of our fellow citizens do not believe them. Obviously, then, our radio, our press and our government still have a job to do in bringing the truth, ugly though it may be, home to the people.

For we citizens of America never really will understand what we are fighting for and sacrificing for until we grasp that this war is utterly unlike any other we have fought. The openly avowed aim of Nazi Germany is not only to defeat us, but to destroy us. There is nothing secret about this aim. There is no earthly reason for us not to believe it. [. . .]

—*New York Herald Tribune*, March 21, 1943, A1, A7.

Pressure to Act

In April 1943, the United States and Great Britain held a conference in Bermuda to discuss rescue and relief of Europe's Jewish refugees. The conference concluded with a joint declaration that confirmed the two nations had "examined the refugee problem in all its aspects, including the position of those potential refugees who are still in the grip of the Axis powers without any immediate prospect of escape."[24] However, the Bermuda conference led to no concrete action; some American Jews and other concerned members of the public became even more frustrated with the US government.

Freda Kirchwey (1893–1976), editor of the liberal *Nation* magazine and a vocal opponent of fascism throughout the 1930s and 1940s, penned multiple articles criticizing the Allied governments' inaction. In an article titled "While the Jews Die," Kirchwey wrote: "Hundreds of thousands of Jews fell into their self-dug graves while our government, with glacial slowness, moved toward a proposal to confer and to explore."[25] She followed that article with this harsh criticism of the Bermuda Conference for its "Program of Inaction," and she proposed rescue measures under the very remote, even far-fetched possibility that Hitler would allow Jews in Nazi-occupied nations to go free.

24. "Joint Communiqué of United States and British Delegations," *Department of State Bulletin* 8, no. 201 (May 1, 1943): 388.
25. Freda Kirchwey, "While the Jews Die," *Nation* (March 13, 1943): 366–67.

19.

A Program of Inaction

BY FREDA KIRCHWEY

The weeks following the end of the Bermuda conference on refugee problems have brought nothing but a series of excuses for the failure of the British and American governments to do anything effective to rescue the victims of Hitler's terror who still remain alive. Indeed, the conference itself seems to have been devoted almost entirely to the formulation of those excuses. You couldn't ask favors of Hitler or of any of the governments under his domination. There wasn't any available transportation even in ships coming back from the war fronts in ballast. The extermination of the Jews seemed only too likely, but still, among all the would-be refugees of Europe, how could one single out the Jews for special treatment? Then, where would they go? England had taken more than its share, and so had the rest of the empire. Palestine's gates had been closed by a White Paper.[26] The quota system in the United States was immutable. The conferees would therefore concentrate most of their effort on the immediate problem of transferring to temporary places of settlement refugees who have succeeded in reaching neutral countries. The Nazi victims in occupied Europe would have to wait for an Allied victory. Wait—above the earth or under it. [. . .]

We should examine the excuses formulated in Bermuda and decide for ourselves whether or not they are sufficient to justify inaction. Certainly it is unlikely that Hitler would yield to any pleas for the release of Jews now under his direct control. But since, in the past, he has been interested in getting rid of Jews and has not always insisted upon slaughtering them, it is barely possible that he might agree to an exodus from the ghettoes of Poland arranged through neutral intermediaries. It is not likely, but it is possible.

But assuming Hitler refused to relinquish his prey, there is still a definite chance that some of the lesser Axis governments might agree to do so. Hungary, Bulgaria, Romania might well choose to dispose of a troublesome problem and at the same time curry favor with the powers that now appear the probable winners. If these Axis satellites would release the Jews within their borders, how many hundreds of thousands could be saved.

But how could these hordes be transported? And where could they go? If Britain would ease the restrictions on immigration into Palestine, refugees admitted there could travel overland. The most desired of all solutions has been flatly refused. Not even to save lives will Britain go beyond the quotas established in 1939. [With] Palestine ruled out, it still might be possible to establish settlements, temporary at least, in other parts of the Near East and in North Africa. Ships carrying war supplies to the Mediterranean could bring refugees back to Britain or the United States.

---

26. Policy issued by the government of the United Kingdom in 1939 that set strict limits on Jewish immigration to Palestine, then under UK administration.

But this suggestion collides with one of the chief obstacles to a solution—the re-luctance of Britain and the United States to admit more refugees. Britain has been far more generous in this matter than we have. The United States has multiplied the complications involved in getting a visa to such a degree that only a fraction of the ex-isting quotas from Nazi-occupied countries are being filled. Without changing the law in any particular we could take in more than 140,000 refugees immediately. And today they could be used to help overcome our growing shortage of industrial man-power.

As for the difficulty, stressed both here and in London, of singling out the Jews for rescue and ignoring the 120,000,000 people who, according to Mr. Peake,[27] would escape from enemy-occupied territories if they could, this is one of those stumbling-blocks set up to serve as an excuse for inaction. Whole populations neither can nor want to escape, however much they may hate the tyrant. The Jews alone represent a group detached by force from their homes and occupations, segregated physically as well as socially, marked as a whole for annihilation. It is disingenuous to pretend that because the entire population of occupied Europe cannot be evacuated, no effort should be made to save any special group.

The difficulties raised at the Bermuda conference are real. But they afford no valid excuse for a policy of sitting back and doing nothing. The process of extermination may be complete long before victory is won. The only hope lies in acting now. A determined effort should be made to carry out at least a limited program of rescue. Even the attempt would bring hope and comfort to the desperate millions marked for slaughter.

—*Nation,* June 5, 1943, 796–97.

Ben Hecht (1893–1964)—a well-known journalist, novelist, and Hollywood screen-writer—had little interest in Jewish affairs until the Nazis seized power. After 1933, Hecht became increasingly involved in antifascist activities. In September 1941, he began working closely with Peter Bergson, a militant activist and Zionist[28] who came to the United States in 1940 to raise support for a Jewish army to join the Allies' fight against Nazism. Most mainstream American Jewish organizations, including some which were Zionist, opposed Bergson's efforts, fearing that his confrontational tactics might spark increased prejudice against Jews.

Bergson gathered many Hollywood producers, actors, and screenwriters to stage *"We Will Never Die,"* a theatrical performance that lamented the murder of Europe's

27. Osbert Peake (1897–1966), an official in the UK Home Office, which oversaw immigra-tion and citizenship for the United Kingdom.

28. Modern Zionism: a prominent Jewish political movement after the first Zionist Congress met in Basel, Switzerland, in 1897. During the 1940s, Zionists sought the reestablishment of a Jewish homeland in the former biblical Land of Israel, which was under the British mandate of Palestine during World War II. The State of Israel was founded in 1948.

Jews. Hecht wrote the script for the pageant, which was staged in six US cities in 1943. For the April performance in Washington, DC—attended by First Lady Eleanor Roosevelt, seven Supreme Court justices, and more than 200 members of Congress—Hecht amended the ending of the script to challenge those in the audience to take action to rescue Europe's Jews.

Hecht also drew on his experience as a journalist to write many confrontational full-page newspaper ads that challenged Americans to act. His haunting "Ballad of the Doomed Jews of Europe," which also appeared in US newspapers, was illustrated by Arthur Szyk.

20.

"Narrators' Pitch" Written for Washington

FIRST NARRATOR

We, the actors who have performed for you tonight are nearly done. But there is another cast of actors involved in this tale whose performance is not done. This cast is our audience. Our audience tonight is a notable cast playing vital roles on the stage of history. It is to this audience more than to any group of human beings in the world that the dead and dying innocents of Europe raise their cry, "Remember Us." And tonight it is not as actors playing parts on a stage soon to be dismantled, but as the spokesmen of a people that is being exterminated, that we stand before you—the official, the accredited, the elected makers of history. Two million Jews have been mercilessly destroyed in Europe. Four million surviving Jews are to be destroyed by Christmas according to the pronouncements of the German government. To utter these miserable words anywhere else in the world would be to cry for pity. To speak them here tonight is a summons to action.

SECOND NARRATOR

Better than we our audience knows the two separate stories of Europe—the story of war and the story of massacre. It knows that as many defenseless men, women and children have been massacred by the Germans as have died on all the battle fronts. The story of the massacre that we have told tonight is incomplete. For we have spoken only of the Jews who lie dead on the steps of civilization. They occupy only part of the massacre ground. Beside them lie millions of Poles, Greeks, Yugoslavs, Czechs, Dutch, French, Norwegians, and others. But we have spoken only of the Jews because the killing of the Jews is a special challenge to history makers. Other people have been villainously slain by the Germans in the effort to reform them, subjugate them, silence them or frighten them. The Germans have no such program for the Jews. They desire neither their reform, nor subjugation. They desire only their extermination. Death to all Jews is their cry. [. . .]

We have come to the great and historic city of Washington to ask the question—what is our answer to this crime? In this city, not far away, are the halls from which

Justice has sounded her loudest battle cries, the chambers from which have issued man's noblest promises to tomorrow. Stranger than the mass murder of the civilian millions of Europe is the silence of these halls today. Stranger than the brutality of the massacre is the quiet of its onlookers in these chambers.

FIRST NARRATOR

For we are more than a nation at war, more than an arsenal, more than a battle line. Above and beyond the valor of our working and fighting millions, America is a dream of justice, a light held aloft to the sacred ways of humanity. It is because of this faith in our country that we have come to the historic capital and speak above the silence of its halls. We have brave soldiers who are fighting to victory. But the massacre of the unarmed civilians is beyond the reach of their guns. The desert and the Mediterranean are their battle front and they are honorably engaged on it. The massacre of Europe is our battle front—and we are not honorably engaged on it.

SECOND NARRATOR

In the historic halls of this city many great deeds and dreams have been forged. We ask that the silence of these halls be broken again. We ask for a second front against the crime of Europe, not a military front of soldiers, tanks and planes. But a second front of the human spirit against massacre. The crime of Europe calls for the mobilization of every shred of righteousness and spiritual power left in the world. [. . .]

   Our valiant solders are using to the last ounce of their power the weapons given them. But we who hold the weapons of morality—the cry of wrath and outrage, the words of righteousness which more than armies have made the shape of the world—we do not use our weapons. We betray our victories by not winning them in the name of decencies for which they are fought. The dead and dying who litter the steps of civilization had only one cry—Remember us. Speak for us, they said, before you become too guilty in your silence even to mourn us. Speak for us and give not only the Jews, but mankind back its fair name.

FIRST NARRATOR

The Jews have only one voice to raise among the notables who act for governments. [. . .] It is an old voice. It is the voice of prayer. Here in the great and historic city of Washington they raise it tonight. Perhaps the dead will hear it and find comfort. Perhaps the dying will hear it and find hope. Perhaps the Four Freedoms[29] will hear it and find their tongue.

   —*"We Will Never Die"* (1943), Ben Hecht Papers, The Newberry Library, Chicago.

---

29. In his State of the Union address to Congress on January 6, 1941, the president spoke of four freedoms that define values of democracy: freedom of speech, freedom to worship, freedom from want, and freedom from fear. (Message to Congress, January 6, 1941, box 58, Master Speech File, 1898, 1910–1945, FDRL.)

21.

BALLAD OF THE DOOMED JEWS OF EUROPE

FOUR MILLION JEWS waiting for death.
Oh hang and burn but—quiet, Jews!
Don't be bothersome; save your breath—
The world is busy with other news.

Four million murders are quite a smear
Even our State Department views
The slaughter with much disfavor here
But then—it's busy with other news.

You'll hang like a forest of broken trees
You'll burn in a thousand Nazi stews
And tell your God to forgive us please
For we were busy with other news.

Tell Him we hadn't quite the time
To stop the killing of all the Jews;
Tell Him we looked askance at the crime—
But we were busy with other news.

Oh World be patient—it will take
Some time before the murder crews
Are done. By Christmas you can make
Your Peace on Earth without the Jews.

ARTHUR SZYK
N.Y. MARCH 1943.

BEN HECHT

After the Bermuda Conference failed to produce any significant change in US government policy regarding refugees, Peter Bergson and his network of activists continued to apply direct pressure on the Roosevelt administration to rescue Jews. In September 1943, Bergson lobbied US senators and representatives to support a resolution that urged the president to establish a government-sponsored commission to make plans for saving Europe's remaining Jews. Bergson's Emergency Committee to Save the Jews of Europe then allied with Vaad ha-Hatzala, an Orthodox Jewish relief organization established in 1939, to plan a protest in Washington, DC.

On October 6, 1943, some 400 Orthodox rabbis marched through the streets of Washington. Rabbi Stephen Wise and other Jewish leaders opposed the march, as did some Jewish members of Congress. The rabbis hoped to speak directly with President Roosevelt, but he would not see them. Instead, Vice President Henry Wallace[30] met with the rabbis and received their petition to the president demanding action on behalf of suffering Jews. Despite the urging of the rabbis, the Roosevelt administration did not commit to supporting any rescue operations. Instead, Wallace reiterated the administration's position, that the best way to stop the murder of Jews in Europe would be through Allied military victory against Nazism.

22.

Rabbis Urge Agency To Aid Jewish People

WASHINGTON, [OCTOBER 6] (AP)—Several hundred somberly clad Jewish rabbis marched to the Capitol steps to deliver a petition to Vice-President [Henry] Wallace urging creation of a special inter-governmental agency "to save the remnants of Israel in Europe, with powers and means to act at once on a large scale."

Several of the older religious leaders sobbed audibly as Rabbi Haron D. Burack, of New York, intoned the petition in the Hebrew tongue. Rabbi Eliezer Silver, copresident of the Union of Orthodox Rabbis, later read it in English to the Vice President and assembled congressional leaders.

Declaring "the Nazis have poured out their rage against our people with a horrible cruelty unequalled by the savages of ancient days," the group asked for adoption of immediate and practical measures of rescue, food and medical supplies for starving German Jews, facilitated entry of oppressed Jews into the United States and the United Nations, and an immediate opening of "the doors of Palestine."

Wallace responded that the United States government "shares with you the great grief of all freedom loving people at the fate which threatens the Jews as well as all the oppressed victims of the Axis powers."

---

30. Henry A. Wallace (1888–1965): served as Secretary of Agriculture during the first two Roosevelt administrations before being nominated as vice president for Roosevelt's third term (1940–44).

Vice President Henry Wallace (second from left) listens to Rabbi
Eliezer Silver read the Orthodox rabbis' petition on the US Capitol
steps, October 6, 1943. Photo by Thomas D. McAvoy/The LIFE
Picture Collection via Getty Images.

"Nazi Germany was born of violence," he declared. "It thrives on hatred, bigotry
and intolerance. Its efforts to destroy the Jews of Europe are only part of the enemy's
attempt to crush the spirit of the common man all over the world.

"We must work and fight and pray for victory."

Standing with Wallace as he heard the petition were Speaker Rayburn,[31] Senate Ma-
jority Leader Barkley, House Majority Leader McCormack, Senate Minority Leader
McNary, Representative Sol Bloom (D-N.Y.),[32] Senators Johnson (D-Colo.), Barbour
(R-N.J.), Wagner (D-N.Y.),[33] Radcliffe (D-N.M.) and others.

—Associated Press, *Richmond (VA) Times Dispatch*, October 7, 1943, 18.

31. Sam Rayburn (1882–1961): twenty-four-term Democratic Congressman from Texas and
three-time Speaker of the US House of Representatives (1940–47, 1949–53, and 1955–61).

32. Sol Bloom (1870–1949): Democratic Congressman from New York (1923–49) and one of the
delegates chosen by Breckinridge Long to represent the United States at the Bermuda Conference.

33. Senator Robert Wagner (1877–1953): Democratic Senator from New York who had sponsored the Wagner-Rogers Bill in 1939.

A "War Refugee Board" for Rescue

In the months following the public release of news about the "Final Solution" in 1942, State Department officials quietly instructed colleagues at the US embassy in Switzerland to stop transmitting reports about the mass murder of Jews either to the US government or to private citizens. They hoped that blocking such reports would suppress pressure to aid Jews.

In 1943, Treasury Department staff discovered that the State Department had deliberately withheld information it had received about the murders and had been obstructing efforts to release private funds from the US for Jewish refugee relief in Europe. They informed Treasury Secretary Henry Morgenthau Jr. that the State Department was "guilty" of "gross procrastination and willful failure to act" and even of "the acquiescence of this government in the murder of the Jews."

Secretary Morgenthau's report to President Roosevelt described the "slaughter" of Europe's Jews as "one of the greatest crimes in history." It explained that the State Department staff had tried to "cover up their guilt" through lies and misrepresentations. In presenting the report, Morgenthau and his colleagues asked President Roosevelt to form an independent government agency to rescue Jews.

23.

SECRET

<u>PERSONAL REPORT TO THE PRESIDENT</u>

One of the greatest crimes in history, the slaughter of the Jewish people in Europe, is continuing unabated.

This Government has for a long time maintained that its policy is to work out programs to save those Jews and other persecuted minorities of Europe who could be saved.

You are probably not as familiar as I with the utter failure of certain officials in our State Department, who are charged with actually carrying out this policy, to take any effective action to prevent the extermination of the Jews in German-controlled Europe.

The public record, let alone the facts which have not yet been made public, reveals the gross procrastination of these officials. It is well known that since the time when it became clear that Hitler was determined to carry out a policy of exterminating the Jews in Europe, the State Department officials have failed to take any positive steps reasonably calculated to save any of these people. Although they have used devices such as setting up inter-governmental organizations to survey the whole refugee problem,[34] and calling conferences such as the Bermuda Conference to explore the

---

34. A reference to the Intergovernmental Committee on Refugees, established at the Évian Conference in July 1938.

whole refugee problem, making it appear that positive action could be expected, in fact nothing has been accomplished.

The best summary of the whole situation is contained in one sentence of a report submitted on December 20, 1943, by the Committee on Foreign Relations of the Senate, recommending the passage of a Resolution (S.R. 203), favoring the appointment of a commission to formulate plans to save the Jews of Europe from extinction by Nazi Germany. [. . .] The Committee stated:

> "We have talked; we have sympathized; we have expressed our horror; the time to act is long past due."

Whether one views this failure as being deliberate on the part of those officials handling the matter, or merely due to their incompetence, is not too important—from my point of view. However, there is a growing number of responsible people and organizations today who have ceased to view our failure as the product of simple incompetence on the part of those officials in the State Department charged with handling this problem. They see plain Anti-Semitism motivating the actions of these State Department officials and, rightly or wrongly, it will require little more in the way of proof for this suspicion to explode into a nasty scandal.

In this perspective, I ask you to weigh the implications of the following two cases[35] which have recently come to my attention and which have not as yet become known to the public. [. . .]

II
SUPPRESSION OF FACTS REGARDING
HITLER'S EXTERMINATION OF JEWS IN EUROPE

The facts are as follows:

<u>Sumner Welles as Acting Secretary of State requests confirmation of Hitler's plan to exterminate the Jews.</u> Having already received various reports on the plight of the Jews, on October 5, 1942, Sumner Welles as Acting Secretary of State[36] sent a cable (2314) for the personal attention of Minister Harrison in Bern[37] stating that leaders of the Jewish Congress had received reports from their representatives in Geneva and London to the fact that many thousands of Jews in Eastern Europe were being slaughtered pursuant to a policy embarked upon the German Government for the complete extermination of the Jews in Europe. [. . .]

<u>State Department receives confirmation that the extermination was being rapidly carried out.</u> Pursuant to Welles' cable of October 5, Minister Harrison forwarded

---

35. The first case (not included here) details the dispute between the Treasury and State departments over procedures to assist the World Jewish Congress's effort to aid refugees in Europe.

36. Secretary of State Cordell Hull was on vacation at the time; hence Welles was the "acting secretary."

37. Leland B. Harrison (1883–1951): US minister to Switzerland from 1937 to 1947.

documents from Riegner confirming the fact of extermination of the Jews (in November 1942), and in a cable of January 21, 1943 ([cable no.] 482), relayed a message from Riegner and Lichtheim[38] which Harrison stated was for the information of the Under Secretary of State [Welles] (and was to be transmitted to Rabbi Stephen Wise if the Under Secretary should so determine). This message described a horrible situation concerning the plight of Jews in Europe. It reported mass executions of Jews in Poland[. . . .]

Sumner Welles furnishes this information to the Jewish organizations. Sumner Welles furnished the documents received in November to the Jewish organizations in the United States and authorized them to make the facts public. On February 9, 1943 Welles forwarded the messages contained in cable 482 of January 21 to Rabbi Wise.

The receipt of this message intensified the pressure on the State Department to take some action.

Certain State Department officials attempt to stop this Government from obtaining further information from the very source from which the above evidence was received. On February 10, the day after Welles forwarded the message contained in cable 482 of January 21 to Rabbi Wise, and in direct response to this cable, a most highly significant cable was dispatched to Minister Harrison. This cable, 354 of February 10, read as follows:

> "Your 482, January 21
>
> In the future we would suggest that you do not accept reports submitted to you to be transmitted to private persons in the United States unless such action is advisable because of extraordinary circumstances. Such private messages circumvent neutral countries' censorship and it is felt that by sending them we risk the possibility that steps would necessarily be taken by the neutral countries to curtail or forbid our means of communication for confidential official matter.
>
> HULL (SW)"

The cable was signed for Hull by "SW" (Sumner Welles). But it is significant that there is not a word in it that would even suggest to the person signing that it was designed to countermand the Department's specific requests for information on Hitler's plans to exterminate the Jews. The cable has the appearance of being a normal routine message which a busy official would sign without question. On its face it is most innocent and innocuous, yet when read together with the previous cables is it anything less than an attempted suppression of information requested by this Government concerning the murder of Jews by Hitler? [. . .]

---

38. Richard Lichtheim (1885–1963): World Zionist Organization representative from Palestine to the League of Nations in Geneva from 1938 to 1946.

The facts I have detailed in this report, Mr. President, came to the Treasury's attention as a part of our routine investigation of the licensing of the financial phases of the proposal of the World Jewish Congress for the evacuation of Jews from France and Romania. The facts may thus be said to have come to light through accident. How many others of the same character are buried in State Department files is a matter I would have no way of knowing. Judging from the almost complete failure of the State Department to achieve any results, the strong suspicion must be that they are not few.

This much is certain, however. The matter of rescuing the Jews from extermination is a trust too great to remain in the hands of men who are indifferent, callous, and perhaps even hostile. The task is filled with difficulties. Only a fervent will to accomplish, backed by persistent and untiring effort can succeed where time is so precious.

[*signed*] Henry Morgenthau Jr.

Jan. 16, 1944.

—Henry Morgenthau Jr., "Personal Report to the President," January 16, 1944, The Morgenthau Diaries, vol. 694 (January 14–17, 1944), 194–202, FDRL.

President Roosevelt signed an executive order on January 22, 1944, that established the War Refugee Board, which was charged with the rescue and relief of victims of Nazi oppression as long as it did not interfere with the war effort.

The board coordinated the work of both US and international refugee aid organizations, sending millions of dollars into German-occupied Europe for relief and rescue. Its representatives abroad pressured neutral nations to provide diplomatic aid to Jews and to welcome refugees.

The War Refugee Board existed from January 1944 to September 1945, less than two years. The board's final report estimated that it had rescued "tens of thousands" of people and assisted "hundreds of thousands" more.

24.

EXECUTIVE ORDER 9417
ESTABLISHING A WAR REFUGEE BOARD.

WHEREAS it is the policy of this Government to take all measures within its power to rescue the victims of enemy oppression who are in imminent danger of death and otherwise to afford such victims all possible relief and assistance consistent with the successful prosecution of the war;

NOW, THEREFORE, by virtue of the authority vested in me by the Constitution and the statutes of the United States, as President of the United States and as

Commander in Chief of the Army and Navy, and in order to effectuate with all possible speed the rescue and relief of such victims of enemy oppression, it is hereby ordered as follows:

1. There is established in the Executive Office of the President a War Refugee Board (hereinafter referred to as the Board). The Board shall consist of the Secretary of State, the Secretary of the Treasury, and the Secretary of War. The Board may request the heads of other agencies or departments to participate in its deliberations whenever matters specially affecting such agencies or departments are under consideration.

2. The Board shall be charged with the responsibility for seeing that the policy of the Government, as stated in the Preamble, is carried out. The functions of the Board shall include without limitation the development of plans and programs and the inauguration of effective measures for (a) the rescue, transportation, maintenance, and relief of the victims of enemy oppression, and (b) the establishment of havens of temporary refuge for such victims. To this end the Board, through appropriate channels, shall take the necessary steps to enlist the cooperation of foreign Governments and obtain their participation in the execution of such plans and programs.

3. It shall be the duty of the State, Treasury, and War Departments, within their respective spheres, to execute at the request of the Board, the plans and programs so developed and the measures so inaugurated. [. . .] The State Department shall appoint special attachés with diplomatic status, on the recommendation of the Board, to be stationed abroad in places where it is likely that assistance can be rendered to war refugees, the duties and responsibilities of such attachés to be defined by the Board in consultation with the State Department.

4. The Board and the State, Treasury, and War Departments are authorized to accept the services or contributions of any private persons, private organizations, State agencies, or agencies of foreign governments in carrying out the purposes of this Order. The Board shall cooperate with all existing and future international organizations concerned with the problems of refugee rescue, maintenance, transportation, relief, rehabilitation, and resettlement.

5. To the extent possible the Board shall utilize the personnel, supplies, facilities, and services of the State, Treasury, and War Departments. [. . .] The Board shall appoint an Executive Director who shall serve as its principal executive officer.[39] It shall be the duty of the Executive Director to arrange for the prompt execution of the plans and programs developed and the measures inaugurated by the Board, to supervise the activities of the special attaches, and to submit frequent reports to the Board on the steps taken for the rescue and relief of war refugees.

6. The Board shall be directly responsible to the President in carrying out the policy of this Government, as stated in the Preamble, and the Board shall report to

---

39. John W. Pehle (1909–99), an assistant to Treasury Secretary Henry Morgenthau Jr., was named the Board's first executive director soon after Roosevelt issued his executive order.

him at frequent intervals concerning the steps taken for the rescue and relief of war refugees and shall make such recommendations as the Board may deem appropriate for further action to overcome any difficulties encountered in the rescue and relief of war refugees.

FRANKLIN D. ROOSEVELT

THE WHITE HOUSE,

January 22, 1944

—President, Executive Order 9417, "Creation of a War Refugee Board," *Federal Register 9*, no. 18 (Washington, DC: USGPO, January 26, 1944): 935–36.

Among the many actions it took to rescue Jews, the War Refugee Board brought 982 refugees from eighteen different countries to the Fort Ontario Emergency Refugee Shelter in Oswego, New York, in August 1944. This was the only time during World War II that the US government bypassed its immigration laws to allow a group of refugees to reach American shores. Instead of welcoming them as immigrants, however, the United States designated them as "guests" being temporarily sheltered at a "free port."

The refugees, most of whom were Jewish, did not have clear legal status in the United States. They were held behind barbed-wire fences at Fort Ontario and were informed that they would be returned to Europe when the war ended. First Lady Eleanor Roosevelt showed her support for the refugees by visiting Fort Oswego and writing about their experiences in her widely published "My Day" newspaper column.

In February 1946, nine months after the defeat of Nazi Germany, the Fort Ontario Emergency Refugee Shelter closed. Most of the refugees were admitted to the United States on immigrant visas. As President Harry S. Truman had explained in December 1945, he believed it would have been "inhumane . . . to require these people to go all the way back to Europe."[40]

25.

MY DAY
Oswego refugee shelter offers a duration home to 982 weary Europeans

by Eleanor Roosevelt

HYDE PARK, [NY,] Thursday—Tuesday evening I went with Mrs. Henry Morgenthau, Jr., to Syracuse, where we spent the night. In the morning [September 20]

40. "Immigration to the United States of Certain Displaced Persons and Refugees in Europe: Statement by the President," *Department of State Bulletin* 13, no. 339 (December 23, 1945): 982.

Mr. Joseph Smart[41] called for us, and we went to Oswego to visit the refugee shelter where the United States is temporarily offering hospitality to 982 refugees from concentration [and refugee] camps in Italy. Our army there was glad to have them come to this country, and since Fort Ontario is not being used at present, they are housed there in soldiers' barracks. Partitions have been put up, affording them some privacy, but only the absolute necessities of life are being provided.

Forty-five cents a day per person is what is allowed for food. Regular iron cots and springs with cotton mattresses, army blankets, an occasional bare table and a few stiff chairs—this is the furniture of what must be considered a temporary home. Restrictions are plentiful, and there is much work to be done around the place; but at least the menace of death is not ever-present. They have elected a committee of their own which decides on questions concerning camp organization and direction, and they work closely with the camp director, Mr. Smart.

Oswego has an advisory committee that works with theirs, and they have set up recreation, education and business sections, so that both the shelter and the city may profit by their contacts. Volunteers come out to teach English; but since most of the people in the shelter are professional people and frequently have many talents, they, too, have much to offer to the community. After lunch, for instance, an opera singer from Yugoslavia sang for us, and I have rarely enjoyed anything more.

I was much touched by the flowers which were given me, and especially by some of the gifts, for these, in the absence of money, represented work. One talented young woman had put a great deal of work into her temporary home. Although clothes have to be hung on hooks in the wall, she had covered them with a piece of unbleached muslin, and up above had painted and cut out figures of animals, stars and angels, which were placed all over the plain surface to become a decorative wall covering.

Brightly colored pictures from magazines and papers had been cut out and pasted elsewhere on the walls, and colorful covers had been made for their beds. The effort put into it speaks volumes for what these people have undergone, and for the character which has brought them through. Somehow you feel that if there is any compensation for suffering, it must someday bring them something beautiful in return for all the horrors they have lived through.

—*Courier-Journal* (Louisville, KY), September 23, 1944, 10.

41. Joseph H. Smart (1900–1993): director of the Ft. Ontario Emergency Refugee Shelter during its operations in 1944 and 1945. He had been a regional director for the War Relocation Authority (1942–44) which oversaw the forced removal of Americans of Japanese ancestry to camps in 1942. After the war, he advocated fulltime for the Fort Ontario refugees to remain in the United States.

26.

On the first anniversary of his arrival at Fort Ontario, refugee
Max Sipser reflected on the stark contrast between the promise
of liberty in New York Harbor and the distant ideal of liberty as
his detainment continued. This untitled drawing appeared in the
August 2, 1945, issue of the *Ontario Chronicle*, a newspaper written
and published by the refugees at Fort Ontario.

USHMM Collection, gift of Richard Lehmann.

Throughout spring 1944, the War Refugee Board received dozens of suggestions
about how to save Jews. Among these were pleas for the Allies to bomb the rail lines
that carried the trainloads of Jews to the Auschwitz-Birkenau killing center in Nazi-
occupied Poland, or bomb its gas chambers or the entire camp.[42] In June, board officials

42. Auschwitz-Birkenau: the second and largest of the three main camps and more than
forty subcamps that composed the Auschwitz complex. Constructed between fall 1941 and
spring 1942, its original three small gas chambers were replaced in spring 1943 with four much

forwarded these requests to the US War Department without endorsing them. The War Department, in response, declared the bombing "impracticable" and a "diversion" from operations "essential to the success" of the war.

In August and September 1944, however, the War Department authorized bombing the I. G. Farben oil and rubber (Buna) works, a strategic German industrial target and forced labor camp about four miles from the Auschwitz-Birkenau site. These were carried out by US long-range heavy bombers based in Foggia, Italy.

In November 1944, after the War Refugee Board had received more detailed information about mass killings at Auschwitz, board director John Pehle concluded that the murder facilities should be destroyed. He urged Assistant Secretary of War John McCloy[43] to authorize "direct bombing action." The War Department again refused, repeating that bombing Auschwitz-Birkenau would divert the military from its main objective—winning the war as quickly as possible.

27.

EXECUTIVE OFFICE OF THE PRESIDENT
WAR REFUGE BOARD

OFFICE OF THE
EXECUTIVE DIRECTOR   Nov 8 1944

Dear Mr. McCloy:

I send you herewith copies of two eye-witness descriptions of the notorious German concentration and extermination camps of Auschwitz and Birkenau in Upper Silesia, which have just been received from the Board's Special Representative in Bern, Switzerland, Roswell McClelland whom we have borrowed from the American Friends Service Committee. No report of Nazi atrocities received by the Board has quite caught the gruesome brutality of what is taking place in these camps of horror as have these sober, factual accounts of conditions in Auschwitz and Birkenau. I earnestly hope that you read these reports.

The destruction of large numbers of people apparently is not a simple process. The Germans have been forced to devote considerable technological ingenuity and administrative know-how in order to carry out murder on a mass production basis, as the attached reports will testify. If the elaborate murder installations at Birkenau were destroyed, it seems clear that the Germans could not reconstruct them for some time.

---

larger gassing and crematoria facilities. An estimated 1.1 million people—90 percent of whom were Jews—died at Birkenau before the Germans destroyed its operations in late 1944 as the Soviet Red Army advanced into Nazi-occupied eastern Europe.

43. John J. McCloy (1895–1986): assistant secretary of war, the second-ranking position, from 1941 to 1945.

Until now, despite pressure from many sources, I have been hesitant to urge the destruction of these camps by direct, military action. But I am convinced that the point has now been reached where such action is justifiable if it is deemed feasible by competent military authorities. I strongly recommend that the War Department give serious consideration to the possibility of destroying the execution chambers and crematories in Birkenau through direct bombing action. It may be observed that there would be other advantages of a military nature to such an attack. The Krupp and Siemens factories, where among other things cases for hand grenades are made, and a Buna plant, all within Auschwitz, would be destroyed.[44] The destruction of the German barracks and guardhouses and the killing of German soldiers in the area would also be accomplished. The morale of underground groups might be considerably strengthened by such a dramatic exhibition of Allied air support and a number of the people confined in Auschwitz and Birkenau might be liberated in the confusion resulting from the bombing. That the effecting of a prison break by such methods is not without precedent is indicated by the description in the enclosed copy of a recent New York Times article of the liberation from Amiens prison of 100 French patriots by the RAF [Royal Air Force of the UK].

Obviously, the War Refugee Board is in no position to determine whether the foregoing proposal is feasible from a military standpoint. Nevertheless in view of the urgency of the situation, we feel justified in making the suggestion. I would appreciate having the views of the War Department as soon as possible.

Very truly yours,
[*signature*] J. W. Pehle
Executive Director

WAR DEPARTMENT
OFFICE OF THE ASSISTANT SECRETARY
WASHINGTON, D. C.

18 November 1944

Mr. John W. Pehle, Executive Director
War Refugee Board
Treasury Department Building, Rm. 3414
Washington 25, D. C.

Dear Mr. Pehle:

I refer to your letter of November 8th, in which you forwarded the report of two eye-witnesses on the notorious German concentration and extermination camps of Auschwitz and Birkenau in Upper Silesia.

---

44. These industrial factories were in detached Auschwitz subcamps and physically at various distances from Birkenau.

The Operations Staff of the War Department has given careful consideration to your suggestion that the bombing of these camps be undertaken. In consideration of this proposal the following points were brought out:

a. Positive destruction of these camps would necessitate precision bombing, employing heavy or medium bombardment, or attack by low flying or dive bombing aircraft, preferably the latter.

b. The target is beyond the maximum range of medium bombardment, dive bombers and fighter bombers located in United Kingdom, France, or Italy.

c. Use of heavy bombardment from United Kingdom bases would necessitate a hazardous round trip flight unescorted of approximately 2000 miles over enemy territory.

d. At the present critical stage of the war in Europe, our strategic air forces are engaged in the destruction of industrial target systems vital to the dwindling war potential of the enemy, from which they should not be diverted. The positive solution to this problem is the earliest possible victory over Germany, to which end we should exert our entire means.

e. This case does not at all parallel the Amiens mission because of the location of the concentration and extermination camps and the resulting difficulties encountered in attempting to carry out the proposed bombing.

Based on the above, as well as the most uncertain, if not dangerous effect such a bombing would have on the object to be attained, the War Department has felt that it should not, at least for the present, undertake these operations.

I know that you have been reluctant to press this activity on the War Department. We have been pressed strongly from other quarters, however, and have taken the best military opinion on its feasibility, and we believe the above conclusion is a sound one.

Sincerely,
[*signature*] John J. McCloy
Assistant Secretary of War

—Letters, November 8 and 18, 1944, box 7, "German Extermination Camps (1)," Records of the War Refugee Board, 1944–1945, FDRL.

Witnesses to the "Final Solution"

Following Germany's invasion of Poland on September 1, 1939, resistance organizations formed a Polish Underground State (*Polskie Państwo Podziemne*) to combat the occupation. Among its early fighters was Jan Karski (1914–2000), a young army officer who helped organize many of the Underground's covert activities. In late 1942, the Underground sent Karski to London to give detailed reports on conditions in Poland to the Polish Government-in-Exile and top British officials. From there, he went to the United States to meet with government and civic leaders. On July 28, 1943, Karski met with President Roosevelt at the White House.

Prior to his travels, Karski had been smuggled into both the Warsaw ghetto and a prisoner transit camp to witness the horrors suffered by Poland's Jews. Among other topics, Karski discussed German atrocities with Roosevelt. He later recalled that the president promised the Allies "shall win the war" but made no mention of rescuing Jews.

Karski's wartime memoir, *Story of a Secret State,* published in November 1944, included searing descriptions of Nazi anti-Jewish brutality. A preview excerpt from the book, similar to the following selection, appeared in the October 14, 1944, issue of *Collier's,* one of the most widely read American magazines. The book gained broad distribution as a selection for the popular Book-of-the-Month Club in January 1945.

28.
"To Die in Agony . . ."

As we approached to within a few hundred yards of the camp, the shouts, cries, and shots cut off further conversation.[45] I noticed, or thought I noticed, an unpleasant stench that seemed to have come from decomposing bodies mixed with horse manure. [. . .] We passed through a small grove of decrepit-looking trees and emerged directly in front of the loud, sobbing, reeking camp of death.

It was on a large, flat plain and occupied about a square mile. It was surrounded on all sides by a formidable barbed-wire fence, nearly two yards in height and in good repair. Inside the fence, at intervals of about fifteen yards, guards were standing, holding rifles with fixed bayonets ready for use. Around the outside of the fence militia men circulated on constant patrol. The camp itself contained a few small sheds or barracks. The rest of the area was completely covered by a dense, pulsating, throbbing, noisy human mass. Starved, stinking, gesticulating, insane human beings in constant, agitated motion. Through them, forcing paths if necessary with their rifle butts, walked the German police and the militia men. They walked in silence, their faces bored and indifferent. They looked like shepherds bringing in a flock to the market or pig-dealers among their pigs. They had the tired, vaguely disgusted appearance of men doing a routine, tedious job.

45. Karski, disguised in a camp guard's uniform, was in the company of a guard bribed to guide this risky visit.

[. . .] To my left I noticed the railroad tracks which passed about a hundred yards from the camp. From the camp to the track a sort of raised passage had been built from old boards. On the track a dusty freight train waited, motionless. [. . .]

The Jewish mass vibrated, trembled, and moved to and fro as if united in a single, insane, rhythmic trance. They waved their hands, shouted, quarreled, cursed, and spat at one another. Hunger, thirst, fear and exhaustion had driven them all insane. I had been told that they were usually left in the camp for three or four days without a drop of water or food.

They were all former inhabitants of the Warsaw ghetto. [. . .]

There was no organization or order of any kind. None of them could possibly help or share with each other and they soon lost any self-control or any sense whatsoever except the barest instinct of self-preservation. They had become, at this stage, completely dehumanized. It was, moreover, typical autumn weather, cold, raw, and rainy. The sheds could not accommodate more than two to three thousand people and every "batch" [of new arrivals] included more than five thousand. This meant that there were always two to three thousand men, women, and children scattered about in the open, suffering exposure as well as everything else.

The chaos, the squalor, the hideousness of it all was simply indescribable. There was a suffocating stench of sweat, filth, decay, damp straw and excrement. To get to my post we had to squeeze our way through this mob. It was a ghastly ordeal. [. . .]

I remained there perhaps half an hour, watching this spectacle of human misery. At each moment I felt the impulse to run and flee. I had to force myself to remain indifferent, practice stratagems on myself to convince myself that I was not one of the condemned, throbbing multitude. [. . .] Finally, I noticed a change in the motion of the guards. They walked less and they all seemed to be glancing in the same direction—at the passage to the track which was quite close to me.

I turned toward it myself. Two German policemen came to the gate with a tall, bulky, SS man.[46] He barked out an order and they began to open the gate with some difficulty. It was very heavy. He shouted at them impatiently. They worked at it frantically and finally whipped it open. [. . .]

The SS man turned to the crowd, planted himself with his feet wide apart and his hands on his hips and loosed a roar that must have actually hurt his ribs. It could be heard far above the hellish babble that came from the crowd:

"*Ruhe, ruhe!* Quiet, quiet! All Jews will board this train to be taken to a place where work awaits them. Keep order. Do not push. Anyone who attempts to resist or create a panic will be shot."

---

46. Since the Nazi regime established its first concentration camp in 1933, the camp system was controlled by the SS (*Schutzstaffel*) under Heinrich Himmler.

He stopped speaking and looked challengingly at the helpless mob that hardly seemed to know what was happening. Suddenly, accompanying the movement with a loud, hearty laugh, he yanked out his gun and fired three random shots into the crowd. A single, stricken groan answered him. He replaced the gun in his holster, smiled, and set himself for another roar:

"Alle Juden, 'raus—'raus!" ["All Jews, out—out!"]

For a moment the crowd was silent. Those nearest the SS man recoiled from the shots and tried to dodge, panic-stricken, toward the rear. But this was resisted by the mob as a volley of shots from the rear sent the whole mass surging forward madly, screaming in pain and fear. The shots continued without let-up from the rear and now from the sides, too, narrowing the mob down and driving it in a savage scramble onto the passageway. In utter panic, groaning in despair and agony, they rushed down the passageway, trampling it so furiously that it threatened to fall apart.

Here new shots were heard. The two policemen at the entrance to the train were now firing into the oncoming throng corralled in the passageway, in order to slow them down and prevent them from demolishing the flimsy structure. The SS man now added his roar to the deafening bedlam.

"Ordnung, ordnung!" he bellowed like a madman.

"Order, order!" The two policemen echoed him hoarsely, firing straight into the faces of the Jews running to the trains. Impelled and controlled by this ring of fire, they filled the two cars quickly.

And now came the most horrible episode of all. [. . .]

The military rule stipulates that a freight car may carry eight horses or forty soldiers. Without any baggage at all, a maximum of a hundred passengers standing close together and pressing against each other could be crowded into a car. The Germans had simply issued orders to the effect that 120 to 130 Jews had to enter each car. These orders were now being carried out. Alternately swinging and firing their rifles, the policemen were forcing still more people into the two cars which were already over-full. The shots continued to ring out in the rear and the driven mob surged forward, exerting an irresistible pressure against those nearest the train. These unfortunates, crazed by what they had been through, scourged by the policemen, and shoved forward by the milling mob, then began to climb on the heads and shoulders of those in the trains.

These were helpless since they had the weight of the entire advancing throng against them and responded only with howls of anguish to those who, clutching at their hair and clothes for support, trampling on necks, faces and shoulders, breaking bones and shouting with insensate fury, attempted to clamber over them. After the cars had already been filled beyond normal capacity, more than another score of human beings, men, women and children gained admittance in this fashion. Then the policemen slammed the doors across the hastily withdrawn limbs that still protruded and pushed the iron bars in place.

The two cars were now crammed to bursting with tightly packed human flesh, completely, hermetically filled. All this while the entire camp had reverberated with a tremendous volume of sound in which the hideous groans and screams mingled weirdly with shots, curses, and bellowed commands.

Nor was this all. I know that many people will not believe me, will not be able to believe me, will think I exaggerate or invent. But I saw it and it is not exaggerated or invented. I have no other proofs, no photographs. All I can say is that I saw it and that it is the truth.

The floors of the car had been covered with a thick, white powder. It was quicklime. Quicklime is simply unslaked lime or calcium oxide that has been dehydrated. Anyone who has seen cement being mixed knows what occurs when water is poured on lime. The mixture bubbles and steams as the powder combines with the water, generating a large amount of heat.

Here the lime served a double purpose in the Nazi economy of brutality. The moist flesh coming in contact with the lime is rapidly dehydrated and burned. The occupants of the cars would be literally burned to death before long, the flesh eaten from their bones. Thus, the Jews would "die in agony," fulfilling the promise Himmler had issued "in accord with the will of the Fuehrer," in Warsaw, in 1942. Secondly, the lime would prevent decomposing bodies from spreading disease. It was efficient and inexpensive—a perfectly chosen agent for their purposes.

It took three hours to fill up the entire train by repetitions of this procedure. It was twilight when the forty-six (I counted them) cars were packed. From one end to the other, the train, with its quivering cargo of flesh, seemed to throb, vibrate, rock, and jump as if bewitched. There would be a strangely uniform momentary lull and then, again, the train would begin to moan and sob, wail and howl. Inside the camp a few score dead bodies remained and a few in the final throes of death, German policemen walked around at leisure with smoking guns, pumping bullets into anything that by a moan or motion betrayed an excess of vitality. Soon, not a single one was left alive. In the now quiet camp the only sounds were the inhuman screams that were echoes from the moving train. Then these, too, ceased. All that was now left was the stench of excrement and rotting straw and a queer, sickening, acidulous odor which, I thought, may have come from the quantities of blood that had been let, and with which the ground was stained. [. . .]

The images of what I saw in the death camp are, I am afraid, my permanent possessions. I would like nothing better than to purge my mind of these memories. For one thing, the recollection of those events invariably brings on a recurrence of the nausea. But more than that, I would like simply to be free of them, to obliterate the very thought that such things ever occurred.

—Jan Karski, *Story of a Secret State* (Boston:
Houghton-Mifflin Company, 1944), 344–50, 352.

Two Slovakian Jews, Rudolf Vrba and Alfred Wétzler, escaped from Auschwitz in April 1944 and, in interviews, provided authorities two of the first eyewitness accounts of mass murder of Jews carried out at Auschwitz-Birkenau. An expanded version of their reports soon began to circulate among neutral governments; it did not reach the United States until late October.

On November 26, 1944, the War Refugee Board released the report to the American press with the following introduction. Both the report and the press coverage about it in the United States furnished detailed, graphic information about the killing process at Auschwitz-Birkenau.

29.

EXECUTIVE OFFICE OF THE PRESIDENT
WAR REFUGEE BOARD
WASHINGTON, D. C.

GERMAN EXTERMINATION CAMPS — AUSCHWITZ AND BIRKENAU

It is a fact beyond denial that the Germans have deliberately and systematically murdered millions of innocent civilians—Jews and Christians alike—all over Europe. This campaign of terror and brutality, which is unprecedented in all history and which even now continues unabated, is part of the German plan to subjugate the free peoples of the world.

So revolting and diabolical are the German atrocities that the minds of civilized people find it difficult to believe that they have actually taken place. But the governments of the United States and of other countries have evidence which clearly substantiates the facts.

The War Refugee Board is engaged in a desperate effort to save as many as possible of Hitler's intended victims. To facilitate its work the Board has representatives in key spots in Europe. These representatives have tested contacts throughout Europe and keep the Board fully advised concerning the German campaign of extermination and torture.

Recently the Board received from a representative close to the scene two eye-witness accounts of events which occurred in notorious extermination camps established by the Germans. The first report is based upon the experiences of two young Slovakian Jews who escaped in April, 1944 after spending two years in the Nazi concentration camps at Auschwitz and Birkenau in southwestern Poland. The second report is made by a non-Jewish Polish major, the only survivor of one group imprisoned at Auschwitz.

The two reports were prepared independently and are reproduced exactly in the form they were received by the War Refugee Board, except for a few deletions necessary for the protection of persons who may be still alive. The figures concerning the size of the Jewish convoys and the numbers of men and women admitted to the two camps cannot be taken as mathematically exact; and, in fact, are declared by the authors to be no more than reliable approximations. They are accepted as such by the Board.

The Board has every reason to believe that these reports present a true picture of the frightful happenings in these camps. It is making the reports public in the firm conviction that they should be read and understood by all Americans.

November, 1944

> —*German Extermination Camps—Auschwitz and Birkenau,*
> November 26, 1944, box 7, "German Extermination Camps (1),"
> Records of the War Refugee Board, 1944–1945, FDRL.

30.

Cabinet Members Submit Report
On Nazi Extermination Camps

WASHINGTON, Nov. 25—(AP)—The War Refugee Board—three members of President Roosevelt's cabinet—sponsored Saturday a 25,000 word detailed report of bestial cruelty and murder by the million in German extermination camps.

Said the board, comprising Secretary of State Hull, Secretary of the Treasury Morgenthau, and Secretary of War Stimson:

"The board has every reason to believe that these reports present a true picture of the frightful happenings in these camps. It is making the report public in the firm conviction that they should be read and understood by all Americans."

The report consisted of two eyewitness accounts of life in the Nazi camps at Auschwitz and Birkenau in [occupied] southwestern Poland, prepared independently but almost precisely parallel.

Each included an estimate that more than a million and a half Jews from various European countries were gassed and their bodies cremated at Birkenau alone between April 1942 and April 1944.

One estimate by two young Slovakian Jews who for two years had clerical posts in the camp through which they could keep fairly close track of events, set the figure at 1,750,000. The second account was by a non-Jewish Polish major. All three escaped. For their protection, their names were withheld by the board which said in an accompanying statement:

"It is a fact beyond denial that the Germans have deliberately and systematically murdered millions of innocent civilians—Jews and Christians alike—all over Europe."

"This campaign of terror and brutality, which is unprecedented in all history and which even now continues unabated, is part of the German plan to subjugate the free people of the world."

The board, of which John W. Pehle is executive director, is responsible for carrying out the policy of the federal government for rescue of the victims of enemy oppression.

Throughout the more detailed story of the two Jews appeared such gruesome statistics as these: "Conservative estimate" that 65,000 to 70,000 of 80,000 persons received at the camp [in a single deportation from western Europe] were gassed; "lowest estimate" 30,000 gassed out of another group; one month's gassings 90,000; total capacity of crematoria 6,000 a day but for a period it was overloaded and bodies burned in great open pits. [. . .]

"Working conditions were inconceivably hard, so that the majority of us, weakened by starvation and inedible food, could not stand it. The mortality was so high that every day our group of 200 had 30 to 35 dead. Many were simply beaten to death by the overseers—the 'capos'[47]—during work, without the slightest provocation." [. . .]

"At the same time, the so-called 'selections' were introduced. Twice weekly, Mondays and Thursdays, the camp doctor indicated the number of prisoners who were to be gassed and then burned. These 'selectees' were loaded into trucks and brought to the birch forest. Those still alive upon arrival were gassed in a big barrack erected near the trench used for burning the bodies." [. . .]

"Large family convoys arrived from various European countries and were at once directed to the birch wood. The special squad ('Sonderkommando'[48]) employed for gassing and burning worked in day and night shifts. Hundreds of thousands of Jews were gassed during this period. . . .

"At the end of February 1943, a new modern crematoria and gassing plant was inaugurated at Birkenau . . . The large ditch was filled in, the ground leveled and the ashes used as before for fertilizer at the farm labor camp of Hermense."

Next to the furnace room was a large "reception hall" arranged to give the impression of the antechamber of a bathing establishment. It holds 2,000 people and apparently there is a similar waiting room on the floor below. From there a door and a few steps lead down into the very long and narrow gas chamber. The walls of this chamber are also camouflaged with simulated entries to shower rooms to mislead the victims.

"The room is fitted with three traps which can be hermetically closed from the outside. A track leads from the gas chamber through the furnace room. The gassing takes place as follows:

47. Camp prisoners, often recruited from among the imprisoned violent criminals, assigned by SS guards to supervise forced laborers. Their brutality was tolerated as part of the SS control by terror.

48. Squads of killing-center prisoners tasked with removing the dead from the gas chambers and operating the crematoria to dispose of the bodies.

"The unfortunate victims are brought into the hall, where they are told to undress. To complete the fiction that they are going to bathe, each person receives a towel and a small piece of soap, issued by two men clad in white coats. Then they are crowded into the gas chamber in such numbers that there is, of course, only standing room.

"To compress this crowd into the narrow space, shots are often fired to induce those already at the far end to huddle still closer together. When everybody is inside, the heavy doors are closed. Then there is a short pause presumably to allow the room temperature to rise to a certain level, after which SS men with gas masks climb on the roof, open the traps and shake down a preparation in powder form out of tin cans labeled 'cyklon [sic; Zyklon]—for use against vermin' which is manufactured by a Hamburg concern. It is presumed that this is a 'cyanide' mixture of some sort which turns into gas at a certain temperature.

"After three minutes, everyone in the chamber is dead."

The bodies are then taken out and burned.

"On principle only Jews are gassed: Aryans very seldom, as they are usually given 'special treatment' by shooting."

—Associated Press, *Billings (MT) Gazette,* November 26, 1944, 10.

By late 1944, more than three-quarters of Americans believed that Germany's mass-murder campaign was occurring, but most could not grasp the scale of the crime. By the time this poll was taken, well over five million Jews had been murdered.

31.

Gallup Polls, November 1944

"Do you believe the stories that the Germans have murdered many people in concentration camps?"

76% Yes
12% No
12% No opinion

"Nobody knows, of course, how many (people in concentration camps) may have been murdered (by Germans), but what would be your best guess?"

36% 100,000 or less
 7% 100,000 to 500,000
 1% 500,000 to 1,000,000
 8% 1,000,000
11% 2,000,000 to 6,000,000

5% 6,000,000 or more

33% Unwilling to guess

—Gallup Organization. 1944. Gallup Poll # 1944-0335: Presidential Election/
Education. Question 22: USGALLUP.120444.R01A, and Question 23:
USGALLUP.120444.R01B. Cornell University, Ithaca, NY: Roper Center for
Public Opinion Research. https://doi.org/10.25940/ROPER-31087318.

"We are in the presence of a crime without a name," declared British Prime Minister Winston Churchill to radio listeners on August 24, 1941.[49] His announcement came two months after British intelligence had received secret information about mass shootings of Soviet Jews by the Nazi regime and its collaborators.

Three years later, Raphael Lemkin (1900–59), a Polish Jewish refugee who had immigrated to the United States, named the crime *genocide*, which he defined as the "deliberate destruction" of a nation or an ethnic group. On December 3, 1944, the *Washington Post* ran an editorial titled "Genocide" that introduced American readers to this new word.

32.

Genocide

No human creature can read the report of the War Refugee Board released last Sunday [November 26, 1944] without a sense of shock and shame. The report presents eyewitness accounts of events which occurred at the German extermination camps of Auschwitz and Birkenau. "So revolting and diabolical are the German atrocities," says the WRB, "that the minds of civilized people find it difficult to believe that they have actually taken place. But the governments of the United States and of other countries have evidence which clearly substantiates the facts." The facts are really quite simple, although perhaps somewhat difficult to grasp: in Birkenau, between April, 1942, and April, 1944, approximately 1,765,000 Jews were put to death by poison gas in ingeniously constructed chambers; their bodies were then burned in specially designed furnaces[. . . .]

It is a mistake, perhaps, to call these killings "atrocities." An atrocity is a wanton brutality. There were unspeakable atrocities at Auschwitz and Birkenau. But the point about these killings is that they were systematic and purposeful. The gas chambers and furnaces were not improvisation; they were scientifically designed instruments

49. Broadcast transcript: University of North Carolina, *ibiblio.org:* https://www.ibiblio.org/pha/policy/1941/410824a.html.

for the extermination of an entire ethnic group. On the scale practiced by the Germans, this is something new. And it is this purpose which human beings find it difficult to believe or understand. Yet it is a purpose which Hitler has openly avowed.

We have never even had a word for it until now. But one has been recently coined by a noted Polish scholar and attorney, Prof. Raphael Lemkin, now on the faculty of Duke University. He has devised the term genocide out of the ancient Greek word *genos* (race, tribe) and the Latin *cide* (killing). "Genocide," he says in a volume, *Axis Rule in Occupied Europe* recently published by the Carnegie Endowment for International Peace, "is directed against the national group as an entity, and the actions involved are directed against individuals, not in their individual capacity, but as members of the national group." Thus Jews were gassed at Birkenau and Aryan Poles and Russians and Slovenes were otherwise butchered, not for any crime or any resistance to Axis authority but because the Nazis wished to exterminate the ethnic groups to which they belonged.

"Generally speaking," says Professor Lemkin, "genocide does not necessarily mean the immediate destruction of a nation, except when accomplished by mass killings of all members of a nation. It is intended rather to signify a coordinated plan of different actions aiming at the destruction of essential foundations of the life of national groups, with the aim of annihilating the groups themselves." In this sense the Germans have committed genocide in virtually all the countries of Europe which they occupied. They have struck deliberately at the culture, language, religious and political institutions and at the economic existence of the peoples they conquered—all with a view to undermining their national identity and weakening them, physically and morally, so that they would become subservient to German rule.

As long ago as 1933 Professor Lemkin proposed the recognition of genocide as a crime under international law. [. . .] One of the vital steps in the punishment of war guilt, we believe, is to secure international agreement now on the outlawing of genocide. If such an agreement is reached, neutrals will feel no violation of their sovereignty in the demand that perpetrators of this crime be handed over to justice. And the execution of justice will be given a firm legal foundation.

—*Washington Post*, December 3, 1944, B4.

April 12, 1945

On January 20, 1945, Franklin Roosevelt was inaugurated to his fourth term as president. Less than three months later, on April 12, 1945, at 3:35 p.m., President Roosevelt died at the age of 63 of a massive cerebral hemorrhage at the Little White House, his long-time personal retreat in Warm Springs, Georgia. He was succeeded that day by his vice president, Harry S. Truman. Roosevelt died twenty-seven days before the end of the war in Europe.

33.

Washington Post, April 13, 1945.

As Allied troops began to push Nazi Germany's forces back into Germany, they encountered concentration camps, mass graves, and other sites of Nazi crimes. Although the Allies' primary objective was winning the war—not liberating Nazi camps—US troops and their British, Canadian, and Soviet allies freed prisoners, provided aid to survivors, and collected evidence.

On April 12, 1945, just hours before the president's death, US Army General Dwight D. Eisenhower, Supreme Commander of the Allied Forces in Europe, toured Ohrdruf, a subcamp of the Buchenwald concentration camp in central Germany. Three days later, Eisenhower described his visit to General George C. Marshall, Chief of Staff of the United States Army in Washington, DC: "The things I saw beggar description. [. . .] The visual evidence and verbal testimony of starvation, cruelty and bestiality were so overpowering as to leave me a bit sick. [. . .] I made the visit deliberately, in order to be in a position to give first-hand evidence of these things if ever, in the future, there develops a tendency to charge these allegations merely to 'propaganda.' "[50]

50. Dwight D. Eisenhower to George C. Marshall, April 15, 1945, *Papers of Dwight David Eisenhower: The War Years* (Baltimore: Johns Hopkins University Press, 1970), 4: doc. 2418.

Eisenhower telegrammed General Marshall on April 19, telling him that everything Americans had heard about Nazi atrocities "to date has been understatement." Eisenhower urged Marshall to arrange visits to the concentration camp by members of the US Congress and "prominent editors" of newspapers. These occurred soon thereafter.

34.

SHAEF[51] MESSAGE FORM

From	Originator	Date
(A) SHAEF FRD	Supreme Commander	19 APRIL 1945

[. . . .]

WE CONTINUE TO UNCOVER GERMAN CONCENTRATION CAMPS FOR POLITICAL PRISONERS IN WHICH CONDITION OF INDESCRIBABLE HORROR PREVAIL. FROM EISENHOWER TO GENERAL MARSHALL FOR EYES ONLY. I HAVE VISITED ONE OF THESE MYSELF AND I ASSURE YOU THAT WHATEVER HAS BEEN PRINTED ON THEM TO DATE HAS BEEN UNDERSTATEMENT. IF YOU WOULD SEE ANY ADVANTAGE IN ASKING ABOUT A DOZEN LEADERS OF CONGRESS AND A DOZEN PROMINENT EDITORS TO MAKE A SHORT VISIT TO THIS THEATER IN A COUPLE OF C-54S,[52] I WILL ARRANGE TO HAVE THEM CONDUCTED TO ONE OF THESE PLACES WHERE THE EVIDENCE OF BESTIALITY AND CRUELTY IS SO OVERPOWERING AS TO LEAVE NO DOUBT IN THEIR MINDS ABOUT THE NORMAL PRACTICES OF THE GERMANS IN THESE CAMPS. I AM HOPEFUL THAT SOME BRITISH INDIVIDUALS IN SIMILAR CATEGORIES WILL VISIT THE NORTHERN AREA TO WITNESS SIMILAR EVIDENCE OF ATROCITY.

—Dwight D. Eisenhower's Pre-Presidential Papers, Principal File, Box 134, Cables Off., George C. Marshall/DDE, April 19–November 10, 1945 (4), Dwight D. Eisenhower Presidential Library, Abilene, KS.

Edward R. Murrow (1908–65), a pioneer in radio journalism during the mid-twentieth century and one of the most trusted voices in the United States, toured the Buchenwald concentration camp on April 12, 1945, the day after troops from the US Third Army reached the camp. Three days later Murrow transmitted one of the first

51. SHAEF: Supreme Headquarters Allied Expeditionary Force, from which the commander of the Allied forces in northwest Europe operated.
52. The C-54 "Skymaster": a military transport aircraft.

eyewitness radio broadcasts from Buchenwald. Likely more than half of all Americans heard Murrow describe the horrors that he encountered in the camp.

Though Murrow spoke eloquently about the atrocities at Buchenwald, he also struggled to convey the enormity of the suffering there. "For most of it," Murrow famously reported, "I have no words."

35.

Radio Broadcast from Buchenwald

[. . .] Permit me to tell you what you would have seen and heard had you been with me on Thursday. It will not be pleasant listening. If you are at lunch or if you have no appetite to hear what Germans have done, now is a good time to switch off the radio. For I propose to tell you of Buchenwald. It is on a small hill about four miles outside Weimar, and it was one of the largest concentration camps in Germany, and it was built to last.

As we approached it, we saw about 100 men in civilian clothes with rifles, advancing in open order across a field. There were a few shots. We stopped to inquire. We're told that some of the prisoners had a couple of SS men cornered in there.

We drove on, reached the main gate. The prisoners crowded up behind the wire. We entered. And now let me tell this in the first person. For I was the least important person there as you can hear.

There surged around me an evil-smelling horde, men and boys reached out to touch me.[53] They were in rags and the remnants of uniforms. Death already had marked many of them, but they were smiling with their eyes. I looked out over that mass of men to the green fields beyond, where well-fed Germans were plowing. [. . .]

As I walked down to the end of the barracks, there was applause from the men too weak to get out of bed. It sounded like the handclapping of babies. They were so weak. [. . .]

In another part of the camp they showed me the children, hundreds of them. Some were only 6. One rolled up his sleeve, showed me his number. It was tattooed on his arm. B-6030, it was.[54] The others showed me their numbers. They will carry

53. At the time of liberation, the small number of women prisoners in the Buchenwald camp had been sent to one of its many female subcamps.

54. The number indicates he was a Hungarian Jew deported to Auschwitz after May 1944. His presence in Buchenwald means he survived the "death march" evacuation of Auschwitz ahead of the Soviet Army's arrival in January 1945.

them till they die. An elderly man standing beside me said: "The children—enemies of the state!" I could see their ribs through their thin shirts. [. . .]

We crossed to the courtyard. Men kept coming up to speak to me and to touch me. Professors from Poland. Doctors from Vienna. Men from all Europe. Men from the countries that made America.

We went to the hospital. It was full. The doctor[55] told me that 200 had died the day before. I asked the cause of death. He shrugged and said, "Tuberculosis, starvation, fatigue, and there are many who have no desire to live. It is very difficult." Dr. Heller pulled back the blanket from a man's feet to show me how swollen they were. The man was dead. Most of the patients could not move. [. . .]

I asked to see the kitchen. It was clean. The German in charge had been a Communist. Had been at Buchenwald for nine years. Had a picture of his daughter in Hamburg. Hadn't seen her for almost twelve years, and if I got to Hamburg, would I look her up. He showed me the daily ration. One piece of brown bread about as thick as your thumb, on top of it a piece of margarine as big as three sticks of chewing gum. That, and a little stew, was what they received every 24 hours. He had a chart on the wall; very complicated it was. There were little red tabs scattered through it. He said that was to indicate each 10 men who died. He had to account for the rations, and he added: "We're very efficient here." [. . .]

Dr. Heller, the Czech, asked if I would care to see the crematorium. He said it wouldn't be very interesting because the Germans had run out of coke[56] some days ago and had taken to dumping the bodies into a great hole nearby. [. . .]

We proceeded to the small courtyard. The wall was about eight feet high. It adjoined what had been a stable or garage. We entered. It was floored with concrete. There were two rows of bodies stacked up like cordwood. They were thin and very white. Some of the bodies were terribly bruised, though there seemed to be little flesh to bruise. Some had been shot through the head, but they bled but little. All except two were naked.

I tried to count them as best I could and arrived at the conclusion that all that was mortal of more than 500 men and boys lay there in two neat piles. There was a German trailer, which must have contained another 50, but it wasn't possible to count them. The clothing was piled in a heap against the wall. It appeared that most of the men and boys had died of starvation; they had not been executed.

But the manner of death seemed unimportant. Murder had been done at Buchenwald. God alone knows how many men and boys have died there during the last 12

---

55. Dr. Paul Heller: a Buchenwald prisoner since 1938 who worked in the camp hospital.
56. A form of coal treated to remove impurities for cleaner burning.

years. Thursday, I was told that there were more than 20,000 in the camp. There had been as many as 60,000. Where are they now?[57]

As I left that camp, a Frenchman [. . .] came up to me and said, "You will write something about this perhaps." And he added, "To write about this, you must have been here at least two years. And after that, you don't want to write anymore."

I pray you to believe what I have said about Buchenwald. I have reported what I saw and heard, but only part of it. For most of it, I have no words. [. . .]

If I have offended you by this rather mild account of Buchenwald, I'm not in the least sorry.

I was there on Thursday [April 12, 1945], and many men and many tongues blessed the name of Roosevelt. For long years, his name had meant the full measure of their hope. These men who had kept close company with death for many years, did not know that Mr. Roosevelt would within hours join their comrades who had laid their lives on the scales of freedom. Back in '41, Mr. Churchill said to me with tears in his eyes, "One day, the world and history will recognize and acknowledge what it owes to your President."

I saw and heard the first installment of that at Buchenwald on Thursday. It came from men from all over Europe. Their faces with more flesh on them might have been found anywhere at home. To them, the name Roosevelt was a symbol, a code word for a lot of guys named "Joe" who are somewhere out in the blue with the armor heading east.

At Buchenwald, they spoke of the President just before he died. If there be a better epitaph, history does not record it.

—CBS News, April 15, 1945.

"Victory" in Europe

The Soviet Red Army encircled Berlin on April 23, 1945, and moved to seize the seat of Hitler's government, the Reich Chancellery. On April 30, Hitler committed suicide in his nearby Führerbunker. A week later, *Time* magazine (overleaf) called him "demonic" and added: "Seldom in human history, never in modern times, had a man so insignificantly monstrous become the absolute head of a great nation."[58]

57. Beginning on April 7, 1945, as Allied armies moved into Germany, tens of thousands of prisoners were marched from Buchenwald to camps away from the battle lines. Thousands died during these so-called death marches.

58. Foreign News, Germany, "The Betrayer," *Time*, May 7, 1945, 29.

36.

Boris Artzybasheff, for *Time* magazine. May 7, 1945.

In the final days of Nazism, American newspapers and newsmagazines covered victories in war alongside some of the first widely circulated photographs from liberated concentration camps. In its May 7, 1945, issue, *Life* magazine published six pages of photographs—including these five—documenting atrocities at the Bergen Belsen, Buchenwald, and Nordhausen camps, and other sites.

37.

A young boy walks along a road near the towns of Bergen and Celle, Germany, lined with the corpses of prisoners who died at the Bergen-Belsen concentration camp. April 20, 1945. Photo by George Rodger/The LIFE Picture Collection via Getty Images.

Women prisoners behind the barbed wire fence of the Bergen-Belsen concentration camp. Mid-April 1945. Photo by George Rodger/The LIFE Picture Collection via Getty Images.

Weak and dying prisoners behind a Bergen-Belsen camp barracks. May 1, 1945. Photo by George Rodger/The LIFE Picture Collection via Getty Images.

Starving inmates on their bunks at the Buchenwald concentration camp near Weimar, Germany. April 1945. Photo by Margaret Bourke-White/The LIFE Picture Collection via Getty Images.

An emaciated male prisoner in a barracks at the Buchenwald concentration camp. April 13, 1945. Photo by Margaret Bourke-White / The LIFE Picture Collection via Getty Images.

The bodies of some 3,000 dead from the Nordhausen slave labor camp laid out for reburial by US troops. April 1945. Photographer unknown. Bettmann / Getty Images.

POSTSCRIPT

After President Franklin D. Roosevelt died on April 12, 1945, Vice President Harry S. Truman became the 33rd president of the United States. Victory over the Nazi regime in Europe came on May 8, 1945, less than one month into Truman's presidency. Victory over Japan followed in August, after President Truman made the fateful decision to drop atomic bombs on Hiroshima and Nagasaki. The postwar peace, however, was far from peaceful, as new challenges arose while reestablishing order.

The International Military Tribunal

On November 1, 1943, ten months after the Allies' joint declaration about the "cold-blooded extermination" of the Jews, President Roosevelt, United Kingdom Prime Minister Winston Churchill, and Soviet Union Premier Josef Stalin issued the Moscow Declaration on Atrocities, stating that perpetrators of these "abominable deeds" would be judged under the laws of the nation in which their crimes were committed; major criminals "whose offenses have no particular geographical location . . . will be punished by a joint decision of the Governments of the Allies."[1] In August 1945, just three months after the war in Europe ended, the liberated Republic of France joined these three nations to establish an International Military Tribunal (IMT) to prosecute the major European Axis war criminals.[2]

The IMT, the best known of the numerous postwar war crimes trials, opened in Nuremberg on November 20, 1945, presided over by judges from the four Allied nations and conducted in German, English, French, and Russian. After much debate, twenty-four defendants had already been selected to represent a cross-section of Nazi diplomatic, economic, political, and military leadership. Adolf Hitler, Heinrich

---

1. "Declaration of German Atrocities," November 1, 1943, in Charles I. Bevans, comp., *Treaties and Other International Agreements of the United States of America*, vol. 3, *Multilateral 1931–1945* (Washington, DC: USGPO, 1969): 834.

2. "Agreement [by the United States, United Kingdom, France, and the Soviet Union] for the Prosecution and Punishment of the Major War Criminals of the European Axis," *US Statutes at Large* 59, pt. 2 (Washington, DC: USGPO, 1946), 1544–89 (in US and British English, French, and Russian).

209

The 21 defendants, including Hermann Göring (front row, far left), in the dock at the International Military Tribunal in Nuremberg, Germany. Guards from the US Army surround the dock.

Himmler, and Joseph Goebbels were not among the defendants; all three had committed suicide. Only twenty-one defendants appeared in court; the most significant figure was Hermann Göring. One defendant was excluded due to age and ill health, one was tried in absentia, and one committed suicide before the trial began.

The IMT indicted the defendants on charges of crimes against peace; war crimes; and crimes against humanity, which it defined as "murder, extermination, enslavement, deportation . . . or persecutions on political, racial, or religious grounds." A fourth charge of conspiracy to commit these three crimes was added to cover related criminal activity committed before the start of World War II.

The trial lasted eleven months, with much international media coverage. Testimony presented at Nuremberg revealed important information about the Nazi regime's crimes, including the details of the death machinery at Auschwitz-Birkenau, the destruction of the Warsaw ghetto, and the estimate of six million Jewish victims of the Holocaust. However, only to a limited extent were the atrocities committed against Europe's Jews a focus of the trial.

The judges delivered their verdict on October 1, 1946. Twelve defendants were sentenced to death and hanged on October 16. Göring escaped the hangman's noose by committing suicide the night before he was scheduled to be executed. The IMT sentenced three defendants to life imprisonment and four to prison terms ranging from ten to twenty years; three were acquitted.

In the decades after the famous Nuremberg IMT, hundreds of trials of perpetrators have continued to take place throughout Europe.

The New Refugee Crisis

When the war ended in spring 1945, an estimated ten- to fourteen-million people across the continent had been uprooted from their native countries and left homeless. Among these "displaced persons" (DPs) were an estimated 50,000 Jews who had survived in the Nazi camps or on the "death march" evacuations. That number nearly doubled by year's end as Jews fled west from violent antisemitism and harsh Soviet control in Eastern Europe.

In late December 1945, six months after the war ended in Europe, President Truman issued a directive intended to urge Congress and the State Department to permit more refugees to enter the United States. Truman's rhetoric and actions aimed to change the minds of many Americans; a public opinion poll taken two weeks before the directive revealed that many Americans still hoped to keep refugees from entering, even after the horrors of the Holocaust were becoming more widely revealed.

Despite not asking for any relaxation of the long-established restrictive immigration quotas, Truman's directive had some effect. Although overall immigration into the United States did not increase, DPs received a greater share of the available visas. About 22,950 DPs, two-thirds of whom were Jewish, entered the United States in 1946 and 1947 under provisions of the Truman Directive. More than 100,000 Jewish DPs settled in the United States in the decade after the war.

1.

Immigration to the United States of Certain Displaced Persons and Refugees in Europe

Statement by the President

December 22, 1945

The war has brought in its wake an appalling dislocation of populations in Europe. Many humanitarian organizations, including the United Nations Relief and Rehabilitation Administration,[3] are doing their utmost to solve the multitude of problems

---

3. UNRRA (1943–47): a refugee relief agency proposed by Roosevelt and backed by forty-three nations to work in lands freed from Axis control. It became part of the postwar intergovernmental organization, the United Nations, after the UN's founding in June 1945.

arising in connection with this dislocation of hundreds of thousands of persons. Every effort is being made to return the displaced persons and refugees in the various countries of Europe to their former homes. The great difficulty is that so many of these persons have no homes to which they may return. The immensity of the problem of displaced persons and refugees is almost beyond comprehension.

A number of countries in Europe, including Switzerland, Sweden, France, and England, are working toward its solution. The United States shares the responsibility to relieve the suffering. To the extent that our present immigration laws permit, everything possible should be done at once to facilitate the entrance of some of these displaced persons and refugees into the United States.

In this way we may do something to relieve human misery, and set an example to the other countries of the world which are able to receive some of these war sufferers. I feel that it is essential that we do this ourselves to show our good faith in requesting other nations to open their doors for this purpose. [. . .]

Very few persons from Europe have migrated to the United States during the war years. In the fiscal year 1942, only ten per cent of the immigration quotas was used; in 1943, five per cent; in 1944, six per cent; and in 1945, seven per cent. As of November 30, 1945, the end of the fifth month of the present fiscal year, only about ten per cent of the quotas for the European countries has been used. These unused quotas however do not accumulate through the years, and I do not intend to ask the Congress to change this rule.

The factors chiefly responsible for these low immigration figures were restraints imposed by the enemy, transportation difficulties, and the absence of consular facilities. [. . .]

I consider that common decency and the fundamental comradeship of all human beings require us to do what lies within our power to see that our established immigration quotas are used in order to reduce human suffering. I am taking the necessary steps to see that this is done as quickly as possible.

Of the displaced persons and refugees whose entrance into the United States we will permit under this plan, it is hoped that the majority will be orphaned children. The provisions of law prohibiting the entry of persons likely to become public charges will be strictly observed. Responsible welfare organizations now at work in this field will guarantee that these children will not become public charges. Similar guarantees have or will be made on behalf of adult persons. The record of these welfare organizations throughout the past years has been excellent, and I am informed that no persons admitted under their sponsorship have ever become charges on their communities. Moreover, many of the immigrants will have close family ties in the United States and will receive the assistance of their relatives until they are in a position to provide for themselves.

These relatives or organizations will also advance the necessary visa fees and travel fare. Where the necessary funds for travel fare and visa fees have not been advanced by a welfare organization or relative, the individual applicant must meet these costs. In this way the transportation of these immigrants across the Atlantic will not cost the American taxpayers a single dollar.

In order to enter the United States it is necessary to obtain a visa from a consular officer of the Department of State. As everyone knows, a great many of our consular establishments all over the world were disrupted and their operations suspended when the war came. It is physically impossible to reopen and to restaff all of them overnight. Consequently it is necessary to choose the area in which to concentrate our immediate efforts. This is a painful necessity because it requires us to make an almost impossible choice among degrees of misery. But if we refrain from making a choice because it will necessarily be arbitrary, no choice will ever be made and we shall end by helping no one.

The decision has been made, therefore, to concentrate our immediate efforts in the American zones of occupation in Europe.[4] This is not intended however entirely to exclude issuance of visas in other parts of the world.

In our zones in Europe there are citizens of every major European country. Visas issued to displaced persons and refugees will be charged, according to law, to the countries of their origin. They will be distributed fairly among persons of all faiths, creeds and nationality.

It is intended that, as soon as practicable, regular consular facilities will be reestablished in every part of the world, and the usual, orderly methods of registering and reviewing visa applications will be resumed. The pressing need, however, is to act now in a way that will produce immediate and tangible results. I hope that by early spring adequate consular facilities will be in operation in our zones in Europe, so that immigration can begin immediately upon the availability of ships.

I am informed that there are various measures now pending before the Congress which would either prohibit or severely reduce further immigration. I hope that such legislation will not be passed. This period of unspeakable human distress is not the time for us to close or to narrow our gates. I wish to emphasize, however, that any effort to bring relief to these displaced persons and refugees must and will be strictly within the limits of the present quotas as imposed by law. [. . .]

[. . .] Our major task is to facilitate the entry into the United States of displaced persons and refugees still in Europe. To meet this larger problem, I am directing the Secretary of State, the Attorney General, the Secretary of War, the War Shipping Administrator and the Surgeon General of the Public Health Service to proceed at once to take all appropriate steps to expedite the quota immigration of displaced persons and refugees from Europe to the United States. [. . .]

---

4. Germany and Austria were each divided into US, British, French, and Soviet "zones" for postwar administration.

I wish to emphasize, above all, that nothing in this directive will deprive a single American soldier or his wife or children of a berth on a vessel homeward bound, or delay their return.

This is the opportunity for America to set an example for the rest of the world in cooperation towards alleviating human misery.

—*Department of State Bulletin* 13, no. 339 (Washington, DC: USGPO, December 23, 1945): 981–82.

2.

Gallup Poll, December 1945

"Should we permit more persons from Europe to come to this country each year than we did before the war, should we keep the number about the same, or should we reduce the number?"

5% More
32% Same
37% Fewer
14% None at all
12% No opinion

—Gallup Organization. 1945. Gallup Poll # 1945-0361: Military Service/Truman's Proposal for Labor Disputes/Pearl Harbor/Television/1948 Presidential Election. Question 54: USGALLUP.011446.RK12A. Cornell University, Ithaca, NY: Roper Center for Public Opinion Research. https://doi.org/10.25940/ROPER-31087344.

Acknowledgments

Americans and the Holocaust: A Reader is one of many educational resources resulting from a multiyear, collaborative initiative of the United States Holocaust Memorial Museum. The initiative—which includes exhibitions, multiple online resources, educational and public programs, and publications—honors the mandate in the institution's founding charter that the Museum put special emphasis on Americans' responses to the Holocaust.

The United States Holocaust Memorial Museum is deeply grateful to the following donors for their generous support of the Museum's Americans and the Holocaust Initiative: lead donors Jeannie & Jonathan Lavine; The Bildners–Joan & Allen *z"l*, Elisa Spungen & Rob, Nancy & Jim; Jane and Daniel Och; Akin Gump Strauss Hauer & Feld LLP; Arnold & Porter Kaye Scholer LLP; Ruth Miriam Bernstein; Joyce and Irving Goldman Family Foundation; In Memory of Simon Konover; Philip and Cheryl Milstein Family; Benjamin and Seema Pulier Charitable Foundation; David and Fela Shapell Family Foundation; Deborah Simon; and Laurie and Sy Sternberg.

Staff across the institution have contributed to the success of this initiative. For assistance with this book, the editors thank USHMM Director Sara Bloomfield, Deputy Museum Director and Chief Program Officer Sarah Ogilvie, and Director of Education Initiatives Gretchen Skidmore. Museum colleagues Rebecca Erbelding, Patricia Heberer-Rice, Steven Luckert, and Gretchen Skidmore reviewed a draft of the manuscript. Belinda Blomberg coordinated permissions and graphics acquisitions. Research contributions to this book came from Ron Coleman, Rebecca Erbelding, and Anna Rennich. Multiple "citizen historians" throughout the United States uploaded useful historical newspaper articles to the Museum's crowdsourced website History Unfolded: US Newspapers and the Holocaust. Education Initiatives staff Stacey Knepp and Bianca Saunders assisted with audience testing, and Brandy Johnson provided administrative support.

Americans and the Holocaust benefitted from the expertise of numerous colleagues outside the Museum. We wish to particularly thank Peter Hayes, Professor Emeritus of History at Northwestern University, for addressing our many questions.

Finally, we're especially thankful to Elisabeth Maselli, assistant to the director and associate editor at Rutgers University Press, for acquiring this book and seeing it through production. We appreciate the work of RUP production editor Vincent Nordhaus, book designer Carey Nershi, copyeditor Leslie Jones, and indexer Elise Hess.

Further Reading

This list is intended to help readers who want to know more about the United States and the Holocaust. It is not comprehensive, and lists only a few of the many survey histories of the Holocaust in Europe.

United States and the Holocaust

Abzug, Robert H. *America Views the Holocaust, 1933–1945: A Brief Documentary History*. Boston: Bedford/St. Martin's, 1999.

Bauer, Yehuda. *Could the US Government Have Rescued European Jewry?* Jerusalem: Yad Vashem, 2017.

Bernstein, Arnie. *Swastika Nation: Fritz Kuhn and the Rise and Fall of the German-American Bund*. New York: Picador USA, 2014.

Breitman, Richard. *Official Secrets: What the Nazis Planned, What the British and Americans Knew*. New York: Hill and Wang, 1998.

Breitman, Richard, and Allan J. Lichtman. *FDR and the Jews*. Cambridge: Belknap Press, 2013.

Casey, Steven. *Cautious Crusade: Franklin D. Roosevelt, American Public Opinion, and the War Against Nazi Germany*. New York: Oxford University Press, 2001.

Doherty, Thomas. *Hollywood and Hitler, 1933–1939*. New York: Columbia University Press, 2013.

Erbelding, Rebecca. *Rescue Board: The Untold Story of America's Efforts to Save the Jews of Europe*. New York: Doubleday, 2018.

Feingold, Henry L. *Bearing Witness: How America and Its Jews Responded to the Holocaust*. Syracuse, NY: Syracuse University Press, 1995.

Feingold, Henry L. *The Politics of Rescue: The Roosevelt Administration and the Holocaust, 1938–1945*. New Brunswick, NJ: Rutgers University Press, 1970.

Fleming, Michael. *Auschwitz, the Allies and Censorship of the Holocaust*. New York: Cambridge University Press, 2014.

Harris, Mark. *Five Came Back: A Story of Hollywood and the Second World War*. New York: Penguin, 2014.

Hart, Bradley. *Hitler's American Friends: The Third Reich's Supporters in the United States*. New York: Thomas Dunne Books, 2018.

Larsen, Erik. *In the Garden of Beasts: Love, Terror, and an American Family in Hitler's Berlin*. New York: Crown, 2011.

Leff, Laurel. *Buried by the Times: The Holocaust and America's Most Important Newspaper*. New York: Cambridge University Press, 2005.

Lipstadt, Deborah E. *Beyond Belief: The American Press and the Coming of the Holocaust, 1933–1945*. New York: Free Press, 1986.

Lipstadt, Deborah E. *Holocaust: An American Understanding.* New Brunswick, NJ: Rutgers University Press, 2016.

Nagorski, Andrew. *Hitlerland: American Eyewitnesses to the Nazis Rise to Power.* New York: Simon & Schuster, 2012.

Neufeld, Michael J., and Michael Berenbaum, eds. *The Bombing of Auschwitz: Should the Allies Have Attempted It?* New York: St. Martin's Press, 2000.

Newton, Verne W., ed. *FDR and the Holocaust.* New York: St. Martin's Press, 1996.

Novick, Peter. *The Holocaust in American Life.* Boston: Houghton Mifflin, 1999.

Power, Samantha. *"A Problem from Hell": America and the Age of Genocide.* New York: Basic Books, 2002.

Pressman, Steven. *50 Children: One Ordinary American Couple's Extraordinary Rescue Mission into the Heart of Nazi Germany.* New York: Harper, 2014.

Ross, Steven J. *Hitler in Los Angeles: How Jews Foiled Nazi Plots Against Hollywood and America.* New York: Bloomsbury, 2017.

Subak, Susan Elisabeth. *Rescue & Flight: American Relief Workers Who Defied the Nazis.* Lincoln: University of Nebraska Press, 2010.

Trachtenberg, Barry. *The United States and the Nazi Holocaust: Race, Refuge, and Remembrance.* New York: Bloomsbury, 2018.

Whitman, James Q. *Hitler's American Model: The United States and the Making of Nazi Race Law.* Princeton, NJ: Princeton University Press, 2017.

Wyman, David S. *The Abandonment of the Jews: America and the Holocaust, 1941–1945.* New York: Pantheon Books, 1984.

Germany and the Holocaust

Bergen, Doris. *War and Genocide: A Concise History of the Holocaust.* New York: Rowman and Littlefield, 2016.

Caplan, Jane. *Nazi Germany: A Very Short Introduction.* Oxford: Oxford University Press, 2019.

Friedländer, Saul. *Nazi Germany and the Jews: The Years of Persecution, 1933–1939.* New York: Harper Collins, 1997.

Friedländer, Saul. *Nazi Germany and the Jews: The Years of Extermination, 1939–1945.* New York: Harper Collins, 2007.

Hayes, Peter. *Why?: Explaining the Holocaust.* New York: W. W. Norton, 2018.

Laqueur, Walter. *The Terrible Secret: Suppression of the Truth about Hitler's "Final Solution."* Boston: Little, Brown, 1980.

Snyder, Timothy. *Bloodlands: Europe Between Hitler and Stalin.* New York: Basic Books, 2010.

American Immigration and Interwar US History

Daniels, Roger. *Guarding the Golden Door: American Immigration Policy and Immigrants since 1882.* New York: Hill and Wang, 2004.

Daniels, Roger. *Prisoners without Trial: Japanese Americans in World War II.* New York: Hill and Wang, 1993.

Dinnerstein, Leonard. *Antisemitism in America.* New York: Oxford University Press, 1994.

Katznelson, Ira. *Fear Itself: The New Deal and the Origins of Our Time.* New York: Liveright, 2013.

Kennedy, David M. *Freedom from Fear: The American People in Depression and War, 1929–1945.* New York: Oxford University Press, 1999.

Lee, Erika. *America for Americans: A History of Xenophobia in the United States.* New York: Basic Books, 2019.

Okrent, Daniel. *The Guarded Gate: Bigotry, Eugenics, and the Law that Kept Two Generations of Jews, Italians, and Other European Immigrants Out of America.* New York: Scribner, 2019.

Refugee Crisis

Breitman, Richard, and Alan M. Kraut. *American Refugee Policy and European Jewry, 1933–1945.* Bloomington: Indiana University Press, 1987.

Dobbs, Michael. *The Unwanted: America, Auschwitz, and a Village Caught in Between.* New York: Alfred A. Knopf, 2019.

Dwork, Debórah, and Robert Jan van Pelt. *Flight from the Reich: Refugee Jews, 1933–1946.* New York: W. W. Norton, 2009.

Lowenstein, Sharon R. *Token Refuge: The Story of the Jewish Refugee Shelter at Oswego, 1944–1946.* Bloomington: Indiana University Press, 1986.

Ogilvie, Sarah A., and Scott Miller. *Refuge Denied: The St. Louis Passengers and the Holocaust.* Madison: University of Wisconsin Press, 2006.

Wyman, David S. *Paper Walls: America and the Refugee Crisis, 1938–1941.* Amherst: University of Massachusetts Press, 1968.

Isolation Versus Intervention

Berg, A. Scott. *Lindbergh.* London: Simon & Schuster, 2013.

Churchwell, Sarah. *Behold, America: The Entangled History of "America First" and "The American Dream."* New York: Basic Books, 2018.

Dunn, Susan. *1940: FDR, Willkie, Lindbergh, Hitler—The Election amid the Storm.* New Haven, CT: Yale University Press, 2013.

Olson, Lynne. *Those Angry Days: Roosevelt, Lindbergh, and America's Fight over World War II, 1939–1941.* New York: Random House, 2013.

Permissions

Texts from newspaper scans online at Newspapers.com, reprinted with the following permissions:

    Pp. 24, 28, 32, 56, 76, 88, 91, 115, 164, 176, 194: Copyrighted 1933–1944. Associated Press. 2161113:0221PF.

    Pp. 27, 118, 119: Reprinted courtesy UPI.

    P. 44: Public domain.

    Pp. 144, 145: Reprinted by permission of Pittsburgh Courier archives.

    P. 183: Reprinted by permission of the Estate of Eleanor Roosevelt.

Texts from images produced by ProQuest LLC as part of ProQuest® Historical Newspapers, and published with permission of ProQuest LLC. www.proquest.com. Further reproduction is with the following permissions:

    P. 9: Public domain.

    Pp. 11, 36: Copyright © 1923, 1933 Chicago Tribune. All rights reserved. Used under license.

    P. 21: Courtesy of the American Jewish Historical Society.

    P. 35: Copyrighted 1933. Associated Press. 2161113:0221PF.

    P. 46: Public domain.

    Pp. 64, 197, 199: Copyright © 1938, 1944, 1945 The Washington Post. All rights reserved. Used under license.

    P. 86: Copyright © 1939 The New York Times Company. All rights reserved. Used under license.

    P. 143: Public domain.

    P. 168: Reprinted by permission of Don Congdon Associates, Inc. on behalf of the William L. Shirer Literary Trust.

P. 14: Copyright © Condé Nast, Inc. Reprinted by permission.

P. 16: Reprinted by permission of *Newsweek*.

Pp. 19, 20, 38, 66, 204: Copyright © 1933, 1935, 1938, 1945 TIME USA LLC. All rights reserved. Used under license.

P. 29: Reprinted by permission of JTA at jta.org. All rights reserved.

P. 43: Reprinted by permission of the United States Olympic & Paralympic Committee.

P. 54: Library of Congress, Prints & Photographs Division, (LC-DIG-hlb-01250). A 1939 Herblock Cartoon © The Herb Block Foundation; reproduced by permission.

P. 70: Reprinted by permission of the *Reading Eagle*.

Pp. 71, 72: *Newspaper image:* Copyright © 1938 The Dallas Morning News, Inc. *Inset photo:* AP Photo. *Text:* Reprinted courtesy UPI.

Pp. 77, 107, 111, 167, 196, 214: Reprinted by permission of the Roper Center for Public Opinion Research.

Index